D0992551

Why Love Hurts

Why Love Hurts

A Sociological Explanation

Eva Illouz

polity

Copyright © Eva Illouz 2012

The right of Eva Illouz to be identified as Author of this Work has been asserted in accordance with the UK Copyright, Designs and Patents Act 1988.

First published in 2012 by Polity Press, 2013

Polity Press
65 Bridge Street
Cambridge CB2 1UR, UK

Polity Press
350 Main Street
Malden, MA 02148, USA

All rights reserved. Except for the quotation of short passages for the purpose of criticism and review, no part of this publication may be reproduced, stored in a retrieval system, or transmitted, in any form or by any means, electronic, mechanical, photocopying, recording or otherwise, without the prior permission of the publisher.

ISBN-13: 978-0-7456-6152-0

A catalogue record for this book is available from the British Library.

Typeset in 10.5 on 12 pt Sabon
by Toppan Best-set Premedia Limited
Printed and bound in the USA by Edwards Brothers, Inc.

The publisher has used its best endeavours to ensure that the URLs for external websites referred to in this book are correct and active at the time of going to press. However, the publisher has no responsibility for the websites and can make no guarantee that a site will remain live or that the content is or will remain appropriate.

Every effort has been made to trace all copyright holders, but if any have been inadvertently overlooked the publisher will be pleased to include any necessary credits in any subsequent reprint or edition.

For further information on Polity, visit our website: www.politybooks.com

ACC LIBRARY SERVICES AUSTIN, TX

Contents

Acknowledgments

In more than one way, I started writing this book in my head many years ago, while still an adolescent. It is the product of hundreds, perhaps thousands, of conversations with close friends and strangers that left me perplexed and puzzled by the chaos that pervades contemporary romantic and sexual relationships. Why is it that despite their strength and autonomy, women in the four countries in which I have lived during my adult life (France, the United States, Israel, and Germany) are baffled by the elusiveness of men? Why do men seem to have become a puzzle and an ongoing source of bemusement for women? And did the men and women of the past agonize about love in the same way as modern men and women do? Most of the surrounding culture instructs us to answer these questions by looking for the hidden history of our flawed childhood and to explain the disarray of romantic lives with flawed psyches. This book wants to question this largely unquestioned assumption. It wants to explain why love hurts by highlighting the social, rather than the psychological, context of men's and women's encounters.

This book, then, emerges from the intimacy of many hours of conversation, but it owes much to other, less intimate but no less important, conversations. My first thanks go to the Wissenshaftskolleg zu Berlin, which during the 2007–8 year provided the peace and quiet of a monastery and the intense conversations of an eighteenth-century salon. I thank Dale Bauer, Ute Frevert, Sven Hillerkamp, Axel Honneth, Tom Laqueur, Reinhart Merkel, Reinhart Meyer-Kalkus, Susan Neiman, John Thompson, and Eitan Wilf for engaging me so compellingly in their thoughts, questions, and often brilliant suggestions. Mattan Shachak has been entirely necessary to the process of writing this book; he has made tangible on a daily basis the joy of being the teacher of an outstanding student and research assistant. Ori Schwarz, Dana Kaplan, and Zsuza Berend have read many chapters; their comments have been crucial in helping me significantly improve the book. I thank them for their remarkable intellectual generosity. Nathalie-Myriam Illouz, my sister and a brilliant psychoanalyst, and Beatrice Smedley, my friend and fellow-writer, have endlessly discussed with me the splendor and misery of love. I can only hope to emulate the subtlety of their analyses.

A book is a special kind of commodity: it must be not only produced by expert heads and hands, but also believed in. Polity Press is unique in its dedication to furthering the global circulation of ideas, and in its intimate, intense care in the process of producing a book. I am privileged to have seen this book endorsed so wholeheartedly by John Thompson. The depth of his care and the precision of his responsiveness make him an exceptional publisher. Justin Dyer has been a superb editor, and Jennifer Jahn and Clare Ansell have been most responsive and helpful as editorial assistant and production editor, respectively.

I thank all the people, close friends and strangers, who confided in me and told me their stories, sometimes in despair, often in hope and trust. I dedicate this book to the men and the women I will keep loving for a long time, painlessly and painfully.

The publishers would like to acknowledge the following for permission to reproduce the epigraphs:

From INDIGNATION by Philip Roth. Copyright (c) 2008, Philip Roth, used by permission of The Wylie Agency (UK) Limited;

Chris Carter, www.catchhimandkeephim.com;

From DISGRACE by J.M. Coetzee, copyright (c) 1999 by J. M. Coetzee. Used by permission of Viking Penguin, a division of Penguin Group (USA) Inc. and of Vintage, a division of Random House;

From LOVE, ETC. by Julian Barnes, copyright (c) 2000 by Julian Barnes. Used by permission of Alfred A. Knopf, a division of Random House, Inc.; published by Vintage Books. Reprinted by permission of The Random House Group Ltd;

I want my works to be read by the far-from-frigid virgin
On fire for her sweetheart, by the boy,
In love for the very first time. May some fellow-sufferer
Perusing my anatomy of a desire,
See his own passion reflected there, cry in amazement:
Who told this scribbler about my private affairs?

Ovid, *Amores*

1

Introduction
The Misery of Love

But Bliss in love is seldom the case: For every successful contemporary
love experience, for every short period of enrichment, there are ten
destructive love experiences, post-love "downs" of much longer duration – often resulting in the destruction of the individual, or at least
an emotional cynicism that makes it difficult or impossible ever to love
again. Why should this be so, if it is not actually inherent in the love
process itself?

> Shulamith Firestone, *The Dialectic of Sex: The Case for
> Feminist Revolution*[1]

Wuthering Heights (1847) belongs to a long literary tradition por-
traying love as an agonizingly painful emotion.[2] The novel's notorious protagonists, Heathcliff and Catherine, develop a strong love for
each other while growing up together, yet Catherine decides to marry
Edgar Linton, a socially more appropriate match. Humiliated when
he accidentally overhears Catherine claim that she would degrade
herself in marrying him, Heathcliff runs away. Catherine looks for
him in the fields, and when she does not find him, she falls ill to the
point of near-death.

In a far more ironic mode, *Madame Bovary* (1856) describes the
unhappy marriage of a romantic woman with a kind-hearted but
mediocre provincial doctor, who cannot satisfy his wife's sappily
romantic and social fantasies. Its eponymous protagonist thinks she
has found the hero she has so frequently read and dreamed about in
the figure of Rodolphe Boulanger, a dashing landowner. After a three-
year-long affair, they decide to elope. On the fateful day, Emma
receives Rodolphe's letter breaking off his promise. Here the narrator

dispenses with his usual irony when describing the romantic feelings of his heroine, instead describing her suffering with compassion:

> She leant against the embrasure of the window, and reread the letter with angry sneers. But the more she fixed her attention upon it, the more confused were her ideas. She saw him again, heard him, encircled him with her arms, and throbs of her heart, that beat against her breast like blows of a sledge-hammer, grew faster and faster, with uneven intervals. She looked about her with the wish that the earth might crumble into pieces. Why not end it all? What restrained her? She was free. She advanced, looking at the paving-stones, saying to herself, "Come! come!"[3]

By our own standards, Catherine and Emma's pain seems extreme, but it is still intelligible to us. Yet, as this book seeks to claim, the romantic agony that both of these women experience has changed its content, color, and texture. First of all, the opposition between society and love which each enacts in her suffering is hardly relevant to modern societies. Indeed, there would be few economic obstacles or normative prohibitions preventing either Catherine or Emma from making their love their first and only choice. If anything, our contemporary sense of appropriateness would command us to follow the dictates of our heart, not of our social milieu. Second, a battery of experts would now be likely to come to the rescue of a hesitant Catherine and of Emma's passionless marriage: psychological counseling, couple therapy, divorce lawyers, mediation specialists, would massively appropriate and adjudicate over the private dilemmas of prospective or bored wives. In the absence of (or in conjunction with) experts' help, their modern counterparts would have shared the secret of their love with others, most likely female friends, or, at the very least, occasional anonymous friends found on the Internet, thus considerably diminishing the solitude of their passion. Between their desire and their despair, there would have been a thick flow of words, self-analysis, and friendly or expert advice. A contemporary Catherine or Emma would have spent a great deal of time reflecting and talking about their pain and likely found its causes in their own (or their lovers') deficient childhood. They would have derived a sense of glory not from the experience of grief, but precisely from having overcome it, through an arsenal of self-help therapeutic techniques. Modern romantic pain generates an almost endless gloss, the purpose of which is both to understand and extirpate its causes. Dying, committing suicide, and running away to a cloister no longer belong to our cultural repertoires. This is not to say, obviously, that we, "post-" or "late" moderns, do not know something about the agony of love. In fact we may possibly know more about it than our predecessors. But what it does suggest is that the social organization of romantic pain has changed profoundly. This book is about understanding the nature of that transformation through an examination of the changes undergone in three different and crucial aspects of the self: the will (how we want something), recognition (what matters for our sense of worth), and desire (what we long for and how we long for it).

In fact, few people living in the contemporary era have been spared the agonies of intimate relationships. These agonies come in many shapes: kissing too many frogs on the way to Prince/ss Charming; engaging in sisyphean Internet searches; coming back lonely from bars, parties, or blind dates. When relationships do get formed, agonies do not fade away, as one may feel bored, anxious, or angry in them; have painful arguments and conflicts; or, finally, go through the confusion, self-doubts, and depression of break-ups or divorces. These are only some of the ways in which the search for love is an agonizingly difficult experience from which few modern men and women have been spared. If the sociologist could hear the voices of men and women searching for love, s/he would hear a long and loud litany of moans and groans.

Despite the widespread and almost collective character of these experiences, our culture insists they are the result of faulty or insufficiently mature psyches. Countless self-help manuals and workshops profess to help us better manage our romantic lives by making us more aware of the ways in which we unconsciously engineer our own defeats. The Freudian culture in which we are steeped has made the forceful claim that sexual attraction is best explained by our past experiences, and that the love preference is formed in early life in the relationship between the child and its parents. For many, the Freudian assertion that the family designs the pattern of the erotic career has been the main explanation for why and how we fail to find or to sustain love. Undaunted by incoherence, Freudian culture even further claims that whether our partner is opposite or similar to our parents, s/he is a direct reflection of our childhood experiences – themselves the key to explaining our romantic destiny. With the idea of repetition compulsion, Freud went one step further and argued that early experiences of loss, however painful, will be reenacted throughout adult life, as a way to gain mastery over them. This idea had a tremendous impact on the collective view and treatment of romantic misery, suggesting it is a salutary dimension of the process of maturation. More: Freudian culture suggested that, by and large, romantic misery was inevitable and self-inflicted.

Clinical psychology has played a uniquely central role in suggesting (and bestowing scientific legitimacy on) the idea that love and its failures must be explained by the psychic history of the individual, and that, as a result, they are within the purview of her/his control. Although the original Freudian notion of the unconscious aimed at dissolving traditional authorial notions of responsibility, in practice, psychology played a crucial role in relegating the realm of the romantic and the erotic to the individual's private responsibility. Whether psychoanalysis and psychotherapy intended to or not, they have provided a formidable arsenal of techniques to make us the verbose but inescapable bearers of responsibility for our romantic miseries.

Throughout the twentieth century, the idea that romantic misery is self-made was uncannily successful, perhaps because psychology simultaneously offered the consoling promise that it could be undone. Painful experiences of love were a powerful engine activating a host of professionals (psychoanalysts, psychologists, and therapists of all kinds), the publishing industry, television, and numerous other media industries. The extraordinarily successful industry of self-help was made possible against the backdrop of the deep-seated belief that our miseries are tailor-made to our psychic history, that speech and self-knowledge have healing virtues, and that identifying the patterns and sources of our miseries helps us overcome them. The agonies of love now point only to the self, its private history, and its capacity to shape itself.

Precisely because we live in a time where the idea of individual responsibility reigns supreme, the vocation of sociology remains vital. In the same way that at the end of the nineteenth century it was radical to claim that poverty was the result not of dubious morality or weak character, but of systematic economic exploitation, it is now urgent to claim not that the failures of our private lives are the result of weak psyches, but rather that the vagaries and miseries of our emotional life are shaped by institutional arrangements. The purpose of this book is thus to vastly shift the angle of analysis of what is wrong in contemporary relationships. What is wrong are not dysfunctional childhoods or insufficiently self-aware psyches, but the set of social and cultural tensions and contradictions that have come to structure modern selves and identities.

As such, this suggestion is not new. Feminist writers and thinkers have long contested both the popular belief in love as the source of all happiness and the psychological individualist understanding of the miseries of love. Contrary to popular mythology, feminists argue, romantic love is not the source of transcendence, happiness, and self-realization. Rather, it is one of the main causes of the divide between men and women, as well as one of the cultural practices through which women are made to accept (and "love") their submission to men. For, when in love, men and women continue to perform the deep divisions that characterize their respective identities: in Simone de Beauvoir's famous words, even in love men retain their sovereignty, while women aim to abandon themselves.[4] In her controversial *The Dialectic of Sex*, quoted at the beginning of this chapter, Shulamith Firestone went a step further: the source of men's social power and energy is the love women provide for them and continue to provide for men, thus suggesting that love is the cement with which the edifice of male domination has been built.[5] Romantic love not only hides class and sex segregation, but in fact makes it possible. In Ti-Grace Atkinson's striking words, romantic love is the "psychological pivot in the persecution of women."[6] The most arresting claim made by feminists is that a struggle for power lies at the core of love and sexuality, and that men have had and continue to have the upper hand in that struggle because there is a convergence between economic and sexual power. Such sexual male power consists in the capacity to define the objects of love and to set up the rules that govern courtship and the expression of romantic sentiments. Ultimately, male power resides in the fact that gender identities and hierarchy are played out and reproduced in the expression and experience of romantic sentiments, and that, conversely, sentiments sustain broader economic and political power differentials.[7]

But in many ways, it is also this assumption about the primacy of power that constitutes a flaw in what has become the dominant strand of feminist critique of love. In periods where patriarchy was far more powerful than it is today, love played a much *less* significant role in the subjectivity of men and women. More than that: the cultural prominence of love seems to have been associated with a decline – not an increase – in men's power in the family and with the rise of more egalitarian and symmetrical gender relationships. Moreover, much of feminist theory is premised on the assumption that in love (and other) relationships, power is *the* primary building block of social relationships. It thus must disregard the vast amount of empirical evidence suggesting that love is no less primary than power, and that it is also a powerful and invisible mover of social relationships. In reducing women's love (and desire to love) to patriarchy, feminist theory often fails to understand the reasons why love holds such a powerful sway on modern women *as well as on* men and fails to grasp the egalitarian strain contained in the ideology of love, and its capacity to subvert from within patriarchy. Patriarchy certainly plays a central role in explaining the structure of relationships between the sexes and the uncanny fascination which heterosexuality still exerts on them, but it alone cannot explain the extraordinary grip of the love ideal on modern men and women.

This book thus wants to outline a framework in order to identify the institutional causes for romantic misery, but it takes for granted that the experience of love exerts a powerful hold that cannot be simply explained by "false consciousness."[8] This would be to foreclose the question before it is even asked. My claim here is that the reason why love is so central to our happiness and identity is not far from the reason why it is such a difficult aspect of our experience: both have to do with the ways in which self and identity are institutionalized in modernity. If many of us have "a kind of nagging anxiety, or unease" about love and a sense that matters of love make us "troubled, restless, and dissatisfied with ourselves," to use the words of philosopher Harry Frankfurt,[9] it is because love contains, mirrors, and amplifies the "entrapment" of the self in the institutions of modernity,[10] institutions, to be sure, shaped by economic and gender relations. As Karl Marx famously put it, "Human beings make their history themselves, but they do not do so voluntarily, not under circumstances of their own choosing, rather under immediately found, given and transmitted circumstances."[11] When we love or sulk, we do so by using resources and in situations that are not of our own making, and it is these resources and situations this book would like to study. Throughout the following pages, my overall argument is that something fundamental about the structure of the romantic self has changed in modernity. Very broadly, this can be described as a change in the structure of our romantic will, what we want and how we come to implement what we want with a sexual partner (chapters 2 and 3); as a change in what makes the self vulnerable, that is, what makes one feel unworthy (chapter 4); and, finally, as a change in the organization of desire, the content of the thoughts and emotions which activate our erotic and romantic desires (chapters 5 and 6). How the will is structured, how recognition is constituted, and how desire is activated constitute the three main lines of analysis of the transformations of love in modernity. Ultimately, my aim is to do to love what Marx did to commodities: to show that it is shaped and produced by concrete social relations; to show that love circulates in a marketplace of unequal competing actors; and to argue that some people command greater capacity to define the terms in which they are loved than others.

The dangers lurking behind such analysis are many. The most obvious one perhaps has to do with the fact that I may have overdrawn the differences separating "us" – moderns – from "them" – premoderns. Undoubtedly, many, if not most, readers will think about their own set of counter-examples questioning the claim made here – that the causes for love pains have to do with modernity. But a few responses to this serious objection may be readily offered. One is that I do not claim that love pain is new, only that some of the ways in which we experience it are. The second response has to do with the ways in which sociologists work: we are less interested in the singular actions and sentiments of individuals than in the structures which organize these actions and sentiments. While the close and distant past may be full of examples seemingly similar to the present condition, they do not point to the large-scale structures that contemporary romantic practices and their suffering point us to. In that sense, then, I hope historians will forgive me for using history less for its thickness, complexity, and movement, than as a background tapestry with fixed motives which help highlight, by contrast, the characteristic features of modernity.

Like other sociologists, I view love as a privileged microcosm through which to understand the processes of modernity, but unlike them, the story I have to tell here is not one of heroic victory of sentiment over reason, and gender equality over gender exploitation, but far more ambiguous.

What is Modernity?

More than any other discipline, sociology was born out of a frantic and anxious questioning about the meaning and consequences of modernity: Karl Marx, Max Weber, Émile Durkheim, Georg Simmel, have all tried to understand the meaning of the transition from the "old" world to the "new." The "old" was religion, community, order, and stability. The "new" was breath-taking change, secularity, dissolution of community ties, increasing claims to equality, and a nagging uncertainty about identity. Ever since that extraordinary period marking the transition from the mid-nineteenth to the twentieth centuries, sociology has been busy with the same daunting questions: Will the dwindling of religion and community jeopardize social order? Will we be able to live meaningful lives in the absence of sacredness? In particular, Max Weber was troubled by Dostoevsky's and Tolstoy's questions: If we are no longer afraid of God, what will make us moral? If we are not engaged in and compelled by sacred, collective, and binding meanings, what will make our lives meaningful? If the individual – rather than God – is at the center of morality, what will become of the "ethic of brotherliness" that had been the driving force of religions?[12] In fact, from the outset, the vocation of sociology has been to understand what the meaning of life could be after the demise of religion.

Modernity, most sociologists agreed, offered exhilarating possibilities, but also ominous risks to our ability to live meaningful lives. Even the sociologists who conceded that modernity meant progress over ignorance, chronic poverty, and pervasive subjection still viewed it as an impoverishment of our capacities to tell beautiful stories and to live in richly textured cultures. Modernity sobered people up from the powerful but sweet delusions and illusions that had made the misery of their lives bearable. Devoid of these fantasies, we would lead our lives without commitment to higher principles and values, without the fervor and ecstasy of the sacred, without the heroism of saints, without the certainty and orderliness of divine commandments, but most of all without those fictions that console and beautify.

Such sobering up is nowhere more apparent than in the realm of love, which for several centuries in the history of Western Europe had been governed by the ideals of chivalry, gallantry, and romanticism. The male ideal of chivalry had one cardinal stipulation: to defend the weak with courage and loyalty. The weakness of women was thus contained in a cultural system in which it was acknowledged and glorified because it transfigured male power and female fraility into lovable qualities, such as "protectiveness" for the one, and "softness" and gentleness for the other. Women's social inferiority could thus be traded for men's absolute devotion in love, which in turn served as the very site of display and exercise of their masculinity, prowess, and honor. More: women's dispossession of economic and political rights was accompanied (and presumably compensated) by the reassurance that in love they were not only protected by men but also superior to them. It is therefore unsurprising that love has been historically so powerfully seductive to women; it promised them the moral status and dignity they were otherwise denied in society and it glorified their social fate: taking care of and loving others, as mothers, wives, and lovers. Thus, historically, love was highly seductive precisely because it concealed as it beautified the deep inequalities at the heart of gender relationships.

High or hyper-modernity – defined in this book narrowly as the period which followed World War I and used throughout as "modernity" – marked a radicalization of the social tendencies inscribed in early modernity, and changed, at times profoundly, the culture of love and the economy of gender identity contained in it. This culture did retain and even amplify the ideal of love as a power that can transcend daily life. Yet, when it put the two political ideals of gender equality and sexual freedom at the center of intimacy, it stripped love of the rituals of deference and the mystical aura in which it had hitherto been shrouded. All that was holy in love became profane, and men were at last forced to face with their sober senses the real conditions of women's lives. It is this profoundly split and dual aspect of love – both as a source of existential transcendence and as a deeply contested site for the performance of gender identity – that characterizes contemporary romantic culture. More specifically: to perform gender identity and gender struggles is to perform the institutional and cultural core dilemmas and ambivalence of modernity, dilemmas that are organized around the key cultural and institutional motives of authenticity, autonomy, equality, freedom, commitment, and self-realization. To study love is not peripheral but *central* to the study of the core and foundation of modernity.[13]

Heterosexual romantic love is one of the best sites to take stock of such an ambivalent perspective on modernity because the last four decades have witnessed a radicalization of freedom and equality within the romantic bond as well as a radical split between sexuality and emotionality. Heterosexual romantic love contains the two most important cultural revolutions of the twentieth century: the individualization of lifestyles and the intensification of emotional life projects; and the economization of social relationships, the pervasiveness of economic models to shape the self and its very emotions.[14] Sex and sexuality became disentangled from moral norms, and incorporated in individualized lifestyles and life projects, while the capitalist cultural grammar has massively penetrated the realm of heterosexual romantic relationships.

For example, when (heterosexual) love became the constitutive theme of the novel, few noticed that it became tightly intertwined with another theme, no less central to the bourgeois novel and to modernity at large: that of social mobility. As suggested by the two examples of Catherine and Emma discussed earlier, romantic love was almost always inevitably interwoven with the question of social mobility. That is, one of the central questions asked by the novel (and later by Hollywood cinema) was and remains whether and under what conditions love can trump social mobility, and, vice versa, whether socio-economic compatibility should be a necessary condition for love. The shaping of the modern individual was at one and the same time emotional and economic, romantic and rational. This is because the centrality of love in marriage (and in the novel) coincided with the waning of marriage as a tool of family alliances and marked the new role of love for social mobility. But far from marking the demise of economic calculus, it in fact deepened it, as women and men would increasingly move up (and down) the social ladder through the social alchemy of love. Because love made the fit between marriage and strategies of economic and social reproduction less explicit and formal, the modern choice of a mate progressively included and mixed both emotional and economic aspirations. Love now incorporated and contained rational and strategic interests, merging the economic and emotional dispositions of actors into one single cultural matrix. One of the key cultural transformations accompanying modernity was thus the co-mingling of love with economic strategies of social mobility. This is also why this book contains a number of methodological biases: it addresses heterosexual love more markedly than homosexual love because the former contains a denial of the economic underpinnings of the choice of a love object, and fuses both economic and emotional logics. These two logics are sometimes harmoniously and seamlessly reconciled, but they equally often splinter the romantic sentiment from within. The co-mingling of love and economic calculus at once makes love central to modern lives and is at the heart of the conflicting pressures to which love has been submitted. This intertwining of the emotional and the economic is thus one of the threads through which I offer to reinterpret love in modernity, showing how choice, rationality, interest, competition, have transformed the modes of meeting, seeking, courting a partner, ways of consulting and making decisions about one's sentiments. Another bias of this book is that it addresses the condition of love more markedly from the standpoint of women than of men, and more especially from the standpoint of those women who opt largely for marriage, reproduction, and middle-class lifestyles. As I hope to show here, it is the combination of these aspirations and their location in a free market of sexual encounters which creates new forms of emotional domination of women by men. This means then that although this book is relevant to many women, it is obviously not relevant to all of them (certainly not to lesbians, women who are not interested in domesticity, married or unmarried, or in children).

Love in Modernity, Love as Modernity

The usual suspects explaining the rise of modernity have been scientific knowledge, the printing press, the development of capitalism, secularization, and the influence of democratic ideas. Absent from most accounts is the formation of a reflexive emotional self, one that, as I have argued elsewhere,[15] accompanied the making of modernity and defined itself and its identity in primarily emotional terms, centered on the management and affirmation of its feelings. This book would like to situate the cultural ideal and practice of romantic love within the cultural core of modernity, most conspicuously in its decisive importance for the shaping of biography and for the constitution of the emotional self. As Ute Frevert put it, "[E]motions are not only made by history, they also make history."[16]

Philosopher Gabriel Motzkin offers a way to start thinking about the role of love in the long process of the formation of the modern individual self. According to him, Christian (Paulinian) faith made the emotions of love and hope both visible and central, thus creating an emotional self (rather than, say, an intellectual or political one).[17] Motzkin's argument is that the process of secularization of culture consisted, among other things, in secularizing religious love. Such secularization took two different forms: it made profane love into a sacred sentiment (later celebrated as romantic love), and it made romantic love into an emotion opposed to the restrictions imposed by religion. The secularization of love thus played an important role in the process of emancipation from religious authority.

If one had to give a more precise time frame to these analyses, the Protestant Reformation seems to have been an important stage in the formation of a modern romantic self, for it marked a novel set of tensions between patriarchialism and new emotional expectations regarding the ideal of companionate marriage. "Puritan writers encouraged the formation of new ideals for marital conduct, emphasizing the importance of intimacy and emotional intensity between married couples. Husbands were encouraged to be mindful of their wives' spiritual and psychological welfare."[18]

Numerous scholars, historians, and sociologists have argued that love, especially in Protestant cultures, has been a source of gender equality because it was accompanied by a strong valuation of women.[19] Through the religious injunction to love tenderly one's spouse, women saw an increase in their status and their ability to make decisions on an equal footing with men. Anthony Giddens and others further suggest that love played a central role in the construction of female autonomy, which had its source in the fact that in the eighteenth century the cultural ideal of romantic love, once severed from religious ethics, enjoined women, no less than men, to choose freely the object of their love.[20] In fact, the very idea of love presupposes and constitutes the free will and autonomy of lovers. Motzkin even suggests that "the development of democratic conceptions of authority is a long-range consequence of the presupposition of the emotional autonomy of women."[21] Eighteenth-century sentimental literature and novels further accentuated this cultural tendency because the ideal of love they promoted contributed, in theory and in practice, to unsettle the power which parents – especially fathers – exerted in their daughters' marriages. Thus, the ideal of romantic love was an agent of women's emancipation in one important respect: it was an agent of individualization and autonomy, however circumvoluted such emancipation might have been. Because in the eighteenth and nineteenth centuries the private sphere became highly valued, women could exert what Ann Douglas, using Harriet Beecher Stowe's expression, dubbed "the pink and white tyranny": that is, the drive of "nineteenth century American women to gain power through the exploitation of their feminine identity."[22] Love put women under the tutelage of men, but it did so by legitimizing a model of the self that was private, domestic, individualistic, and, most of all, that demanded emotional autonomy. Romantic love thus reinforced within the private sphere the moral individualism that had accompanied the rise of the public sphere. In fact, love is the paradigmatic example and the very engine of a new model of sociability dubbed by Giddens as that of the "pure relationship,"[23] based on the contractual assumption that two individuals with equal rights unite for emotional and individualistic purposes. It is established by two individuals for its own sake and can be entered and exited at will.

However, while love has played a considerable role in the formation of what historians call "affective individualism," the story of love in modernity tends to present it as a heroic one, from bondage to freedom. When love triumphs, so this story goes, marriages of convenience and interest disappear, and individualism, autonomy, and freedom are triumphant. Nevertheless, while I agree that romantic love challenged both patriarchy and the family institution, the "pure relationship" also rendered the private sphere more volatile and the romantic consciousness unhappy. What makes love such a chronic source of discomfort, disorientation, and even despair, I argue, can be adequately explained only by sociology and by understanding the cultural and institutional core of modernity. This is also why I believe this analysis to be relevant for most countries involved in the formation of modernity, based on equality, contractualism, integration of men and women in the capitalist market, instutionalized "human rights" as the central core of the person: this transcultural institutional matrix, to be found in many countries worldwide, has disrupted and transformed the traditional economic function of marriage and the traditional modes of regulation of sexual relationships. This matrix enables us to reflect on the highly ambivalent normative character of modernity. While my analysis of love in the conditions of modernity is *critical*, it is critical from the standpoint of a *sobered modernist* perspective: that is, a perspective which recognizes that while Western modernity has brought about a vast amount of destruction and misery, its key values (political emancipation, secularism, rationality, individualism, moral pluralism, equality) remain with no superior alternative currently in sight. Yet, endorsing modernity must be a sobered enterprise because this Western cultural form of modernity has brought about its own forms of emotional misery and destruction of traditional life-worlds, has made ontological insecurity a chronic feature of modern lives, and increasingly impinges on the organization of identity and desire.[24]

Why Sociology Is and Remains Necessary

The grandfather of modern psychology, William James, claimed that the first fact for psychologists to consider is that "thinking of some sort goes on," and thinking, he said, is personal: every thought is part of a personal consciousness that leads the individual to choose which experiences of the outside world to deal with or reject.[25] In contrast, from its inception, the main vocation of sociology has been to debunk the *social* basis of belief. For sociologists, there is no opposition between the individual and the social, because the contents of thoughts, desires, and inner conflicts have an institutional and collective basis. For example, when a society and culture promote both the intense passion of romantic love and heterosexual marriage as models for adult life, they shape not only our behavior but also our aspirations, hopes, and dreams for happiness. But social models do more: by juxtaposing the ideal of romantic love with the institution of marriage, modern polities embed social contradictions in our aspirations, contradictions which in turn take a psychological life. The institutional organization of marriage (predicated on monogamy, cohabitation, and the pooling of economic resources together in order to increase wealth) precludes the possibility of maintaining romantic love as an intense and all-consuming passion. Such a contradiction forces agents to perform a significant amount of cultural work in order to manage and reconcile the two competing cultural frames.[26] This juxtaposition of two cultural frames in turn illustrates how the anger, frustration, and disappointment that often inhere in love and marriage have their basis in social and cultural arrangements. While contradictions are an inevitable part of culture, and while people typically move effortlessly in-between them, some are more difficult to manage than others. When contradictions touch upon the very possibility to articulate experience, their smooth integration in everyday life is less easy.

That individuals vary in their interpretations of the same experiences, or that we live social experiences mostly through psychological categories, does not entail that these experiences are private and singular. An experience is always contained and organized by institutions (a sick person in a hospital; an unruly teenager in a school; an angry woman in a family, etc.); and experiences have shapes, intensities, textures, which emanate from the way in which institutions structure emotional life. For example, much of the anger or disappointment in marriage has to do with the way in which marriage structures gender relations and mixes institutional and emotional logics: say, a desire for genderless fusion and equality, and the distance that inevitably emanates from the performance of gender roles. Finally, to be intelligible to oneself and to others, an experience must follow established cultural patterns. A sick person may explain his disease as God's punishment for his past misdeeds, as a biological accident, or as caused by an unconscious death wish; all of these interpretations emerge from and are situated within elaborate explanatory models used and recognizable by historically situated groups of people.

This is not to say that I deny the idea that there are important psychic differences between people, or that these differences do not play an important role in determining our lives. Rather, my objection to the current dominant psychological ethos is three-fold: that what we take to be individual aspiration and experience have in fact much social and collective content to them; that psychic differences are often – though not always – nothing but differences in social positions and social aspirations; and, finally, that the impact of modernity on the formation of the self and identity is precisely to lay bare individuals' psychic attributes and to grant them a crucial role in determining their destinies, both romantic and social. The fact we are psychological entities – that is, that our psychology has so much influence on our destiny – *is itself a sociological fact*. In diminishing the moral resources and the set of social constraints which shaped individuals' maneuvering within their social environment, the structure of modernity exposes individuals to their *own* psychic structure, thus making the psyche both vulnerable and highly operative in social destinies. The vulnerability of the self in modernity can thus be summarized as follows: powerful institutional constraints shape our experiences, yet individuals cope with them with the psychic resources they have amassed in the course of their social trajectory. It is this dual aspect of modern social experiences – ensconced between the institutional and the psychic – that I wish to document in reference to love and love sufferings.

Sociology and Psychic Suffering

From its inception, sociology's main object of study has been collective forms of suffering: inequality, poverty, discrimination, diseases, political oppression, large-scale armed conflicts, and natural disasters have been the main prism through which it has explored the agonies of the human condition. Sociology has been very successful in analyzing these collective forms of suffering, yet has neglected the analysis of the ordinary psychic suffering that inheres in social relationships: resentment, humiliation, and unreciprocated desire are only a few among the many examples of its daily and invisible forms. The discipline has been reluctant to include within its purview emotional suffering – rightly viewed as the mainstay of clinical psychology – lest it be dragged into the murky waters of an individualist and psychic model of society. But if sociology is to remain relevant to modern societies, it must imperatively explore the emotions that reflect the vulnerability of the self in conditions of late modernity, a vulnerability that is at once institutional and emotional. This book contends that love is one such emotion and that a careful analysis of the experiences it generates will take us back to the primary and still much needed and acutely relevant vocation of sociology.

The notion of "social suffering" may seem a welcome means of thinking about the modernity of love suffering. Yet, such a notion is not very useful for my purposes because, as anthropologists understand it, social suffering designates the large-scale visible consequences of famine, poverty, violence, or natural disasters,[27] thus omitting the less visible and less tangible forms of suffering such as anxiety, feelings of worthlessness, or depression, all embedded in ordinary life and ordinary relationships.

Psychic suffering has two cardinal features. First, as Schopenhauer has suggested, suffering derives from the fact that we live through "memory and anticipation."[28] In other words, suffering is mediated through imagination: the images and ideals that make up our memories, expectations, and longings.[29] A more sociological way of saying this is to suggest that suffering is mediated by cultural definitions of selfhood. Second, suffering is characteristically accompanied by a breach in our capacity for sense-making. As a result, Paul Ricoeur says, suffering often takes the form of a lamentation about its blindness and arbitrariness.[30] Because suffering is the irruption of the irrational within everyday life, it demands a rational explanation, an account about desert.[31] In other words, an experience of suffering will be all the more intolerable to the extent that it cannot be made sense of. When suffering cannot be explained, we suffer doubly: from the pain we experience and from our incapacity to bestow meaning on it. Thus any experience of suffering always points us to the systems of explanation that are deployed to account for it. And systems of explanation of suffering differ in the ways in which they make sense of pain. They differ in the ways they allocate responsibility, in the aspects of the experience of suffering they address and stress, and in the ways in which they convert (or not) suffering into another category of experience, be it "redemption," "maturation," "growth," or "wisdom." I would add that *modern* psychic suffering, while it may involve a range of responses, physiological and psychological, is characterized by the fact that the self – its definition and sense of worth – is directly at stake. Psychic suffering contains an experience which threatens the integrity of the self. Suffering in contemporary intimate interpersonal relationships reflects the situation of the self in conditions of modernity. Romantic suffering is not parenthetical to presumably more serious forms of suffering because, as I hope to show, it displays and performs the dilemmas and forms of powerlessness of the self in modernity. As I document by analyzing a variety of sources (in-depth interviews, Internet sites, the *New York Times*' "Modern Love" column, the *Independent*'s sex column, novels of the eighteenth and nineteenth century, self-help books to dating, love, and romance)[32] experiences of abandonment and unreciprocated love are as crucial to one's life narrative as other (political or economic) forms of social humiliation.

Skeptics could rightly claim that poets and philosophers have long been aware of the devastating effects of love and that suffering has been and is still one of the main tropes of love, culminating in the Romantic movement, in which love and suffering mutually reflected and defined each other. Yet, this book claims there is something qualitatively new in the *modern* experience of suffering generated by love. What is properly modern in modern romantic suffering are: the de-regulation of marriage markets (chapter 2); the transformation of the architecture of choice of a mate (chapter 3); the overwhelming importance of love for the constitution of a social sense of worth (chapter 4); the rationalization of passion (chapter 5); and the ways in which the romantic imagination is deployed (chapter 6). But if this book is then about understanding what in romantic suffering is properly new and modern, it does not aim to cover exhaustively the many forms which romantic agony takes, but only some of them; nor does it exclude the fact that many live happy love lives. The claim made here is that both romantic misery and happiness have a specific modern form, and it is to this form that this book wants to pay attention.

2

The Great Transformation of Love or the Emergence of Marriage Markets

"Why do you not come in PERSON to see me?" Dear one, what would people say? I should have but to cross the courtyard for people to begin noticing us, and asking themselves questions. Gossip and scandal would arise, and there would be read into the affair quite another meaning than the real one. No, little angel, it were better I should see you tomorrow at Vespers.

Fyodor Dostoevsky, *Poor Folk*[1]

[I]t was 1951 [...]. What girl found a boy "desirable" at Winesburg College? I for one had never heard of such feelings existing among the girls of Winesburg or Newark or anywhere else. As far as I knew, girls didn't get fired up with desire like that; they got fired up by limits, by prohibitions, by outright taboos, all of which helped to serve what was, after all, the overriding ambition of most of the coeds who were my contemporaries at Winesburg: to reestablish with a reliable young wage earner the very sort of family life from which they had temporarily been separated by this attending college, and to do so as rapidly as possible.

Philip Roth, *Indignation*[2]

Love has long been portrayed as an experience that overwhelms and bypasses the will, as an irresistible force beyond one's control. Yet, in this and the next chapter I make a counter-intuitive claim: one of the most fruitful ways to understand the transformation of love in modernity is through the category of choice. This is not only because to love is to single out one person among other possibilities and thus to constitute one's individuality in the very act of choosing a love object, but also because to love someone is to be confronted with questions of choice: "Is s/he the right one?" "How do I know this person is right for me?" "Won't there be a better person along the way?" These questions pertain both to sentiments and to choice, as a differentiated type of action. To the extent that modern selves are defined by their claim to exercise choice – most glaringly in the two realms of consumption and politics – love can give us important insights into the social basis of choice in modernity.

Choice is the defining cultural hallmark of modernity because, at least in the economic and political arenas, it embodies the exercise not only of freedom, but also of two faculties that justify the exercise of freedom, namely rationality and autonomy. In this sense, choice is one of the most powerful cultural and institutional vectors shaping modern selfhood; it is both a right and a form of competence. If choice is intrinsic to modern individuality, *how* and *why* people choose – or not – to enter a relationship is crucial to understanding love as an experience of modernity.

Economists, psychologists, and even sociologists tend to think of choice as a natural feature of the exercise of rationality, a kind of fixed, invariant property of the mind, defined as the capacity to rate preferences, to act consistently based on these hierarchized preferences, and to make choices by using the most efficient means. Yet, choice is far from being a simple category and is no less shaped by culture than are other features of action. To the extent that choice implies a hierarchy between rational thought and emotions – and among the kind of rational thoughts and emotions which can impel a choice – and to the extent that it presupposes the very capacity for choice, and cognitive mechanisms to organize the process of choice, we may say that it is culturally and socially shaped, a simultaneous property of the environment and of the person's thoughts and beliefs *about* choice.[3]

One of the main transformations undergone by love in modernity has to do with the very conditions within which romantic choices are made. These conditions are of two kinds. One concerns the *ecology of choice*, or the social environment that compels one to make choices in a certain direction. For example, endogamic rules are a very good example of how choice might be constrained within and by a social environment, excluding as potential partners members of the same family or members of different racial or ethnic groups. Alternatively, the sexual revolution transformed the ecology of sexual choice in removing a considerable number of prohibitions on the choice of a sexual partner. The ecology of choice might be the outcome either of an intended and consciously designed policy[4] or of unplanned social dynamics and processes.

But choice has another aspect as well, which I suggest calling the *architecture of choice*.[5] Architecture of choice has to do with mechanisms that are internal to the subject and shaped by culture: they concern both the criteria with which one evaluates an object (piece of art, toothpaste, prospective spouse), and the modes of self-consultation, the ways in which a person consults his or her emotions, knowledge, and formal reasoning to reach a decision. The architecture of choice consists in a number of cognitive and emotional processes, and, more especially, it has to do with the ways in which emotional and rational forms of thinking are valued, conceived of, and monitored in making a decision. A choice can be the outcome of an elaborate process of self-consultation and exposition of alternative courses, or of an "instantaneous" snap decision, but each of these routes has specific cultural pathways, which remain to be elucidated.

Six cultural components of the architecture of choice are most salient. First, does choice include thought about the remote consequences of one's decisions,[6] and if yes, which consequences are thought about and imagined? For example, the increased rate of divorce is likely to have introduced a new perception of the consequences of marriage in the decision to marry. Aversion of risk and anticipation of regret can in turn become culturally salient features of some decisions (e.g., marriage), thereby transforming the process of choice. Conversely, some decisions can be made with or without thinking about the remote consequences of one's actions (e.g., Wall Street's financial wizards before the 2008 crisis probably became far more aware of the perceptions of the consequences of their own choices after the financial collapse). Whether consequences are foregrounded in the process of making the decision, and with what consequences, is thus culturally variable.

Second, how formalized is the process of consultation used to make a decision? For example, does one follow explicit rules or one's intuition? Does one consult an expert (oracle, astrologer, rabbi, priest, psychologist, lawyer, financial consultant) in order to make the decision, or does one follow peer pressure and communal norms? If one consults an expert, what exactly is clarified in a formal process of decision-making: one's "future" (as with an astrologer), the law, one's true unconscious desires, or one's rational self-interests?

Third, what are the modes of self-consultation used to make a decision? One could rely on one's intuitive, habitual knowledge of the world, or alternatively one could conduct a systematic search and evaluation of various courses of action, with or without a mental map of the available options. Or one could make a decision following an epiphanic revelation. For example, modern men and women increasingly introspect about their emotions by using models of psychology to understand the reasons for them. Such processes of self-consultation vary historically and culturally.

Fourth, are there cultural norms and techniques to hold one's desires and wants in suspicion? For example, Christian culture contains a built-in suspicion of one's own (sexual and other) wants and desires, whereas a culture of consumer self-realization, on the contrary, encourages the view of desire as the legitimate grounds for choice. Culturally designed suspicions (or lack of them) are likely to shape the course and outcome of decisions.

Fifth, what are the accepted grounds for making a decision? Are rational or emotional modes of evaluation the legitimate rationales for choice, and in which area of choice are they most likely to be operative? For example, the purchase of a house and the choice of a mate are viewed as differently regulated by rational cognition and emotions. Even if in practice we are a great deal more "emotional" in a real estate market or more "rational" in the marriage market than we would like to acknowledge, cultural models of affectivity and rationality influence the ways in which we make and perceive our decisions.

Finally, is choice as such valued for its own sake? Modern consumer and rights-based culture differs significantly from pre-modern cultures in this respect. Moreover, in, for example, Taiwan as opposed to the United States, commitment to another person in the mate selection process is far more often based on factors that are unrelated to the couple (social norms, social networks, or circumstances).[7] The very category of choice differs profoundly in the two cultures.

What people understand to be their preferences, whether they conceive of them in emotional, psychological, or rational terms, the ways in which they introspect about preferences, are shaped by languages of the self that constitute the architecture of choice.[8] If the cognitive and emotional nuts and bolts that form the architecture of choice vary historically and culturally, then the modern self may be usefully characterized by the conditions and ways in which choices are made. In this and the following chapter, I attempt to characterize the transformations in the ecology and architecture of romantic choice.

Character and the Moral Ecology of Romantic Choice

To understand the *differentia specifica* of modern contemporary love choices, I want to proceed *a contrario* and focus on a cultural prototype that is modern enough to fit the patterns of affective individualism and yet different enough from ours to help make more salient the relevant features of what characterizes our own contemporary romantic practices. In order to undertake such an analysis, I focus on literary texts because they articulate, better than other data, cultural models and ideal-types. In particular, I have chosen the literary world of Jane Austen, notoriously concerned with matrimony, love, and social status.

I use these texts not as actual historical documents of romantic practices, but as cultural testimonies of the assumptions that organized the self, morality, and interpersonal relationships of early to mid-nineteenth-century England. These novels are thus not used as evidence of the historical complexity of Regency matrimonial practices. Nor do I intend to highlight the multi-faceted aspects of Austen's plots and characters, as a conventional literary reading of her novels would undoubtedly prefer to do. My own reductive approach ignores the multi-layered complexity of her texts and prefers to focus on the *system* of cultural assumptions that organize the middle-class matrimonial-romantic practices discussed in the Austenian world. Austen notoriously criticized the rampant self-interest that governed matchmaking, and promoted a view of matrimony based on affection, mutual respect, and sentiments (albeit grounded in socially accepted norms). But her texts are interesting precisely because they offer a conscious reflection on class-regulated matrimony and on emotional individual choice, because they offer a form of "compromise" between these two forms of action, and because they offer a good point of entry to understand the cultural system within which early to mid-nineteenth-century English romantic feelings were organized: that is, the rituals, the social rules, and the institutions which constrained the expression and experience of sentiments.

To the extent that literary texts contain systematically encoded cultural assumptions – about selfhood, morality, or rituals of conduct – they can help us construct cultural models alternative to ours – what sociologists call ideal-types – which by way of contrast may help us probe an analysis of our own romantic practices. In drawing parallels between Austen's cultural model and the actual courtship practices of the nineteenth-century middle and upper-middle classes, I hope to understand some elements of the modern social organization of matrimony. In the same way that painters use bright background colors to throw into sharper relief the objects at the forefront of their painting, the Austenian world is used here as a colored canvas to better expose the social organization and underlying structure of pairing in modern contemporary romantic practices. The following analysis thus highlights structural tendencies and changing cultural patterns rather than fine-grained analysis of particular cases.

The Love of Character, the Character of Love

In her masterpiece *Emma* (1816), Jane Austen explains the nature of Mr Knightley's love for Emma:

> She [Emma] had often been negligent or perverse, slighting his [Knightley's] advice, or even wilfully opposing him, insensible of half his merits, and quarrelling with him because he would not acknowledge her false and insolent estimate of her own – but still, from family attachment and habit, and thorough excellence of mind, he had loved her, and watched over her from a girl, with an endeavour to improve her, and an anxiety for her doing right, which no other creature had at all shared.[9]

The vision of love outlined here emanates directly from what nineteenth-century men and women called "character." In contradistinction to a long Western tradition that presents love as an emotion that overtakes one's capacity to judge and that idealizes the object of love to the point of blindness, love is here solidly anchored in Knightley's capacity for discernment. This is why Emma's faults are no less emphasized than her virtues. The only person who loves Emma is also the only one to see her faults. To love someone *is* to look at them with wide-opened and knowing eyes. And, contrary to what we would expect today, such capacity for discernment (and awareness of another's flaws) does not entail any ambivalent feeling toward Emma. On the contrary, Knightley's own excellence of character makes him forgive her faults, discern (what will later prove to be) her own "excellence of mind,"[10] and strive to improve her character with fervor and even passion. Understanding Emma's faults is not incompatible with being thoroughly committed to her because both emanate from the same moral source. Knightley's love itself is supremely moral not only because he makes the object of his love accountable to a moral code, but also because to love Emma is intertwined with the moral project of shaping her mind. When he looks at her anxiously, it is not lust that burns in him, but rather his desire to see her do the right thing. In this particular conception of love, it is not the unique originality of the person that we love, but rather the person's capacity to stand for those values we – and others – revere. More interestingly: far from feeling humiliated or diminished by Knightley's rebukes, Emma accepts them. In fact, we may speculate that she respects and loves Knightley precisely because he is the only one to hold her accountable to a moral code that transcends them both. So committed to this moral code is Emma that she accepts what we would call today the narcissistic wounds inflicted by Knightley and his challenge to her good opinion of her self, in the name of a definition of virtue that she shares with him. To be loved by Knightley is to be challenged by him and to rise to the challenge of upholding his and her own moral standards. To love another is to love the good in him and through him. Indeed, "[i]n the Christian and Hebrew traditions [...] character (or 'excellence' of character) was defined as a consistency of virtue and moral purpose in guiding one toward a good life,"[11] and this consistency was expected in all matters, including matters of the heart. Unlike the conception that had come to prevail since the seventeenth century (in France most noticeably), the heart here is not a realm of its own, unintelligible and unaccountable to reason and to morality. It is instead tightly intertwined with and regulated by them. Finally, this is a love that grows out of "attachment and habit," a far cry from the instantaneous attraction that characterizes love at first sight. Love is experienced not as a rupture or a breach in one's existence. Rather, it develops with time, familiarity, knowledge of and tight entanglement with each other's family and everyday life. So close is the familiarity that from the standpoint of modern sensibility there is something vaguely incestuous in Knightley's "watching [Emma] from a girl." It is a love in which one is already incorporated in one's daily life and family and in which one has many opportunities to observe, know, and test another's character through time. As James Hunter put it, "Character [...] resists expedience."[12] The metaphor Kierkegaard uses to speak of character is that of being engraved in the person.[13] Because it depends on character, love is not here an irruptive event but rather a cumulative one, inscribed in the *longue durée*.

A contemporary interpretation of such love might perhaps indict Knightley's feelings for Emma for being paternalistic and controlling and would view "character" or "virtue" as code words for patriarchal control of women. But such an interpretation would have to ignore Austen's heroines' uncanny *souveraineté* in matters of the heart. Such *souveraineté* is a recurrent feature of Austen's women, and the key to deciphering it is to be found in the deep cultural assumptions that organize these women's selfhood. Why does Elizabeth Bennet, the heroine of *Pride and Prejudice* (1813), greet Darcy's arrogant and dismissive comments about her appearance ("she is tolerable; but not handsome enough to tempt *me*..."[14]) neither with dejection nor with a sense of humiliation but rather with wit and spirit? Because his scorn does not shape or affect her sense of self and value. Although Darcy is by far the most attractive marriage prospect available in her immediate environment, Elizabeth remains utterly in control of her feelings, allowing them to be expressed only when he conforms to *her* vision and definition of love.

Anne Elliot, the main protagonist of *Persuasion* (1818), finds out that Captain Wentworth, who has not seen her for nine years, thinks her beauty is lost. Anne is still in love with Wentworth, but instead of being devastated, as we would expect, she "began to rejoice that she had heard [these words]. They were of sobering tendency; they allayed agitation; they composed, and consequently must make her happier."[15] It is difficult to think of a reaction more self-possessed than rejoicing in the fact that the man one is in love with finds one less attractive.

Or, to take a final example, Elinor Dashwood – the heroine of *Sense and Sensibility* (1811) – is in love with Edward Farrars. Only after falling in love with him does she discover that he is secretly engaged to another woman, Lucy. When later she is told that Edward has not broken his engagement to Lucy (which means he is about to marry her), she rejoices in *his* moral glory because breaking his promises to another would have made him morally unworthy. Clearly, Elinor's allegiance to her moral principles has precedence over her love for Edward, in the same way that his engagement to Lucy must take precedence over his feelings for Elinor. Characters such as Knightley, Wentworth, and Anne Elliot do not conduct themselves as if there was a conflict between their sense of moral duty and their passion. There is indeed no such conflict in their behavior, "because the whole personality is integrated."[16] It is, in other words, impossible to separate the moral from the emotional, because it is the moral dimension that organizes emotional life, which thus has also here a public dimension.

From the standpoint of modern sensibility, Jane Austen's heroines are not only uncannily self-possessed but also strangely detached from the need to be, as we would say in modern parlance, "validated" by their suitors. Consider, for example, how Anne reacts to Wentworth's evaluation of her lost beauty. To that extent, their selfhood seems to be less dependent on a man's gaze than is the selfhood of modern women (see chapter 4). Given the state of legal dependency and disenfranchisement of women at that time, this may seem surprising. One easy answer to this puzzling fact may be offered: it lies precisely in their character – that is, in their capacity to mold their inner and outer self to a moral purpose that transcends both their desires and their interests. Their sense of inner self and value is not bestowed on them by anyone, but rather derives from their capacity to recognize and enact moral imperatives that have a quasi-objective existence. In this view, inner value derives precisely from the capacity to bracket their own personal desires and to see their moral principles impeccably enacted, whether by themselves or by others, in love and in other matters. In a sense, then, "character" consists precisely in the coincidence of desire and moral purpose. Character is thus a sort of objectified and externalized version of the values held by the group. It does not rest on an essential, ontological definition of the self, but is rather performative: it must be by definition visible, so that others can witness it and approve of it; it consists not in a unique psychological make-up and feelings (or at least not essentially so) but in acts; it is not about uniqueness and originality of the self but rather about the capacity to display publicly recognizable and tested virtues. Character is thus less about interiority than about the capacity to bridge between the self and the public world of values and norms. It requires that the self depend on reputation and honor regulated by public rules of conduct – and not so much on the private emotional "validation" bestowed by one particular individual. In the context of love and courtship, character designates the fact that both lovers derive their personal sense of value directly from their capacity to enact moral codes and ideals, rather than from the value bestowed on their inner self by a suitor. A woman's value seems to be established quite independently from the value her suitor bestows on her (or not). In this moral economy, both the suitor and the woman know who they are, what their social and moral worth is; and it is from this knowledge that their mutual love is established (see chapter 4 for a useful contrast). They may, obviously, differentiate between similar options through attraction, liking, or love. But choice occurs by conforming to pre-existing moral codes, social rules, and it is from their capacity to enact these codes successfully that actors derive a sense of value. In this sense, the value they bestow on each other is, if not entirely objective, at least grounded in objective anchors.

But the suggestion that these women's selves are explained by their character only invites a further question: what enables such separation of inner value and the courtship process?[17] It is tautological to claim, as some philosophers and communitarian sociologists do, that this is what character consists of. The assertion that character reflects the dispositions of persons, and that it consists in the capacity to have a self-generated sense of value, only raises the still further question of just *how* it does that. Against the somewhat naïve view that character consists of inner dispositions that in turn explain the capacity to adhere to publicly shared moral codes, I suggest that the capacity to derive a sense of value from moral codes, and the display of moral character, are both made possible by a series of *social*, not psychological or moral, mechanisms. Character is not simply a set of inner dispositions and habits of the mind that result from the straightforward internalization of moral norms. Rather, character, even of the moral variety, reflects and is made possible by the deployment of specific social arrangements in the person and more particularly by the ways in which emotions are integrated in an overarching ecology of choice. While a philosopher or historian might be content with the observation that love is intertwined with moral frameworks, for a sociologist it is precisely that fact that needs to be explained. *How* are love and morality intertwined with each other: that is, which social mechanisms make possible the harnessing of love to a moral project of the self? I argue that what we call a moral self and sentiments consist in a specific *ecology and architecture of choice*, in which there is a high degree of congruence between private and public choices, and in which private emotions radiate from a self as a public unit. While Austen's characters had, of course, a great deal of interiority, such interiority differs from ours in that it strove to congruence with a public world of rituals and roles. Which social mechanisms enable such congruence remains to be specified.

Courtship as a Social Web

Like other Austen novels, *Emma* shows courtship to be a process conducted within the framework of one's kin and neighbors. The point here is not that such supervision exerted control and constrained choices, although it obviously also did that. Rather, the point is that it made courtship into an activity in which the woman's self was naturally enmeshed within and protected by her social network and kin. In the courtship process described by Austen (and many other novelists), it is not so much the woman who is observed and scrutinized as the man. The man conducts his courtship under the watchful eyes of others and thus comes to the woman "mediated" by a variety of social relationships. As literary critic James Wood observes, in *Sense and Sensibility* we are told that Elinor "was resolved not only upon gaining every new light as to his [Willoughby's] character which her own observation or the intelligence of others could give her, but likewise upon watching his behaviour to her sister."[18] To know a man was often to know him through the eyes of others. Mollie Dorsey Sanford, who resided on the frontier in Colorado, wrote in her diary in 1860: "Grandma has taken it into her dear old head that he is my lover, and [...] I believe he is myself. I knew today when he came, and I had not seen him for so long, that I cared a great deal for him."[19] Her love is a revelation to her as mediated by her grandmother; and such revelation derives from the fact that he has become a part of her daily life and of her relationships with her family. Such intimate knowledge of a prospective spouse was necessary to gain confidence about the social and psychological compatibility of two people. For example, in *Persuasion* Anne Elliot is heavily influenced by Lady Russell, who deems her first true (and only) love, Captain Wentworth, inappropriate. Our modern sensibility can only relate to the fact that her negative evaluation of Wentworth forced Anne to renounce the object of her love. But from another perspective, Lady Russell's mistake derived from the fact that Anne's self was tightly protected because it was embedded in kin relationships. It is true that Austen shows the limits of this system by suggesting that Anne's social milieu is unable to distinguish social status from inner value. Yet, Anne and the reader can gain such confidence in their judgment of Wentworth only because they have had many opportunities to verify this. Indeed, courtship, both in England and in the United States, often entailed a process of verification of the claims and credentials of suitors. "[Courtship] was a game filled with deceit, superficial trickery and blandishments. Yet it was necessary to uncover the frauds and to make sure the 'other' was indeed the person who through the long years would remain one's closest friend."[20]

This careful monitoring of men is illustrated by the practices of prospective in-laws checking suitors' reputations. For example, before he could court and propose to Olivia Langdon, Samuel Clemens (later Mark Twain) had to submit letters of recommendation about him to the family, at their request. After the process was completed, Clemens could say about himself,

> I think all my references can say I never did anything mean, false, or criminal. They can say that the same doors that were open to me seven years ago are open to me yet; that *all* the friends I made in seven years, are still my friends; that wherever I have been I can go again – & enter in the light of day & hold my head up.[21]

This example illustrates the fact that during courtship the woman's self was solidly "encased" in her close relationships, and that these played an active role in the process of evaluating the suitor and forging a bond with him. Because several people participated in the social task of evaluating and judging a suitor and potential husband, the woman's opinion was a reflection and extension of her social network. A woman's sentiments for a man were activated along with the opinion that others expressed about him. The intertwining of sentiment and judgment, of individual feelings and collective observation, implies that when loving someone and ultimately making a decision about a prospective spouse, one was incessantly immersed in the moral universe of norms and taboos of the group and that one's romantic involvement was entangled with the web of one's commitment to others. The lovers' selves – that of the man and the woman – were contained in and protected by the thick presence of others who acted as arbiters and enforcers of moral and social norms.[22] This state of affairs was prevalent well until the nineteenth century.

Acknowledged, Unacknowledged Rules

Courtship in the Austenian world is structured by myriad invisible rules. Non-sociologists tend to think of rules as limiting. But for sociologists, rules are also enabling, the medium through which actors relate to each other, build expectations about each other, and trudge well-known paths with each other.[23] Rituals – a set of rules known to actors in order to engage in or disengage from relationships – are similar to a well-drawn pathway in a jungle of possibilities. They create expectations about what can and should happen next.[24] To put it differently, rituals are a powerful symbolic tool to ward off anxieties created by uncertainty. Thus, in the nineteenth century among the propertied classes, there were, if not scrupulously observed rules, at least codes and rituals of conduct that organized encounters and that needed to be respected in order for men and women to be proved worthy of each other. In this romantic order, actors derive a sense of propriety from the rules of conduct they observe.

Calling was such a ritual. It took place at the girl's home (when she was still young enough to be called a "girl"), which therefore made it inappropriate for a man to take the initiative in calling. A man could show a girl that he liked her, but it was the girl's "privilege" to ask a man to call.[25] The middle-class practice of calling on a woman gave the parents and the woman herself control over the courtship process,[26] and this control was not contested. Similarly, if a gentleman was introduced to a lady at a party for the purpose for dancing, he could not automatically resume their acquaintance on the street. He had to be re-introduced by a mutual friend and be permitted by the woman to resume contact. More crucially for my argument, once the courtship was conducted, it advanced by subtle gradations, with couples first speaking, then walking out together, and finally keeping company once their mutual attraction had been confirmed. In other words, emotional involvement was carefully monitored, as it had to follow well-known ritual sequences.

In this ritualized romantic order, emotions followed actions and declarations (or were closely concomitant), but were not strictly speaking the precondition for them. I call this organization of emotions a *regime of performativity of emotions*: that is, a regime in which emotions are induced by the ritualized actions and expressions of sentiments. In a way, our emotions are always induced by those of others.[27] But the romantic interaction poses a different problem because the question of reciprocity is crucial in it, and because in exposing one's sentiments, one runs the risk of seeing those sentiments unreciprocated. In a performative (i.e., ritualized) regime of emotions, one not only reveals but also comes to feel sentiments after the performance of rituals of conduct and the decoding of their meaning. It is thus an incremental process, often induced by another's use of appropriate signs and codes of love. It is the result of a subtle exchange of signs and signals shared by two people. In such a regime, one of the two parties took on the social role of inducing the emotions of the other, and this role fell on the man. In a performative regime of emotions, the woman was not and perhaps could not be overwhelmed by the object of love; courtship followed rules of engagement such that the woman was drawn in a close and intense bond progressively. She responded to signs of emotions whose patterns of expression were well rehearsed.

Studying courtship practices during the nineteenth century, historian Ellen Rothman quotes Eliza Southgate writing that "no woman suffers herself to think she could love any one before she has discovered an affection for her." Rothman continues: "A woman would wait to be sure that her feelings were reciprocated before admitting them even to herself."[28] The fact that love was highly ritualized protected women from the realm of emotions, which could overwhelm them. In fact, the whole novel *Sense and Sensibility* is precisely about the question of the *gradation* with which one ought to proceed in the affairs of the heart. Elinor is not the preacher of reason against passion; rather, she embodies and defends the ritualized version of love, in which intense feelings are disclosed and expressed only after they have followed a proper sequencing of attraction, courtship, and commitment. In the ritualized version of love, emotion confirms commitment as much as commitment confirms emotion. That is, although questions about sincerity and true feelings are obviously present in a performative/ritualized romantic order, they are often superseded by a concern with the right sequencing of emotions: "Once a man had gotten sufficient encouragement from the girl he was courting, it was considered proper for him to ask for the father's consent before he made a proposal. [...] [T]he woman was to wait for the man to declare his love before she revealed her true feelings."[29]

This regime is in contrast with a *regime of emotional authenticity*, which pervades modern relationships. Authenticity demands that actors know their feelings; that they act on such feelings, which must then be the actual building blocks of a relationship; that people reveal their feelings to themselves (and preferably to others as well); and that they make decisions about relationships and commit themselves based on these feelings. A regime of emotional authenticity makes people scrutinize their own and another's emotions in order to decide on the importance, intensity, and future significance of the relationship. "Do I *really* love him, or is it just lust?" "If I love him, how deep, intense, and real is my love?" "Is this love healthy or narcissistic?" These are questions that belong to a regime of authenticity. In contrast, in traditional societies, "authenticity has no place in the vocabulary of human ideals. Here men are satisfied with the life options which their social system provides for them: they conceive of their highest good [...] as 'the fulfillment of a determinate social function.'"[30] Authenticity presumes there is a real (emotional) ontology that precedes and exists beyond the rules by which the expression and experience of feelings in general and love in particular are organized and channeled. In the regime of authenticity, commitment does not precede but rather follows emotions that are felt by the subject and that become the alternate motivation for the commitment. A regime of authenticity thus demands two possible courses for the subject to gain certainty about his or her feelings: either through a great deal of self-scrutiny as the question of the nature and "true" causes of emotions becomes crucial to the subject; or, conversely, through an overwhelming revelation that imposes itself by its intensity ("love at first sight," for example). Self-scrutiny presupposes that reflexive self-understanding will help to understand the "true nature" of our emotions; the epiphanic mode presupposes that the intensity and irrationality of one's feelings are an adequate indication of one's true feelings. These two modes to ascertain the authenticity of one's romantic feelings coexist side by side in contemporary culture and, when followed, result in a romantic bond that is dependent less on ritual rules than on emotional interiority.

Semiotic Consistency

Central to the performative regime of emotions is the crucial social rule that one's actions converge with one's intentions. For example, an 1879 etiquette manual offered these instructions:

A gentleman's conduct toward Ladies. Gentlemen are at liberty to invite their lady friends to concerts, operas, balls, etc., to call upon them at their homes, to ride and drive with them, and make themselves agreeable to all young ladies to whom their company is acceptable. In fact, they are at liberty to accept invitations and give them ad libitum. As soon, however, as a young gentleman neglects all others, to devote himself to a single lady, he gives that lady reason to suppose that he is particularly attracted to her, and may give her cause to believe that she is to become engaged to him, without telling her so. A gentleman who does not contemplate matrimony should not pay too exclusive attention to any one lady.[31]

This moral order was essentially underpinned by a semiotic order in which actors had to make their actions reflect not only their emotions but also their intentions. As *Sense and Sensibility* illustrates amply, incongruence between words and actions, on the one hand, and intentions, on the other, was deemed to be a source of moral and social wreckage (the problem of Willoughby is not his lack of emotions, as he loved Marianne, but rather the fact that his behavior did not *signal* his actual intentions). A morally adequate suitor strove for maximum consistency between outer actions and inner intentions. To take another example of the ways in which morally praiseworthy characters strove for such congruence: in *Persuasion*, thinking himself unloved by Anne, Wentworth courts Louisa. Yet, as the plot progresses, the reader and Wentworth himself come to understand that he still loves Anne and wants to remain faithful to her. But because his behavior had given the appearances of courting Louisa, he feels compelled to leave the city in which he had temporarily taken residence. "He found too late, in short, that he had entangled himself; and that precisely as he became fully satisfied of his not caring for Louisa at all, he must regard himself as bound to her, if her sentiments for him were what the Harvilles supposed."[32] Because courtship is here so well codified, and because the signifiers he used do not correspond to his feelings, Wentworth, having courted someone without following suit, knows that he has committed a dishonorable act. Such codes were taken very seriously, especially among the English gentry. Unsurprisingly, these codes had crossed the Atlantic.

In his analysis of courtship practices among Boston's elite, Timothy Kenslea discusses the "friendlies," a group of young women who thought and talked a great deal about courtship practices. In this group, "a premature gesture or expression, or even an inappropriate tone of voice, could be read as a pledge of commitment where none was intended."[33]

The minute codification of love rituals had one main effect: to deflect or diminish uncertainty by binding the realm of emotions tightly to a clear system of signs. Emotions both fed the signs and were fed by them, in the sense that the adequate production of signs generated emotions, both in the performer of ritual and in the receiver, and vice versa. Such minute codification and ritualization of signs of feelings is likely to have created a closely regulated emotional dynamic of incremental reciprocity: that is, a subtle gradation of expressions of feelings, which in turn generated further feelings and further ritual expression of feelings, in another and in oneself.

Interest as Passion

Pre-modern courtship was taken very seriously because it was the most significant economic operation of many people's lives, especially as a woman's property went to her husband upon marriage. This had three important implications.

First, whatever emotions one had were organized within a broad frame of social and economic interest. A commonly received view, both within and outside sociology, holds that acting on one's interests is inimical to passion. In contrast, I argue that, far from being incompatible with passion, interests actually provide the impetus activating and maintaining it. As economist Robert Frank suggests, emotions play a crucial role in signaling our commitment to our interests and to carrying out appropriate actions to defend these interests. "[P]assions often serve our interests very well indeed," he writes.[34] What made Austenian emotions particularly intense was *precisely* the fact they were solidly anchored in reason and interest, which in turn acted as powerful catalysts of emotions. This remark can be generalized to other classes: because marriage was crucial to economic survival, it generated emotional structures of commitment. This is an order in which passions and interests, while held in theory to be separate, can mutually reinforce each other: contempt (of Darcy's variety, for example) or love (of Emma and Knightley's variety, for example) served as a tool for maintaining class endogamy.

The second implication of the anchoring of marriage in economic interest was that a marriage offer was often rejected or accepted because of social position or fortune. Among the popular and middle classes in the seventeenth, eighteenth, and nineteenth centuries, "[p]arents typically rejected prospective husbands because they were not rich enough."[35] If in Austen's courtship system, the self – as the repository of one's identity and value – is less vulnerable than the modern self, it is because it is *a priori ranked*, to use the terminology of the French anthropologist Louis Dumont.[36] In fact, the characters whom Austen presents as devoid of a sense of social place are characters who repeatedly suffer humiliations and border on the ridiculous or the immoral (e.g., Harriet Smith in *Emma*, or William Elliot in *Persuasion*). In the romantic order Austen describes, the romantically successful are those who know their social place and do not aspire to reach above that place, or to go beneath it. In other words, because the criteria to rank people were known and shared and because the decision to marry was explicitly based (at least partially) on social class, being rejected as a marriage prospect did not hinge on the inner essence of the self, only on its position. When Austen herself was asked not to meet again with Tom Lefroy, by whom she was courted and of whom she was obviously fond, she accepted the verdict without any protest, because she knew both of them lacked money. When the philosopher Thomas Carlyle's proposal was politely rejected at first by Jane Welsh, he could – and in fact did – impute her rejection to his precarious financial prospects, not to his personality or attractiveness. In contrast, when the self becomes essentialized,[37] when love is defined as addressing the innermost essence of the person, not his/her class and position, love becomes a direct bestowal of value on the person, and a rejection becomes a rejection of the self (see chapter 4).

Finally, in pre-modern courtship the prevalence of economic considerations also means that the modes of evaluation were more "objective" – that is, they relied on the prospective partner's (more or less) objective status and ranking, as it was known and accepted by his or her social environment. Thus, a woman's dowry determined her value in a marriage market. "The dowry was the most significant factor in a young woman's marriageability and, hence, in affecting her future."[38] The dowry played a key role in bestowing status and forging alliances. "The size of the dowry indicated a bride's social and economic standing."[39] In most cases, even women who did not have direct control over their dowries "could claim them in case of separation or divorce," a fact that, according to Marion Kaplan, may have inhibited "male whim and protected women."[40] The fact that dowries played an important role in mate selection meant that female marriageability was based on "objective" criteria: that is, criteria independent of one's unique sense of self. Emma, Jane Austen's heroine, who tries to match her friend Harriet Smith to the vicar Elton, a social climber, is guilty not of having misjudged Harriet's looks or character, but rather of having misjudged her *objective* compatibility with Elton's ambition to move upward. Emma's failure is to not use objective criteria to evaluate compatibility, thus suggesting that Austen's romantic courtship is solidly organized in the framework of class endogamy. The use of objective criteria hence anchored a private choice in a public order of ranks and worth. In that sense, evaluating the social appropriateness of a partner was a public act of evaluation, not a private one. The uncertainty that always lurks behind evaluation was assuaged by the fact such evaluation was the work of many people and was grounded on well-known criteria (see chapter 5 for a further elaboration of these criteria).[41]

Reputation and Promise-Keeping

At the center of this moral, semiotic, and economic system was promise-keeping. Because most people had typically few choices to marry someone in a lifetime, and because undoing a match could have severe consequences, reputation was a central tool for mate selection. The capacity to keep promises was a central component of such reputation. To the extent that promises bind one's self-interest to that of another – to recall Hume's claim[42] – promise-keeping functioned as a mechanism that made people settle for the first "good enough" choice. In fact, the variety of unpalatable characters in Jane Austen all have one thing in common: they all break their promises in order to improve and maximize their marriage prospects. Isabella Thorpe in *Northanger Abbey* (1818) and Lucy and Willoughby in *Sense and Sensibility* are all characterized by their inability to keep their promises, itself the result of their desire to maximize their self-interest through marriage. This is congruent with Steven Shapin's description of the moral order of the English gentleman in the seventeenth and eighteenth centuries as being characterized by his capacity to keep his word and be truthful.[43]

In the Austenian world, to break a promise is a serious infringement upon one's reputation and honor, both men's and women's. The most glaring Austenian example is that of Anne Elliot in *Persuasion*, who, prior to the beginning of the action of the novel, had been engaged to Captain Wentworth but, as we have seen, he was thought to be unsuitable by her friend and protector, Lady Russell, thereby breaking her engagement to him. Anne now gets the attentions of her rich and noble cousin, William. This is how she reacts: "How she might have felt, had there been no Captain Wentworth in the case, was not worth enquiry; for there was a Captain Wentworth: and be the conclusion of the present suspense good or bad, her affection would be his for ever. Their union, she believed, could not divide her more from other men, than their final separation."[44] This is a manifesto against utility-seeking and utility-maximizing behavior in the realm of sentiments, calling on men and women to keep their promises regardless of whatever better financial prospect may have appeared on the way. Wentworth is the masculine counterpart of Anne's loyalty and constancy. Indeed, consistent with Anne's behavior and sentiments, we learn that

> [s]he [Anne] had never been supplanted. He never even believed himself to see her equal. Thus, much indeed he was obliged to acknowledge – that he had been constant unconsciously, nay unintentionally; that he had meant to forget her, and believed it to be done. He had imagined himself indifferent, but he had only been angry; and he had been unjust to her merits, because he had been a sufferer from them. Her character was now fixed on his mind as perfection itself, maintaining the loveliest medium of fortitude and gentleness.[45]

Or to give a final example of how prevalent this code of promise-keeping was until well into the early decades of the twentieth century: when Charity Royall, the heroine of Edith Wharton's *Summer* (1917), discovers that the man she is in love with, Harney, and whom she hoped to marry, is actually engaged to Annabel Balch, she writes to him: "I want you should marry Annabel Balch if you promised to. I think maybe you were afraid I'd feel too bad about it. I feel I'd rather you acted right. Your loving CHARITY."[46] Here again the woman prefers to forgo her own love and future happiness for the sake of keeping intact the man's promise, because promise-keeping is the ultimate mark of character and fundamental to the moral and social order.

At the heart of promise-keeping lies an important assumption about the capacity of the self to display temporal continuity. Thus, Samuel Clemens, writing to Jervis Langdon, Olivia's father, declared: "It is my desire as truly as yours that sufficient time shall elapse to show you, beyond all possible question, what *I have been, what I am*, and what I am *likely to be*. Otherwise you could not be satisfied with me, nor I with myself."[47] Clemens is obviously trying here to display and prove his character, precisely by displaying the temporal continuity of his self, its capacity to be in the future what he already is (or an improved version of it). Character proves itself by constancy and by the capacity to unite within the center of volition who one was, who one is, and who one will be.

In the Austenian world, such constancy proves itself by the almost ostentatious way in which characters pass up "better" opportunities, preferring instead their earlier and more modest objects of commitment. As a mechanism that stopped the search for a partner and the desire to maximize one's interests, promise-keeping was at the foundation of commitment. Obviously, in practice, some did not honor their engagements, as witnessed by the fact that, for example, the nineteenth century in England witnessed breaches of promise of marriage,[48] which were adjudicated by courts. However, that these breaches of promise were prosecuted is in itself proof of how seriously they were viewed. They were, moreover, relatively rare because a man's or a woman's reputation was crucially dependent on how he or she behaved in matters of matrimony. A breach of matrimonial promise was considered such a severe infraction of the moral order that in Anthony Trollope's *Doctor Thorne* (1858), when Henry Thorne abandons Mary Scatcherd after he seduced and promised to marry her, he is killed by Mary's brother. When the brother is arraigned, Trollope/the narrator muses ironically: "[H]e was found guilty of manslaughter, and sentenced to be imprisoned for six months. Our readers will probably think that the punishment was too severe."[49] Such social order connected between emotions, moral self, and time in a single axis.

Roles and Commitment

In Edith Wharton's celebrated book *The Age of Innocence* (1920), the hero, Newland Archer, decides to forgo his intense passion for Ellen Olenska and to respect his previous commitment to marry May Welland. This is thus how he views his prospective marriage with a woman who corresponds to the morality of his class:

> [H]e had long since discovered that May's only use of the liberty she supposed herself to possess would be to lay it on the altar of her wifely adoration. [...] [W]ith a conception of marriage so uncomplicated and incurious as hers such a crisis could be brought about only by something visibly outrageous in his own conduct; and the fineness of her feeling for him made that unthinkable. *Whatever happened, he knew, she would always be loyal, gallant and un-resentful; and that pledged him to the practice of the same virtues.* (emphasis added)[50]

The drama that unfolds throughout the novel stages an opposition between Archer's commitment to marry May and his private, anti-institutional desire to live his passion for Ellen. In this model of matrimony, sentiments located in the interiority of the person are not the legitimation, or at least not the only legitimation, of marriage. Rather, sentiments are experienced through well-known roles and through one's capacity to play these roles consistently throughout one's life. Moreover, what will decide the value and quality of this marriage is not whether each character will express in it his or her authentic self and realize his or her own buried interiority. A good marriage consisted in the capacity to play one's role successfully, namely to feel and display the emotions attendant to the role. The overall cultural and moral frame guiding this enactment of roles was the imperative of commitment, the capacity to uphold one's promises to another, to play one's social role, to feel the (real) emotions attendant to it.

Commitment was thus a moral structure that guided emotions both before and during marriage and made actors dwell on their interiority through the question of what they ought to do. This does not mean that people had no interiority or emotions, but rather that such interiority was deontologically structured, determined by what they should do and who they ought to be. For example, the same Mollie Dorsey Sanford who resided at the frontier where she went for the sake of her husband wrote in 1860 in her diary (from Colorado): "I am ashamed to be so homesick. Of course I do not *say* all that I inscribe here. [...] I try to be cheerful for By's [her husband's] sake, for fear he might think I wasn't happy with him. He hasn't the family ties that I have and cannot understand."[51] What makes these short lines foreign to our modern sensibility is the fact that they are motivated not by what we would call her authentic self but by her commitment to her role as a wife. Indeed, it is highly unlikely a modern young woman would be ashamed of being homesick. Mollie's shame here comes essentially from her sense of not living up to her *role* as a wife. Undoubtedly, this is an example of the way in which "the traditional Victorian division of labor and authority between husbands and wives remained the backbone of marriage from the Atlantic to the Pacific."[52] A modern woman's feelings would, on the contrary, be profusely acknowledged and would take precedence over her role. More than that: in modern definitions of marriage, the husband is expected to actively take notice of such feelings and support them: that is, to pay attention to them, to acknowledge them, and to accept their validity. Modern intimacy includes verbal disclosure of emotions, but also and maybe even more crucially the act of sharing such emotions with a partner, with an expectation that the emotional self be revealed and laid bare, in order to get "support" and recognition. Thus, another noticeable difference with modern sensibility is that this woman does not think it proper to communicate her inner authentic feelings. On the contrary, to be adequate is to be able to hide these feelings and to disguise them under an appearance of cheerfulness. Being able to play her role convincingly consists in helping her husband play his own role, and it is from this that she derives a sense of fulfillment and adequacy. Furthermore, it is likely that this woman is not even trying to understand and express her true feelings. She is more concerned by the fact that in expressing her negative feelings, she might make her husband feel inadequate in his capacity to make her happy. In other words, she views it as *her* responsibility to maintain his own sense of adequacy, defined as his capacity to make her happy. Finally, and perhaps most interestingly, we may notice how she states in a neutral way that he cannot understand her. In fact, she invokes this as a way to explain and excuse the fact that he cannot be made a part of her private distress. This is in stark contrast with the way in which modern men but especially women expect to reveal their intimate self and to intertwine it with that of their partner. Pre-modern conjugal relations presuppose intricately connected selves, but in this interconnectedness the self is neither naked nor authentic. The two selves displayed here are, by modern standards, emotionally distant (they do not let each other peek at the content of their thoughts and emotions); yet, they are inextricably intertwined and interdependent. In contrast, modern selves expect each other to be emotionally naked and intimate, but independent. In a modern marriage, it is two highly individuated and differentiated selves that come together;[53] it is the fine-tuned compatibility of two constituted selves that makes up a successful marriage, not the display of roles. The fine-tuning of the emotional makeup of two persons becomes the basis for intimacy.

To further understand the nature of commitment, we may use Amartya Sen's interesting distinction between sympathy and commitment. If I am deeply disturbed by the idea of others being tortured, writes Sen, this is a case of sympathy. If, on the other hand, this idea does not make me personally uncomfortable or distressed, but still makes me think there is something deeply wrong with it, it is a case of commitment. An action based on commitment is thus truly non-egoistic in the literal and non-moral sense that it does not affect the very center of the self, the core from which it radiates.[54] Following such definition, commitment is not primarily or chiefly motivated by individualized sentiments. A similar difference characterizes commitment-based marriage and one based on emotional authenticity. The latter is based on the attempt to reconcile and harmonize two independent emotional selves and must continuously create and re-create the emotional conditions and reasons for coming together in the first place. Commitment, by contrast, does not radiate from the individualized emotional self and does not aim at satisfying ongoing emotional aspirations. Emotions are the effects of social roles and not their *a priori* preconditions.

Thus, the "character" and commitment that regulated courtship and matrimonial practices should be viewed neither as psychological properties of actors, nor as the sign of a more moral culture, but as the result of specific social mechanisms:[55] the dense social networks encasing and buffering the self; the objective (i.e., relatively non-subjective) criteria for selecting a mate; explicitly endogamic criteria to choose a mate – that is, socioreligious–economic status as an overt and legitimate choice for mate selection; a regime of performativity of emotions regulated by rituals; the role of promise-keeping for reputation-building; the fact that commitment was facilitated by social roles. The point of these claims is emphatically *not* to praise the past and even less to claim that nineteenth-century people were better or more moral; rather, it is to suggest that what moral philosophers or communitarians may view as moral dispositions are explained by social mechanisms that organize, even if partially, men's and women's emotional interactions into public rituals and roles. As a result, the self was less vulnerable to others' gaze and to their validation, precisely because the actors' sentiments did not radiate from the interiority of their self. The modes and criteria of evaluation, the capacity to sustain love, the total thrust of the self in the experience of love, are thus shaped by social mechanisms, which turn dispositions into "virtues." It is these mechanisms, at once social and moral, private and public, that regulated the middle- and upper-middle-class choice of a mate well into the nineteenth century, at least in the English-speaking world. What changed in modernity are precisely the conditions within which love choices are made.

The Great Transformation of Romantic Ecology: The Emergence of Marriage Markets

It is a truism to claim that societies in which marital choices are based on love tend to be individualistic: that is, to make individuals – not their clan or family – the bearers of the decision to marry, thereby legitimizing emotional autonomy. But given that affective "individualism" has been around Western Europe for at least three hundred years,[56] this notion is too broad and imprecise to describe and characterize modern emotional transactions. The nineteenth-century English and American culture of romantic choice was individualistic, but the form and meaning of that individualism are significantly different from our own. I argue that this difference is better captured if we focus on the cultural organization of choices. What I have described so far are the social mechanisms that compelled men and women to settle with each other without a protracted bargaining, without a formal and rule-bound process of introspection, without the mental construct of a large degree of choice of potential partners in an open market, and with criteria of evaluation that reflected the community's standards. What has changed profoundly, as I document below and in the following chapters, are the very conditions within which choices are made: that is, *both the ecology and architecture of romantic choice*.

Let me make a bold suggestion: the transformation undergone by romantic choices is akin to the process that Karl Polanyi has described for economic relationships and that he dubbed the "great transformation."[57] The "great transformation" of economic relations refers to the process by which the capitalist market dis-embedded economic action from society and from moral/normative frameworks, organized economy in self-regulated markets, and came to subsume society under economy. What we call the "triumph" of romantic love in relations between the sexes consisted first and foremost in the dis-embedding of individual romantic choices from the moral and social fabric of the group and in the emergence of a self-regulated market of encounters. Modern criteria to evaluate a love object have become disentangled from publicly shared moral frameworks. This disentanglement occurred because of a transformation of the content of the criteria for selecting a mate – which have become both physical/sexual and emotional/psychological – and because of a transformation of the very process of mate selection – which has become both more subjective and more individualized.

The "great transformation" of love is characterized by a number of factors: (1) the normative deregulation of the mode of evaluation of prospective partners – that is, its disentanglement from group and communal frameworks and the role of mass media in defining criteria of attractiveness and worth; (2) an increasing tendency to view one's sexual and romantic partner simultaneously in psychological and sexual terms (with the former being ultimately subsumed under the latter); (3) and, finally, the emergence of sexual fields, the fact that sexuality as such plays an increasingly important role in the competition between actors on the marriage market.

The Sexualization and Psychologization of Romantic Choices

"Character" expressed an interiority that enacted a world of public values. In that sense, although the evaluation of someone's "character" was an individual act, it was also public, shared, and approved by concrete others.

The individualization of the criteria of choice of a mate, and its disentanglement from the moral fabric of the group, is illustrated by the emergence and prevalence of two criteria to evaluate a prospective partner: "emotional intimacy and psychological compatibility," on the one hand, and "sexiness," on the other. The notion of "emotional intimacy" differs from love based on character because its goal is to make compatible two unique, highly differentiated, and intricate psychological makeups. "Sex appeal," "sexual desirability," or "sexiness" reflects a cultural emphasis on sexuality and physical attractiveness as such, detached from a moral world of values.

History is full of examples of the power of erotic attraction, and of the importance of beauty for falling in love. However, although "sexiness" has probably been somewhat implicitly present throughout history as an aspect of attraction and love, its deployment as an explicit, pervasive, and legitimate cultural category and criterion of evaluation is essentially modern in that it is underpinned by a vast economic and cultural organization codifying sexual allure and sexiness. As a cultural category, sexiness is distinct from beauty. Nineteenth-century middle-class women were viewed as attractive because of their *beauty*, less because of what we would call today their sexual appeal. Beauty was viewed as a physical and spiritual attribute.[58] (This is why Robert Browning could fall in love with Elizabeth Barrett, who was an invalid, precisely because he could subsume her physical appearance under her inner beauty. Her invalidity did not seem to pose a particular problem in his account of his love for her.[59]) Sexual appeal *as such* did not represent a legitimate criterion for mate selection and in that respect represents a new criterion of evaluation,[60] detached both from beauty and from moral character, or rather in which character and psychological makeup are ultimately subsumed under sexiness. "Sexiness" expresses the fact that in modernity, men's and especially women's gender identity has been transformed into a sexual identity: that is, into a set of self-consciously manipulated bodily, linguistic, and sartorial codes geared to elicit sexual desire in another. Sexiness in turn has become an autonomous and decisive criterion in the selection of a mate. This transformation emerged as a result of the conjunction of consumerism and of the increasing normative legitimation of sexuality by psychological and feminist cultural worldviews.

Undoubtedly, along with the feminist and bohemian claims to sexual freedom, consumer culture has been the most significant cultural force that has contributed to the sexualization of women, and later of men. Writing about the 1920s, John d'Emilio and Estelle Freedman argue that "American capitalism no longer required an insistent ethic of work and asceticism in order to accumulate the capital to build an industrial infrastructure. Instead, corporate leaders needed consumers. [...] An ethic that encouraged the purchase of consumer products also fostered an acceptance of pleasure, self-gratification, and personal satisfaction, a perspective easily translated to the province of sex."[61] Consumer culture put desire at the center of subjectivity, and sexuality became a sort of generalized metaphor of desire.

The history of cosmetics is illustrative of this process. Nineteenth-century notions of beauty drew a clear separation between fashion or cosmetics – changing, mutable, and driven by external sources – and what was then called "moral beauty" – which had a "timeless" and "inner" quality.[62] Thus, nineteenth-century notions of beauty did not contain an explicit reference to sex or sexuality. Quite the contrary, beauty was relevant only to the extent that it reflected character. Victorian morality viewed cosmetics with suspicion because they were perceived to be an illegitimate substitute for "real" inner moral beauty. At the beginning of the twentieth century, however, perfumes, makeup, powders, cosmetics, and creams flooded the emerging markets of consumption, and in trying to promote these goods, advertisers disentangled beauty from character. "Released from the Victorian underworld, painted women now paraded through advertisers' imaginary worlds. Scenes depicted them swimming, sunbathing, dancing, and motoring – pictures of healthy, athletic, and fun-loving womanhood."[63]

Following a managerial system which devised new methods to package and distribute goods, an industry of cosmetics promoted the body as an aesthetic surface, detached from moral definitions of personhood. This process was accelerated and generalized as across all social classes the cosmetics industry collaborated with the fashion and movie industries.[64] The cosmetics and fashion industries became all the more powerful because they received the endorsement of the cultural industries of movies, modeling, and advertising and were amplified by them.[65] The movie studios, women's magazines, advertisers, and billboards functioned as popularizers, codifiers, and amplifiers of new ways to put forth the body, foreground the face, and eroticize the flesh. Women were incorporated in consumer culture as sexed and sexual agents through the ideal of sexualized beauty that was aggressively promoted by the conjunction of economic sectors that solicited and constructed a self based on eroticism. The new cult of beauty in women's magazines and movies "explicitly connected make-up and sex appeal"[66] in seamlessly weaving together cosmetics, femininity, consumption, and eroticism.[67] In other words, an array of new industries helped promote and legitimize the sexualization of women and, later, of men. The body was apprehended as a sensual body, actively looking for sensuous satisfaction, pleasure, and sexuality. Such search for sensuous satisfaction gave way to the sexualization of the body: the body could and should evoke sexuality and eroticism, arouse it in another, and express it. The construction of eroticized female bodies, across all social classes, was thus one of the most formidable cultural accomplishments of early twentieth-century consumer culture.

The two signifiers of youth and beauty became signifiers of eroticism and sexuality. The commodification of the body through the signifiers of youth and beauty entailed its intense eroticization, and its close proximity to romantic love as well. The association between beauty, eroticism, and love was straightforward: Not only did "[p]aint no longer disqualif[y] respectable women from romance or marriage,"[68] but it also seemed to lead straight to it. "[C]osmetics figured prominently in everyday tableaus [*sic*] of love and rejection, triumph and humiliation."[69] In fact, a rather blatant rationale for the cultivation of beauty was the hope to find one's true love. "The real end" of (women's) beauty was "to secure a husband."[70] It promised women of lower extraction the opportunity to rise above their condition through upwardly mobile marriage. Beauty and a type of femininity that emphasized sexuality were intimately associated with the image of romance because both romance and beauty were thought to be sure sellers by advertisers, studio owners, and cosmetics manufacturers. Romance enacted gender divisions, demanded that men and women ceaselessly perform these differences; yet it also promised to abolish them in a utopia of genderless intimacy.

Men's bodies were also subject to this process of sexualization. Although men were slower in being incorporated into consumer culture, one can find seeds of a masculine identity based in consumer culture, hedonism, and sexuality already in the nineteenth century.[71]

> At the seamier end of the scale were brothels, bloodsports and other illicit pleasures but also significant were an array of businesses that catered to men's consumer demands. Indeed, [...] an extensive "bachelor subculture" formed around the network of eating houses, barber shops, tobacconists, tailors, city bars, theatres and an array of other commercial ventures that thrived on the patronage of affluent, young "men about town."[72]

But it was in the 1950s that a full-fledged consumer culture targeted at men's bodies appeared. The best symbol of such a consumer culture was the magazine *Playboy*, which was first published in 1953. The magazine marked the rise of a "'playboy ethic' that prioritized personal gratification in a sparkling world of endless consumption, leisure, and lascivious indulgence."[73] The commodification of men's bodies initially relied not on beauty and on cosmetics but rather on sports and tapped directly into men's sexual fantasies. In its promotion of a sexual model of masculinity, it promoted the same sense of erotic allure, with one interesting difference, however: namely that the themes of love and romance were far less salient than for women.

From the middle of the nineteenth century onward, photography, and subsequently movies, standardized men's and women's new canons of erotic allure[74] and simultaneously increased their awareness of their own and others' appearance. These homogeneous standards of beauty made widely available new norms and codes of sexual attractiveness, and thus contributed to transforming the criteria for choosing a mate.

The foregrounding of the body in US culture and the intense commodification of sex and sexuality made "sexual attractiveness" a cultural category in itself, detached from moral value *per se*. The cult of beauty, and later of fitness, and the definition of masculinity and femininity in terms of erotic and sexual attributes were relentlessly promoted by the cultural industries and had the effect of progressively transforming sexual attraction and sexiness into positive cultural categories in their own right, making sexual desirability one of the central criteria for choosing a mate and for shaping one's own personhood. The commodification of sex and sexuality – their penetration into the very heart of the capitalist engine – made sexuality into an attribute and experience increasingly detached from reproduction, marriage, long-lasting bonds, and even emotionality.

Consumer culture proved immensely successful at the formidable task of dispensing with traditional sexual norms and prohibitions and of sexualizing bodies and relationships because it relied on the authority and legitimacy of experts who came from the ranks of psychoanalysis and psychology. Indeed, these professions ascribed two fundamental roles to sexuality in their redefinition of selfhood. First, they viewed the psychic history of the individual as being organized around (infantile) sexuality, and in this respect, sexuality became an essential feature of what defined a person, his/her psychic essence, so to speak. But, second, sexuality also quickly became the sign and site of a "healthy" self. A vast industry of clinical psychologists and counselors claimed that a good sexual life was crucial to well-being. Sexuality thus came to stand squarely at the very center of the project of having a good life and a healthy self, paving the way for the positive notion of "sexual experience." In putting sexuality at the center of the subject – that is, in making the self carry its private and unique truth in its sex and sexuality, and in making the good self lean on healthy sexuality – psychology put sex and sexuality on both ends of the narrative temporal line constituting the story of a self: one's past and one's future now revolved around sex and sexuality. The self not only told to itself its story as a sexual story, but it made sexuality itself, as a practice and an ideal, into the *telos* of this narrative.

This message of psychology became particularly amplified with the cultural and sexual revolution brought about by second-wave feminism from the 1960s onward. Indeed, what made second-wave feminism so powerful was its reconceptualization of sexuality as political. Orgasmic sexuality and mutual pleasure were now moral acts of affirmation of autonomy and equality. Sexual pleasure became a way of affirming women's access to full equality with men, as free and equal subjects,[75] thus making sexuality into the repository of a positive and even moral affirmation of the self. Although it was not directly aligned with the feminist movement, the gay movement further contributed to naturalizing the equation between sexuality and political rights, closely associating sex with the central values of democratic polities, namely choice, self-determination, and autonomy. In becoming subsumed under political rights, sexuality became both a naturalized and normative dimension of the self, however, now detached from the set of regulations that had subsumed it under the moral definitions of femininity and masculinity. These cultural forces combined made sex, sexuality, and sexual desirability not only legitimate but also central to the choice of a mate, ultimately granting this criterion an autonomous power of its own. To be "sexually attracted" to someone would become a condition *sine qua non* of romantic partnership.

These various processes and transformations of the meaning of sexuality became palpable in the emergence of the categories of "*sexy*" and "*sexiness*" as new modes of evaluating oneself and others, especially in the realm of romantic relationships. As cultural categories, sex appeal and sexiness were the result of the ways in which consumer culture disentangled beauty from character and morality, progressively autonomized sexuality as a signifier for personhood, and made orgasmic sexuality into a form of competence aspired to by lovers and couples. As documented by the *Oxford English Dictionary*, well until the 1920s the word "sexy" had negative connotations. When used for persons, only around the 1950s does the language register the modern meaning of "sexy" as being both positive and disconnected from beauty and morality. For example, in 1957, William

Camp writes in his *Prospects of Love*: "There must be something about her which screams that she's beddable. A girl doesn't have to be pretty to be sexy."[76] In becoming culturally pervasive, sexiness came to refer to much more than simple appearance; it designated an essence of the person, which includes but extends beyond the sheer physical. As Sophia Loren put it: "[T]he quality of sexiness comes from within. It is something that is in you or it isn't and it really doesn't have much to do with breasts or thighs or the pout of your lips."[77] Here sexiness becomes a general trait inhering in the person and marking her as attractive. More to the point: it becomes the central trait in the selection of a mate. For example, a 52-year-old man, Alan, a pharmaceutical sales manager, is representative of a large class of people when he makes the following claim:

Alan: A basic requirement for me is the looks; not only her face but also her waist, she's got to have a thin waist, nice, full breasts, flat tummy, uhmmm, and long legs. But you know, maybe more important than how she looks is that she is sexy.

Interviewer: What do you mean?

Alan: Like, you've got to feel she's hot, that she likes sex, that she likes giving pleasure and being pleasured.

Interviewer: And are there many women who correspond to this?

Alan: Uhmmm.... well, not a whole lot, of course, but yes, some, I would say so, no doubt about it, but you've got to find the one that truly excites you. That's more difficult to put into words, although you know it when you see it. Sexiness is very important but it's difficult to define. You just know it when you see it.

Clearly, this man's sense of sight is geared to identifying conventional traits of sexual attractiveness and cues and signals that the body is sexualized. He illustrates the paramount importance of sexiness in the choice of a mate, and the ways in which actors develop elaborate criteria to capture the sexiness of others.

The point of this is obviously not to claim that sexiness as such is new or that people of the past were not attracted to something similar to "sexiness." Rather, the point is to suggest that physical attraction has become a conscious, explicit, legitimate, and commandable criterion for mate selection and that modern societies offer many more ways for men and women to translate their sexual attractiveness into the field of romance and matrimony. "Physical attractiveness of the partner was found to be the most significant predictor of liking, while such factors as academic achievement, intelligence, and various personality measures were unrelated to degree of liking."[78] An indication that physical attractiveness is playing an increasingly important role in mate selection is the fact that recent research has found that *both men and women* give much importance to this characteristic,[79] thus suggesting that women also are now joining men in the premium they have traditionally put on it. In a large-scale study of trends for criteria of choice of a mate that spans half a century, David Buss and his associates find very convincing evidence that sexual attractiveness as a criterion to choose a mate has steadily grown for over a period of fifty years in the United States, both for men and for women.[80] In other words, the importance of physical attractiveness has clearly grown with the expansion of media, cosmetics, and fashion industries.[81]

The changes in sexuality after World War I, but more clearly after World War II, were interpreted by many scholars as leading to "recreational sexuality,"[82] in turn a sexuality that was alienated, commodified, and narcissistic. I suggest it is more useful to view sexuality as having become, like beauty, a "diffuse status characteristic":[83] that is, a characteristic which conferred status. One may speculate on the many consequences of the fact that "sexiness" has become an important, and even crucial, criterion with which to select a mate. First, the intertwining of beauty and moral character meant that it was more likely to be closely related to social class ("morality" consisted in the display of class-based manners and a class-based sense of propriety).[84] Because sexiness was shaped by the media–fashion–cosmetics industries in such a way to appeal to a wide variety of women, it has become relatively independent of moral codes, and thus of social class. Angelina Jolie embodies classless codes of sexiness: that is, codes that can in principle be imitated by and accessible to any woman. One obvious implication is thus that sexiness is potentially disruptive of traditional patterns of homogamy. That is, given that beauty and sexiness do not necessarily overlap with social stratification and can in fact constitute for less wealthy and educated women an alternative route to have access to powerful men, the legitimation of sexiness represents a multiplication of modes to enter marriage, a way of undermining traditional hierarchy of rank according to money. "In the lowest classes of society this [erotic] hierarchy might be more salient than elsewhere simply because the poor, powerless, and uneducated have bottom positions in all other respects and, thus, may turn more to the rewards offered by erotic ranks."[85] This ultimately implies that the marriage market interferes with, overlaps, and is sometimes even replaced by a sexual social arena – an arena where sex occurs for its own sake – and that there are many more contestants competing with each other in this sexual arena: say, the wealthy, the educated, and the sexually attractive who may or may not belong to the former.

Second, the multiplication of criteria for choice also implies the possibility of many more contradictions in a choice of a mate. That is, if homogamy constitutes the strongest sociological pull for marriage – marrying others of comparable education and socio-economic status – sexiness introduces a dimension that may potentially – and often does – conflict with the "normal" logic of social reproduction.[86] While attraction to non-homogamic partners was obviously not unknown in the past, this was accorded far less legitimacy. This also means that the attempt to combine equally legitimate criteria that do not necessarily overlap will complexify the search process, and make choosers more likely to have to navigate between (and sometimes choose between) conflicting attributes. In sociological terms, we may say that the modern choice of a mate, based on *habitus* – or the set of bodily, linguistic, and cultural dispositions acquired during socialization – becomes more complex because it now has to internalize different sets of evaluations, some pulling toward the reproduction of social class, others pulling toward media culture which produces a large array of classless images. A romantic *habitus* is an inherently complicated one.

A third and maybe most obvious effect of multiple criteria of choice has to do with the fact that they have legitimized sexuality as a goal in itself, detached from marital purposes. This disentanglement is made obvious in the emergence of the category of "sexual experience," in which a sexual life separate and autonomous from an emotional life is increasingly lived and experienced for its own sake. Such disentanglement implies a much greater distance between emotional intentions and sexual actions, between current emotions and the moral imperative to translate them into future commitments. More: sexiness points to the disentanglement of sex from emotions, because most emotions are organized and generated by moral frameworks and sexiness presents itself as a cultural category and behavior that is not morally coded. This is a general trend but more true for men than for women, as evidenced by the fact that men account for 72% of total visitors of pornography sites and more than 95% of total paid-for pornography, while women are still more likely to mix emotions and sexuality. Moreover, the predominance of sex detached from emotions implies much greater difficulty in the interpretation of each sexual protagonist's actual feelings and intentions.

A fourth consequence has to do with the fact that sexiness makes the process of falling in love entirely subjective, sexual attraction or chemistry being notoriously unaccountable to objective criteria (and this despite criteria of beauty having become standardized). Whereas in Austen's world the criteria for choosing a mate are known, shared, and objectified, they have now become subjectivized because based on inexplicable (in principle) attraction. Individuals, by and large, must rely only on themselves to figure out whether they are attracted to someone, and whether they should love someone, making the choice of a partner the result of an individual decision-making reached through a complex process of emotional and cognitive evaluation.

A fifth consequence is that sexiness makes attraction increasingly dependent on the iconic and the visual,[87] and thus conflicts with the rational and linguistically formulatable criteria that have also come to dominate the process of choice of a mate. The attraction to someone becomes subject to reasons that are not cognitively, consciously, or rationally justifiable. Attractiveness is based on a rapid judgment of strangers in short interactions, and thus gives rise to a cultural scenario of quick forms of pairing (the famous "one-night stand" or, more recently, "hooking up"). "Sexiness" as a mode of evaluation thus marks the rise of the sexual experience acquired for its own sake, which may in turn be lived with no reference to domestic or long-lasting frameworks.

The final consequence, adjacent to the previous one, is that sexiness entails an increasing uniformization of physical looks and appearance, owing to the wide distribution and standardization of images of beauty and sexiness. The sexualization of the romantic encounter has been standardized by typecasting certain body and facial features as desirable. In this process, the models put forward by the fashion and cultural industries come to occupy a privileged role. The standardization of beauty and sexiness in turn has the effect of delineating a *hierarchy* of sexual attractiveness: some people are clearly sexually more attractive than others according to well-rehearsed cultural codes. Because criteria of sexiness are codified, they can be used to evaluate and rank prospective partners, thus making one rank some people higher on a "sexual attractiveness" scale than others. Consequently, the subjectivization of choices – making the self into the only valid source of evaluation – goes hand in hand with the standardization of sexy looks and the capacity to rank them.

These changes set up the conditions for and set the background of what economists call *marriage markets*: that is, encounters which seem to be monitored by individual choice and taste and in which individuals seem to choose and exchange freely the attributes desired in another – typically, attractiveness for women, exchanged for men's status. For economist Gary Becker, the pioneer of the concept of the marriage market, since marriage is always voluntary, the theory of preferences applies, as in any other realm of economic action. More-over, because men and women compete to seek a mate, marriage can be said to be a market,[88] in which the person with most attributes to offer will command a greater power over others. Becker's notion accurately captures the commonly accepted view that marriage is the result of free choice and that criteria for choice are varied. Becker, however, makes a few important mistakes: he views decisions as the outcome of preferences, and views preferences as equivalent, and thus does not distinguish between parents' or the prospective partners' choice of a mate. From a sociological standpoint, however, the two are significantly different in that *individual choice* for one's own self is likely to be a more complicated operation of choice, as one is likely to want to satisfy multiple utilities: that is, have multiple preferences that may in turn conflict with each other. Moreover, Becker is oblivi-ous to the fact that the marriage market, and the conditions for search and choice of a mate, differ significantly according to the ways in which marriage is or is not regulated: that is, according to what I called earlier the ecology of choice. Economists assume that prefer-ence induces choice, and do not ask what the conditions for the formation of preference are. Finally and maybe most crucially, econo-mists are oblivious to the fact that marriage markets are not natural or universal, but rather are the result of a historical process of deregu-lation of romantic encounters – here, of the disentanglement of the romantic encounter from traditional moral frameworks that regu-lated the process of choice. The "great transformation" of romantic encounters is thus the process by which no formal social boundary regulates access to partners and an intense competition comes to prevail in the process of meeting others. What economists view as the natural category of "marriage market" has in fact a historical genesis, linked to the disappearance of formal rules of endogamy, to the individualization of romantic choices, and to the generalization of competition. The conditions for a marriage market emerge only with modernity and are intrinsic to it. In that respect, it would be more appropriate to speak of "sexual fields" than of marriage markets, for fields presuppose that actors have unequal resources to compete on a given social place.

Marriage Markets and Sexual Fields

The eroticization of romantic relations was concomitant with the disappearance of formal mechanisms of endogamy and the deregula-tion of romantic love relations under the banner of individualization. By individualization, I mean that individuals, not families, become carriers of personal, physical, emotional, and sexual attributes that are supposed to constitute and define their particularity and uniqueness and that individuals take charge of the process of evaluating and choosing. The self, thus constituted as unique and individualized, pairs up with another unique person, viewed in possession of unique attributes. The process of choosing a mate becomes defined by the dynamic of taste: that is, becomes the result of the compatibility of two highly differentiated individualities, each looking for specific attributes in a free and unconstrained way. In becoming more subjective, the choice of a mate places individuals in a situation of overt competition with others. This has the result of structuring the encounter with prospective mates in and by an open market in which people meet and pair up according to their "taste" and compete with others on their capacity to access the most desirable mates. This transforms the terms of the exchange between men and women. In Austen's world, men and women are exchanging similar attributes in the form of wealth, status, education, and general pleasantness of their personality. Romantic choices, for the most part, most of the time, reflect and reproduce social stratification and the morality attached to a class. In modernity, the exchange can in principle become asymmetrical: that is, men and women can "exchange" different attributes – beauty or sexiness for, say, socio-economic power.

Viewed sociologically, a marriage market has a number of characteristics. First, the pre-modern search for a mate was (more or less) horizontal: that is, it happened within one's own group. In modernity, on the other hand, given that race, socio-economic status, and religion are no longer formal obstacles to the choice of a mate, the competition becomes both horizontal and vertical, within one's social group, but often and quite typically outside of it, thus becoming in principle open to everyone. The competition over a partner becomes generalized. This is because social classes and social groups do not provide formal and formalized mechanisms for selection of a mate. The result is thus that the pool of potential partners becomes considerably enlarged and that everyone in principle competes with everyone else for the most desirable partners in a given social field, where desirability is simultaneously defined in individualized and irrational terms ("I don't know why I am so attracted to him") and in standardized terms ("She is the kind of woman every man would want for himself").

Second, meeting another becomes a matter of personal taste (taste includes socio-economic factors, as well as less formulatable ones, such as "charm" or "sexiness"). The criteria for selecting a partner, ranging from physical attractiveness and sexual preference to personality and social status, become subjectivized and can now be "traded," according to a privatized dynamic of individual taste. That is, attributes such as sexiness or attractiveness can be "traded" for economic status, precisely because the market of marriage becomes seemingly open to private choice and preferences. The trading of assets is thus the result of a historical transformation of the structure of marriage markets.

Third, because there are no more formal mechanisms by which to pair people up, individuals internalize the economic dispositions that also help them make choices which must be at once economic and emotional, rational and irrational. The romantic *habitus* has thus the characteristic of operating at once economically and emotionally. Sometimes this *habitus* makes choices in which economic calculus is harmoniously reconciled with emotions, but sometimes this *habitus* is subject to internal tensions, as when one has to choose between a "socially appropriate" and a "sexy" person. This is why the sexual-romantic *habitus* has become a very complicated one, precisely because it contains a variety of dispositions.

Fourth, the fact that, in modernity, the selection of a partner is more subjective also means that it is based on qualities that (presumably) inhere in the self, and reflect its "essence": physical attractiveness and personality become indexes of one's inner value. If premodern marriage was established by one's objective standing, and therefore value, it is now almost the reverse: because marriage markets are competitive, because a variety of attributes in them can be traded, because how well one does in this market points back to one's value, one's position in a marriage market is thus also a way of establishing one's general social value, as deduced from how well one does on the sexual market: that is, from the number of partners and/or their desire to commit to oneself. Being successful at the dating game bestows not only popularity, but also, more fundamentally, social value (see chapter 4 for an analysis of this process). Erotic attractiveness and sexual performance mark the rise of new ways of bestowing social value in marriage markets. Sexuality thus becomes closely intertwined with social value.

In short, when social rank is the most important criterion with which to choose a mate, competition among men and women is far more restricted and occurs only within members of the same class. In modernity, in contrast, the competition increases in a significant way, because there are no longer formal mechanisms with which to pair people through their social status, because the criteria for mate selection become both diverse and refined, and mostly because they become integrated in the private dynamic of taste. Modernity marks an important transformation in the criteria for mate selection in that it makes the specifications for physical and character attractiveness far more central, detailed, and, most of all, subjective. There is thus an affinity between the process of individualization of a choice of a mate, the "deregulation" of marriage markets, and the fact that the search process is structured as if on a market, each freely exchanging attributes of his or her self, conceived as an accretion of social, psychological, and sexual traits.

Feminist scholars have sharply (and rightly) criticized the devastating aspects of the sexualization of women,[89] pointing to the ways in which it subordinates women both to men and to the enormous economic machine fed by the beauty industry. The intense commodification of the sexualized body has led many to argue that we live in a pornified culture, in which the boundary between public and private sex, commodified and emotional sex, has eroded.[90] Yet, this critique does not address the more complicated question of how beauty, sexual attractiveness, and sexuality may interact with class structure and may in turn constitute a new mode of stratification. In particular, the feminist critique may miss the fact that beauty and sexiness undercut traditional hierarchies of status and represent the possibility for new social groups (the young and beautiful, the poor and beautiful) to compete with groups in possession of greater social and economic capital and even to constitute a new form of social hierarchy. The sexualization of men and women's identities thus changes importantly the terms of the entry into the marriage markets, since beauty and sexual attractiveness, because they are only loosely correlated to social class, enable the entry of actors hitherto excluded from middle- and upper-middle-class marriage markets. Of course, I do not deny that the body is groomed according to class-based codes, but beauty and sexiness that are cultivated by ubiquitous media are more autonomous dimensions of class than, say, linguistic and cultural codes, thus making the pairing process, at least potentially, far less tightly connected with class structure.

The deregulation of the matching process and the valorization of sexiness give rise to what we may call, paraphrasing Bourdieu, *sexual fields*: that is, social arenas in which sexual desire is autonomized, sexual competition is generalized, sexual appeal is made into an autonomous criterion for selection of a mate, and sexual attractiveness is made into an independent criterion by which to classify and hierarchize people. Sexual attractiveness – either combined with other attributes or alone – becomes an autonomous dimension of pairing. It is activated by traditional class *habitus* – which makes us find attractive the people we can pair with – but because sex is increasingly organized as an autonomous social sphere, it can also disrupt class *habitus* and demand other forms of evaluation (e.g., King Edward VIII abdicating his crown for the commoner divorcee Wallis Simpson, etc.)

This historical process is at the heart of what sociologist Hans Zetterberg has called "erotic ranking," or the probability that one person will induce in others an "emotional overcomeness."[91] According to Zetterberg, people not only differ in their capacity to create that overcomeness, but are also secretly ranked according to it. Given the year he wrote this, 1966, it may not be surprising that he thought this ranking had to be secret. Forty years later, that secret ranking had become quite public, so that we may now call sexual attractiveness, as noted above, a diffuse status characteristic.[92] It is this underlying historical process that has led some sociologists to speak about the emergence of "erotic" or "sexual" fields.

The autonomization of sexual desire creates a "social space" designed to engineer the sexual and romantic encounter in formal venues, such as bars, nightclubs, bathhouses, sex Internet sites, dating Internet sites, personal ads, and match-making companies. These sites are designed for the organization of romantic/sexual encounters and stratified according to the logic of consumer tastes and niches (e.g., *New York Review of Books* personals, an S&M club located in downtown Manhattan, etc.).[93]

If sexual encounters are now organized as a field, then it means, following field analysis, that some actors are more successful than others at defining who an attractive/desirable mate is, and that relatively few members are at the top of the sexual pyramid, that they are the object of competition by a larger number of people than others are. One may wonder, in particular, if the rise of sexual fields has given rise to new forms of domination of women by men. In the pre-modern economy, men and women were exchanging economic assets that were often similar. Because patriarchy meant control over children, a woman, and servants, men wanted to enter matrimony. Both men and women were normatively constrained to enter marriage (except in the case of religious vocation and vows of chastity). In that sense, men and women were emotional equals. In capitalist economies, by contrast, most property and flows of capital are controlled by men, thus making marriage and love crucial to women's social and economic survival. As I document in the next two chapters, the deregulation of marriage markets has entailed new forms of control of the sexual field by men.

Thanks to the demise of formal mechanisms of endogamy, through the transformation and individualization of sexual practices, and through the intense valorization of sex and beauty via the media, the twentieth century witnessed the formation of a new capital circulated in sexual fields that we may call "erotic capital." "Erotic capital can be conceived of as the quality and quantity of attributes that an individual possesses, which elicit an erotic response in another."[94] But I argue that erotic capital takes two forms or paths, which correspond to different gender strategies to accumulate erotic capital in the sexual field.

In its most simple and masculine form, erotic capital is made visible and manifest in the quantity of sexual experiences one has accumulated. For example, Charles is a 67-year-old French journalist living in Paris. He says: "When I was 30–40, having a lot of lovers was very important to me. You see, this was almost a case where quantity was quality. If I had a lot of lovers, then I felt myself to be qualitatively a different, more successful kind of man." Or, in his autobiographical account of how he developed an active gay sexual life, Josh Killmer-Purcell writes:

> I knew I should be having a lot more sex. As a gay man, the world was supposed to be my prurient playground. What was I doing wrong? How was I going to become a good gay? [...] Which is why, at the stroke of midnight on August 28, 1994, my twenty-fifth birthday, I decided to fuck my age in strangers.[95]

This gay man feels inadequate in showing a poor sexual experience, and decides to augment the numbers, which then become a source of pride, which is a way of accruing social value to the self. The writer Greta Christina recounts her sexual experience as follows: "When I first started having sex with other people, I used to like to count them. I wanted to keep track of how many there had been. It was a source of some kind of pride, or identity anyway, to know how many people I'd had sex with in my lifetime."[96] Charles, Killmer-Purcell, and Christina view large sexual experience, accounted for by numbers of partners, as a source of self-value. They behave as sexual capitalists. In these accounts, erotic capital is displayed by the pride they take in the large number of their sexual conquests. That is, sexual desire is contained in a dynamic of ostentatious display of self-value through sexual abundance, which signals that one is in possession of sexual/erotic capital, the capacity to elicit overcomeness in others. This cumulative – or serial – sexual strategy has been adopted by women, but, culturally and historically, as an imitation of men's behavior.

Erotic capital has an additional meaning. Some sociologists even refer to the formation of erotic capital that can be converted, like other forms of capital, into other fields, such as better occupations and higher grades. As Dana Kaplan, quoting a researcher in the field, argues: "[B]eing a sexually-oriented person might signal a whole range of other accumulated skills directly marketable in the labor-force [...] such as sophistication, flexibility, creativity, self-presentation and promotional ability."[97] This form of capital may be said to correspond to the female sexual strategy of pairing, the exclusivist one.

Undoubtedly, the realm where erotic capital has the most directly tangible outcomes and benefits is that of choice of a mate. As Catherine Hakim suggests, the girls thought to be more attractive in high school were more likely than others to marry, to marry young, and perhaps even more surprisingly to have a higher household income (measured fifteen years after initial measurement). Hakim goes as far as to suggest that women can exploit erotic capital for upward social mobility instead of, or as well as, turning to the labor market. One hopes she is not suggesting that "exploiting" one's erotic capital is as commendable a route for social mobility as developing skills in mathematics or weaving, but her findings are useful in that they imply that marriage markets are analogous to labor markets in enabling women to gain social status and wealth in modern societies through their sexual personas.[98] In such a view, then, erotic capital is a part of women's economic capital in the twenty-first century. Obviously, women of the past also used their erotic capital to gain social status and assets they were otherwise deprived of, but what is new is that the current social structure and media culture enable and facilitate the conversion of erotic capital to social capital.

Such transformations explain the rise of a new cultural motive that swept our television screens in the 1990s, namely that of the *search* for a partner in an invisible but powerful marketplace of competing actors. This underlying motive structures the worldwide successful TV series *Sex and the City* and such reality shows as *The Bachelor.* Indeed, *Sex and the City* and *The Bachelor* stage and perform the themes documented in this chapter: the intense sexualization of romantic relations, the individualization and complexification of the search process, the generalized competitiveness of the pairing process, the transformation of sexuality into capital via sexual experience and success, with the result that the *search* for and *choice* of a partner have become an intrinsic segment of the life-cycle, with its own sociological complex forms, rules, and strategies. Much of the self-help literature and the television series thus takes place against the background of the fact that the romantic *search* has become objectively a highly complex sociological endeavor, with its own autonomous economic field, social actors, and social rules. More crucially: it is now sociologically split: sexuality, desire, and love have become tightly intertwined with social stratification – they emanate from social class, they provide status, and often end up conforming to educational homogamy; yet a choice of a mate happens in the context of recreational sexuality based on classless experience of shared pleasure and pure sexuality. Recreational sexuality and the choice of a mate thus frequently constitute opposite sociological pulls.

Conclusion

In documenting the passage from pre-modern to modern choice of a mate, the shift to affective individualism has often been emphasized by historians. While such a characterization is not inaccurate, it hides a far more significant process, namely that the modality of choice has changed: that is, the very relationship between emotion and rationality and the ways in which competition between claimants on the field is organized. Mate selection now takes place in a highly competitive market in which romantic and sexual success is an effect of prior modes of stratification and which also, in turn, has stratifying effects. Such romantic stratification has several components. One concerns the ways in which social stratification harks back and shapes erotic desire: that is, the ways in which social status feeds and shapes erotic desire, the libido being a channel of social reproduction (finding "sexy" the most powerful man in the room). Desirability is intertwined with one's socio-economic status. Another aspect concerns the fact that sexual attractiveness *per se* constitutes an independent dimension of erotic worth and becomes a criterion of stratification in its own right, which may or may not interfere with social stratification. Physical attractiveness becomes an independent criterion for mate selection, which can thus undermine other criteria for mate selection or work in tandem with them.

The triumph of love and sexual freedom marked the penetration of economics into the machine of desire. One of the main transformations of sexual relationships in modernity consists in the tight intertwinement of desire with economics and with the question of value and one's worth. In its very erasure, it is economics that now comes to haunt desire. By this, I mean that generalized sexual competition transforms the very structure of the will and desire, and that desire takes on the properties of economic exchange: that is, that it becomes regulated by the laws of supply and demand, scarcity, and oversupply. How the economic machine transforms and structures the will becomes clearer in the next chapter.

3

Commitment Phobia and the New Architecture of Romantic Choice*

The breeding of an animal that *can promise* – is not this just that very paradox of a task which nature has set itself in regard to Man? Is not this the very problem of man?

Friedrich Nietzsche, *The Genealogy of Morals*[1]

"Women are getting unhappier," I told my friend Carl. "How can you tell?" he deadpanned, "It's always been whine-whine-whine." Why are we sadder?" I persisted. "Because you care," he replied with a mock sneer. "You have feelings." "Oh, that."

Maureen Dowd, "Blue Is the New Black"[2]

Freedom has been the quintessential trademark of modernity, the rallying cry of oppressed groups, the glory of democracies, the pride of capitalist economic markets, and the reproof to authoritative regimes. It has been and remains the great accomplishment of modern political institutions.[3]

Yet, the reference to freedom as a yardstick to evaluate polities should not be oblivious to two important difficulties: competing and incommensurable goods (as solidarity) challenge the idea that freedom should be the ultimate end to our practices,[4] and the exercise of freedom can and does generate forms of distress, such as ontological insecurity and meaninglessness.[5] Although this book is modernist in its endorsement of freedom, it aims to question its consequences because, as will become apparent in the succeeding analysis, sexual and emotional freedom generate their own forms of suffering.

* With Mattan Shachak.

However, "freedom" might be too capacious a concept since it carries different meanings and has different effects in different institutional contexts. The freedom of the capitalist market contains such meanings as "self-interest" and "fair competition"; freedom in the realm of interpersonal relations rests on expressive individualism; in the consumer sphere it resides in the right to choose; and the freedom postulated by civil rights rests on a concept of dignity that is ignored by the other spheres. The practice of freedom is institutionalized in different spheres with different practical and moral consequences.

Thus, although sexual freedom historically is articulated as a political right,[6] freedom in the political and sexual realms differs. Political freedom is activated by a large and sophisticated legal apparatus ensuring the relative orderliness and predictability of its exercise. In interpersonal and sexual relations, "freedom" is not constrained by an institutional apparatus. Except for the legal constraints of "consent" (age of consent, sexual act out of consent, flirtation out of consent, etc.), sexual freedom has progressed in a linear direction of increased emancipation from legal and moral prohibitions, aimed at rendering it devoid of taboos. Transgressive and anti-institutional forms of individuality increasingly are expressed in the realm of sexual relations, making it – perhaps more than the realm of politics – a site for the exercise of pure individuality, choice, and expressiveness. The "pornification" of culture takes place in a context of the commodified emancipation of sexual desire and fantasies, free from the shackles of moral regulation.[7] The morality of modern sexuality consists now in affirming mutual freedom, symmetry, and autonomy, rather than in respecting, say, sexual honor or norms of monogamy.

In the realm of sexual relations, the most obvious expressions of freedom are exemplified in the changes in the meaning of marriage and of sexuality. In the early twentieth century, for most, marriage was a lifetime commitment. Statistics show that the divorce rate in the US was low until 1960, when, over a period of twenty years, this more than doubled.[8] It continues to be high. Research reveals that during the 1960s, attitudes to divorce changed dramatically.[9] In 1981, Daniel Yankelovich reported an important change in the normative fabric of marriage and heterosexual relationships.[10] In a piece of longitudinal research, he compared answers given in the 1950s to those given in the late 1970s. In the 1950s he asked young single and married women why they valued marriage and family. Their responses reflected a deep-seated belief that marriage was both necessary and unavoidable and provided membership in society as well as a sense of normalcy. Some twenty-five years later, in the late 1970s, attitudes had changed: marriage was now one among several options for young women. So-called "deviant" behaviors such as singlehood, homosexuality, or out-of-wedlock pregnancy had become significantly de-stigmatized.[11] Unmarried cohabitation had increased,[12] and led to marriage in only 50% or less cases.[13] Since the end of the 1970s, marriage and stable relationships have become optional, and are often achieved only after exhaustive search, counseling, and expense.[14] In a pioneering study of commitment in marriage and romantic relations conducted in the 1980s, Ann Swidler found that that decade witnessed significant changes in the patterns of cultural and emotional commitment prior to and within marriage.[15] Contraceptive methods and changing moral standards accentuated and normalized the separation between sex and marriage exemplified by the radical change in attitudes to premarital sex after the 1960s.[16] These changes were the tangible results of an increased freedom in intimate relationships. The affirmation of freedom in the sexual sphere was one of the most significant sociological transformations that occurred in the twentieth century. In this chapter, I try to show how this freedom led to a transformation in the emotional transactions between heterosexual couples, and, most conspicuously, in the phenomenon known popularly as "commitment phobia."[17]

As argued in chapter 2, the exercise of freedom occurs always in a social context, and it is this context we need to investigate in order to understand the aporias freedom has generated in the realm of intimate relationships. Sexual and romantic freedom is not an abstract practice, but rather is institutionalized and embedded in a contested but still powerful patriarchy. This has generated new forms of suffering in the shape of inequalities arising from the different ways that men and women feel, experience, and monitor their sexual freedom in competitive sexual fields. Similar to the realm of the market, sexual freedom entails a cultural recoding of gender inequalities, which have become invisible because romantic life follows the logic of entrepreneurial life in which each partner prioritizes his or her freedom and attributes his or her miseries to a flawed *self*. Yet, as I try to show, sexual freedom is similar to economic freedom in that it implicitly organizes and even legitimizes inequalities.

From Female Reserve to Male Detachment

By contemporary standards, eighteenth- and nineteenth-century courtship constrained the sexual behavior of women and, to a lesser degree, men. Middle- and upper-middle class women were more likely than men to be reserved in expressing their romantic emotions and sexual longing. There were two main reasons for a woman's reserve: she had to express sexual reticence, and in the early stages of courtship her behavior was mostly reactive – that is, to accept or reject male courtship. This reticence was the result of changes that occurred in the eighteenth century in terms of views on women's sexuality. During the Christian centuries, although sexual abstinence was imposed on men and women, women were thought to have the greater sexual appetites. "If anything, the daughters of Eve were considered more prone to excess of passion [than men] because their rational control was seen as weaker."[18] During the eighteenth century, however, the belief emerged that women could *naturally* resist sexual temptation. Samuel Richardson's novel *Pamela* (1740) is illustrative.[19] It is the story of a young maid courted aggressively by her master almost to the point of rape. She repeatedly resists his advances, but starts to have fond feelings for him. Ultimately, he respects her virtuous resistance to his advances and asks her to marry him,[20] an offer she gladly accepts. This novel signaled a new way of conceiving of women's nature and of splitting male and female gender identities around the practice of abstinence: for women, abstinence began to be a test and a mark of their virtue, helping to establish a reputation in the marriage market; for men, it allowed them to show their masculinity in their capacity to desire and win over that which the woman was supposed to refuse.

This equation of womanly abstinence with virtue became prominent in American culture. The image and ideal of abstinence, part of a general economy of appropriateness and self-control, served to assign women a higher moral and social status: "By elevating sexual control highest among human virtues, the middle-class moralists made female chastity the archetype for human morality."[21] According to Nancy Cott, the clergy's raising of women to the highest moral status removed their sexuality. This new ideology was helpful for women since sexual abstinence and purity were the prices for "moral equality," for "power and self-respect."[22] Cott shows that in the nineteenth century, women's sexual freedom had been exploited by men and that the imposition of abstinence endowed them with more power and more equality: "The belief that women lacked carnal motivation was the cornerstone of the argument for women's moral superiority, used to enhance women's status and widen their opportunities."[23]

Sexual reticence gave women a reason to refuse a suitor, but did not allow them to pursue one,[24] which meant that men had to be more active and were more exposed during courtship. As we saw in chapter 2, the historian Ellen Rothman suggests that it was too risky for a woman to express her feelings before a marriage offer: "A woman would wait to be sure that her feelings were reciprocated before admitting them even to herself."[25] Rothman stresses that it was imperative that the woman should avoid being the first to show her feelings: "[I]t was a rare woman who was willing to expose herself to rejection by a lover."[26] Thus, women waited for evidence of a man's intentions and affections. The man's affections, his capacity to show and prove love, were of paramount importance in the decision to marry: "When a man proposed marriage, love was his most important qualification; when a woman responded, love was her first consideration."[27] Rothman also states that the man could not be certain whether his offer would be accepted: "Men were more likely than women to complain that letters were answered too slowly or too cursorily."[28] As the initiators of marriage, men were the more vulnerable in the transaction: they had to prove their ardor and strength of feeling, on the one hand, but, on the other, exert some self-control to protect themselves from being too open in the face of possible rejection.[29] While women were largely disenfranchised in most areas of social life, their position in the courtship process seems to have been strong, at least on the level of emotional power defined as the capacity to withhold the expression of emotions and to compel the man to reveal his emotions and then to decide on the response.

Rothman also argues that once a man had made his choice, he rarely wavered: "He showed little ambivalence in the pursuit of his goal. Women, on the other hand, vacillated and wavered as they took the last steps to the altar."[30] Rothman provides a broad description of patterns of courtship in the early US Republic: "[A] young man who was eager to overcome any obstacles; a young woman who often shied at the gate. Because men expected marriage to enrich rather than restrict their daily lives, they were more eager than women to have the wedding take place. [...] [The man] could, however, expect resistance and procrastination on his fiancée's part."[31] The world described here is one where it was more common for a man to disclose his heart, to proclaim the intensity of his feelings, and to try to "win over" the woman – in other words, a world where commitment was not a problem for the man because men's social existence depended on being married. Another example of the steadfastness required of men in matters of the heart is the story of Theodore Sedgwick, son and namesake of the more famous federalist, and his courtship of Susan Ridley. Sedgwick junior proposed in 1805, but he withdrew after Susan's stepfather opposed the match. He re-established a relationship with Susan the following year and was chastised by his brothers for his irresolution: "They say you have not got the *grit* to ax a gal."[32] Resoluteness and determination were prized male qualities in many domains, but particularly in the matrimonial realm. Consider also the courtship of Nathaniel Hawthorne and Sophia Peabody. Less than four months after meeting Sophia, and before any commitment to marry, Hawthorne wrote in a letter:

> [M]y soul yearns for the friend whom God has given it – whose soul He has married to my soul. Oh, my dearest, how that thought thrills me! We *are* married! I felt it long ago; and sometimes, when I was seeking for some fondest word, it has been on my lips to call you –"Wife"! [...] Often, while holding you in my arms, I have silently given myself to you, and received you for my portion of human love and happiness, and have prayed Him to consecrate and bless the union.[33]

Emotional speed, emotional intensity and a desire to commit were as much (if, at times, not more) the prerogative of men as women, at least among nineteenth-century middle-class men and gentry. Nineteenth-century middle-class masculinity was defined in terms of the capacity to feel and express strong feelings, make and keep promises, and to commit to another with determination and resolution. As suggested in chapter 2, steadfastness, commitment, and reliability were the marks of a manly character. Karen Lystra, another specialist of nineteenth-century courtship practices, confirms that "middle- to upper-middle-class men were allowed a range of expression that paralleled, if it did not precisely duplicate, women's."[34] Certainly, such emotional definitions of masculinity were the combined outcomes of the moral code of Victorian culture and the economic character of the transaction: "[M]arriage [...] always involved a transfer of significant amount of real or personal property from the family of the bride to that of the groom, with a reverse commitment in the future of a significant proportion of the annual income."[35] The dowry acted as a device for male commitment to a wife and anchored the interpersonal commitment of the new couple in a wider system of familial, economic, and social obligations. It reinforced family relations between parents and daughters and shaped the social relations among kin to increase ties of affection and interest.[36] In short, male commitment was embedded in a moral and economic ecology based around the dowry. This did not mean that men never broke their commitment and never deserted an impregnated woman or a marriage;[37] but such behavior was perceived as deviant and dishonorable in the context of the propertied classes, at least in Protestant Western Europe and the US.[38] For example, when Søren Kierkegaard broke off his engagement to Regine Olsen in 1841, he had to suffer the wrath and contempt of both her family and his for what they saw as this discreditable act.[39]

This definition of masculinity differs significantly from the ways that men and their commitment to women are depicted in the early twenty-first century. Christian Carter is the web name adopted by the author of a successful series of ebooks on relationships and a weekly electronic newsletter to which I subscribed for more than a year. In a piece advertising his book *From Casual to Committed*, in which he is obviously addressing a hypothetical female readership, he writes:

You meet a guy that seems to have something "special" about him.

And I'm not talking about just "another" guy here...I'm talking about a guy who is RELATIONSHIP material.

He's not only funny, charming, intelligent and successful...he's also actually *normal*!

Better yet, other people have nothing but great things to say about him.

The better you get to know him, the more you begin to REALLY feel the connection...and it seems like he feels it too. And when you finally do get together...it *feels like "magic" is in the air...*

You intuitively "know" you both feel a unique connection that could lead to something *really* special.

Then you start spending more and more time together, and your "dates" start to blend together. And you can't help but feel like you're spending time with someone you've known and been close to for years...

You can't keep your hands off of one another when you're in the same room...and people even stop you in the street to tell you how the two of you seem *perfect*...

Life is wonderful...and although you know it's a little soon, you start to feel like this actually could be "it."

There's fun, passion, romance. Amazing conversations, laughs, inside jokes...

It all feels so "right" that it wouldn't surprise you if you two could spend the rest of your love lives together and stay deeply connected and in love.

While you know it's a little soon to start thinking "that way"...you make up your mind that you're definitely ready for a committed relationship with him...You want him and no one else. And you'd like him to *only* be with YOU.

But the reality is that you don't know *exactly* how to tell him the way you're feeling, or to find out if he *really* feels the same way too.

Although, after all the things he's said and done with you, and all the time you've spent together, you're pretty sure he feels the same about you.

You decide to "play it cool" and see where this leads...

But as the days pass, you find yourself hoping he will say something to you...picturing the moment when he will finally open up, share his deeper feelings, and ask you to be "his"...

But before you know it...weeks have gone by...*and nothing*...

Soon a few months have gone by...and you're starting to wonder what's *really* going on...

Sure...it's still fun...but where are things going?

You find your head filling with unanswered questions...

Where are we going with this?

Does he feel it too?

Why hasn't he asked me to be his girlfriend?

Is he seeing other people?

Is this all a game to him?

Maybe he's not feeling as serious about this as I am!?

WHAT THE HELL IS GOING ON HERE???

You've been patient, but it's driving you nuts...*you have to know*.

You decide to bring it up, in the most casual way possible...

But when you do, he just doesn't seem to "get it."

Maybe he says a few shallow things like, "What do you mean? We've only been dating for a few months!" or..."Everything is great the way it is now!"

Or worse yet...he completely avoids the conversation, won't open up, and acts like YOU are the one being difficult.

Then...over the next few days, he becomes more and more distant...things definitely aren't the same.

The phone calls aren't as frequent...communication seems "forced" and awkward...

And eventually...it stops completely...and the "unthinkable" happens...he's gone. One minute he seemed to be Mr Right, and the next he's gone. And all you have to show for it is a cold, empty feeling in the pit of your stomach.[40]

This advertising blurb manages to capture some of the "primal" motifs structuring the real and imaginary landscapes of relationships between men and women in the late modern era. That stable, intimate relationships are difficult to achieve, especially for women, because men are emotionally elusive and routinely resist women's attempts to commit to a long-term relationship. That a woman's desire to commit to a man is as self-evident as is the male's resistance to it. That a display of care and love, far from enticing a man, often makes him "run away"; only exceptionally are "normal" men willing to commit to a relationship. The obvious implication of this vignette, and its marketing strategy, is that women need psychological advice to recognize commitment-phobic men, to avoid them, and to make reluctant men want to commit to a relationship. In the context of this chapter, the most interesting aspect of this vignette is that it assumes that "commitment" is a male problem and a widespread one. In the US context, commitment phobia – especially among men – has taken on the proportions of a moral panic and is the subject of a seemingly endless series of television soaps, movies, and self-help titles. So widespread is the perception that commitment is a male problem that a site that provides a lexicon of relationships proposes the following definition of commitment: "Currently, the word Commitment (also the word L_O_V_E, a word that some men have even been known to self-strangulate in an attempt to say i.e., lying to get laid for example) has absolutely no relevance to the male species."[41]

If we examine the data, we can find ample, albeit indirect, evidence of changes in the nature of men's and women's commitment. The major trends in marriage in the US since the beginning of the 1980s include an increase in the average age at marriage (27 years for men and 25 years for women in 2003):[42] that is, people are deferring the decision to marry.[43] The percentage of men and women who remain unmarried has also increased. In fact, since the 1970s the number of single-person households has risen hugely,[44] particularly in the US, but also in Europe. This is due to later age on marriage and greatly increased divorce rates. The duration of marriage has decreased: of the men who married in 1955–9, 76% remained in the marriage for at least twenty years, while only 58% of men who married in 1975–9 remained married for the same length of time. The percentage of men reaching shorter anniversaries (as short as five, ten, or fifteen years) fell in this period as well. There has also been a decrease in the number of second marriages.[45] New categories have appeared, too, such as LAT (living apart together),[46] which refers to a pattern of social intimate relations between couples who do not live together because they are unwilling or unable for various reasons to commit to sharing an abode. Finally, the popularity and even relative legitimacy of non-monogamous behavior such as "hooking up" or polyamory, the latter being consensual, ethical, or responsible non-monogamy, suggests that exclusivity – a traditional feature of commitment – is being challenged and replaced by more casual or multiple forms of commitment or even random behavior. The data indicate, albeit imperfectly, that traditional patterns of commitment have undergone a profound transformation as marriage is less readily chosen as a life option than in the past, and as relationships are organized under the aegis of greater flexibility, short-term contractualism, greater capacity to bail out of them, and *a priori* total lack of commitment.[47] Undoubtedly, the demise of commitment is connected to greater individual freedom to enter and leave relationships. However, although commitment phobia seems to apply to both men and women, it appears to be, chronologically and culturally, a male prerogative.[48]

So how can we explain this? Taken at face value, the idea of *male* commitment phobia contradicts a number of the findings in the literature. For example, research shows that men benefit more from marriage than women do.[49] Given that, in most marriages, women tend to serve the man, this is hardly surprising.[50] Moreover, women not only serve their husbands, they encourage their "kin-keeping": that is, they keep intact men's relationships to their children and to other family members. Finally, marriage provides the incentive for men to earn more and remain healthy.[51] Based on these benefits of marriage, men ought to be more eager than women to marry. Indeed, in a study of men's and women's perceptions of marriage, Gayle Kaufman and Frances Goldscheider find that while 37% of men felt that a man could have a full and satisfying life without being married, the proportion was 59% for women. In other words, at least on the level of perception, men are more likely than women to view marriage as an attractive option (and to see the state of not being married as significantly less attractive).[52] Women, by contrast, are more likely to perceive an unmarried life as attractive and full.

It is even more puzzling that women's supposed greater willingness to commit contradicts economic theory and sociological findings that would predict the opposite. One of the dominant explanations for declining rates of marriage is proposed by the economist Gary Becker, who argues that marriage is based on a trading off of mutual advantages, and that higher rates of employment among women should make marriage a less desirable option for them, a fact that also explains the decline in the number of marriages.[53] In this view, women will be more "choosy" and will be able more easily to reject offers from men perceived to be inadequate, in the hope of finding someone better. In other words, a stable marriage market is connected to women being more dependent on marriage for their economic survival. In this view, it is women not men who are responsible for the declining rates of marriage and who should be the ones displaying a pattern of commitment phobia.[54] Although this undoubtedly applies (i.e., women's improved economic opportunities are responsible for declining rates of marriage), women are much less reluctant to commit, and men, even if they view marriage positively, are more hesitant and ambivalent toward commitment and long-term stable relationships.

There are some popular explanations for this state of affairs. The most conspicuous one is that men have deficient psyches and lack the basic capacity for monogamous connectedness, for psychological or evolutionary reasons. Their psychological, biological, and evolutionary makeup makes them prone to sexual multiplicity because masculinity is promiscuous and because evolution demands men spread their sperm, rather than care for their offspring.[55] Such explanations cannot be used by sociologists, because of their tautological character, explaining a given state by simply postulating that necessity inscribed it in the genes or evolution. A different explanation for this state of affairs is that men are confused by their traditional role being challenged by the new power of women. Men withhold their commitment because they are afraid of women and their increasing power threatening their identities.

More psychoanalytic explanations suggest that commitment phobia is the result of the masculine gender identity being built against the feminine: "Masculine identity is born in the renunciation of the feminine, not in the direct affirmation of the masculine, which leaves masculine gender identity tenuous and fragile."[56] In this view, inspired by psycho-dynamic models of the male psyche as in the need to separate from the mother, male gender identity forges itself in opposition to female, and to the need for dependence and sharing, making the man less able to create or to desire a long-lasting bond. From the eighteenth to the mid-nineteenth century, sentiment was as much the prerogative of males as females; after the mid-nineteenth century, it became a mainly female prerogative.[57] Women took over responsibility for caring, for feeling and expressing emotions geared toward the creation and maintenance of close relationships. Nancy Chodorow famously and brilliantly argued that men's and women's different emotional makeups are the result of the structure of the modern nuclear American family, in which women are responsible for the care of children, with the result that girls grow up with no break in identification with their mothers and strive throughout their adult lives to reproduce fusional relationships with others, while boys develop with a sharp sense of separateness, and strive for autonomy. Boys learn to separate; girls learn to bond.[58] A more political variation of this explanation is that men and women, in their intimate relations, play out the inequality that characterizes their relations in society at large. Shulamith Firestone, for example, argues that men use various strategies to maintain control over relationships, such as not wanting to commit and displaying unpredictable behavior (e.g., standing up women, being vague about future dates, making work a priority, etc.). She suggests that "[male] culture was (and is) parasitical, feeding on the emotional strength of women without reciprocity."[59] In this view, then, boys/men are "emotional parasites": that is, they can take love, but not generate or return it to provide the kind of emotional sustenance women need. Following this line of thought, commitment phobia can be viewed as an aspect of "compulsory heterosexuality," one of the main institutionalized descriptions of the ways in which women are systematically humiliated, dismissed, and ignored by men.[60]

These explanations are crucial for situating love in the context of asymmetrical power relations. But a flaw common to all of them is their pathologizing of male behavior and their concomitant affirmation and praise of the female psyche and of the (presumably female) model of intimacy. Sociologists should be suspicious of explanations that *a priori* pathologize forms of behavior. Psychological explanations in particular are suspect because they implicitly rely on a model of the healthy psyche which assumes that intimacy is the "normal" and "healthy" state to which we should aspire and thus denies the empirical and normative possibility that individuals or groups can reject intimacy and not be psychically flawed. In other words, even though as a feminist I find the current state of heterosexuality oppressive, I want to analyze it in ways that do not presume that the woman's way of managing interpersonal relationships is the norm, the yardstick by which men's behavior should be measured. Such an assumption might obscure what to the cultural sociologist is the more interesting question, namely: which are the social conditions men express and perform when they resist commitment? Taking "intimacy" as the normative yardstick prevents us from questioning whether (male) behavior is a strategic and rational response to the new social conditions, more specifically the new ecology of sexual encounters and the architecture of romantic choice. If we take seriously the assumption shared by feminists and sociologists that the psyche is plastic and that intimacy is an institution rather than a measure of a mature psyche, then we should not use this model to measure psychodynamically men's reluctance to commit.

These observations are inspired by Bruno Latour, who claims that in exploring a scientific controversy, the sociologist/anthropologist should view all sides in the controversy as symmetrical.[61] When examining the scientific theory around the theory of germs in late nineteenth-century France, Latour does not presume to know that Pasteur "won."[62] The principle of symmetry helps us avoid the pitfalls of romanticizing or blaming one position compared to another.

Instead of pathologizing men's behavior, we should ask what kind of social relations make possible and even desirable men's "fear" of or lack of commitment and which cultural frames make such behavior meaningful, legitimate, and pleasurable. To clarify the emotional mechanisms of choice and commitment, we need to approach male reluctance to commit *and* women's readiness to commit as two symmetrical phenomena, both puzzling and both in need of explanation. Sociology is primarily interested in the social conditions that make some models of the self more available than others, and the kind of dilemmas that these cultural models may be responding to strategically. What are these conditions?

If the problem of commitment derives neither from a negative perception of marriage nor from the fact that men are more selective than women, it can plausibly be argued that it derives from the ways in which men and women monitor and construct their choices to enter relationships: that is, from the ways in which freedom is institutionalized. Commitment is a response to a structure of opportunities which, in turn, affect the process of attachment: that is, its speed, intensity, and capacity to project itself into the future. The question can thus be reformulated as: to which structure of opportunities is "fear of commitment" a response? If, as I argue, commitment is a strategic response to opportunities, then it would seem plausible to argue that the emotional organization of commitment phobia is shaped by transformations in the ecology and architecture of choice: that is, the social conditions and the cognitive modes through which people make choices and bind themselves to others.

Masculinity and the Demise of Commitment

The historian John Tosh claims that in Western societies, masculinity "occurs in three arenas: home, work, and all-male associations."[63] Authority in the household, the capacity to earn a wage in a non-servile independent way, and the capacity to form meaningful bonds in voluntary associations, taverns, and clubs that effectively excluded women are traditionally the three pillars of masculinity. Capitalism and democratic polities mark a very important change in this tripartite structure: since the twentieth century the feminist movement and its impact on the political, economic, and sexual spheres have consistently and effectively challenged and eroded male authority in the household. Also, the rise of bureaucratic organizations and salaried work has curtailed men's independence, with most men now working under the supervision of other men and/or women, and most all-male sites for homosocial association (with the notable exception of sport) have diminished, with heterosocial leisure the norm in the majority of venues. Thus, if, as Tosh suggests, masculinity is a "social status, demonstrated in specific social contexts,"[64] then clearly some constitutive elements of that status and those contexts have been seriously eroded with the advent of modernity. Independence, authority in the household, and male solidarity have all been undermined, with traditional masculinity even becoming an inverse signal of status – culturally coded working-class masculinity. It is precisely in this context that sexuality has become one of the most significant *status markers* of masculinity. As argued in chapter 2, sexuality confers status. Sex appeal and sexuality have become attributes of gender identity and of what within that identity takes the form of status.[65]

To an extent, sexuality has always been associated with masculinity, but in many societies, male social power is a condition for obtaining access to women. Men affirm their social power over women and over other men by exercising sexual domination over numerous women. That is, if sexuality is a field of struggle, then in traditional societies, powerful men are clearly those who dominate it, because male power is usually translated into greater sexual access to a wider variety of women. As Francis Fukuyama puts it: "Casual access [i.e., casual sex within the framework of marriage] to multiple women has been enjoyed by powerful, wealthy, high-status men throughout history."[66] In other words, sexuality continues to be a reflection of and is directly indexed to socio-economic status. These multiple relationships have often entailed obligations to support the women in various ways, either by eventually marrying them or by providing economic advantages.

Chapter 2 discusses how in the twentieth century the impetus of the consumer culture and clinical psychology led to the autonomization of the sexual sphere from moral regulation and from formal class endogamy, and to the emergence of sexual fields. The results have been significant: men no longer need to be powerful and dominant to have sexual access to women. This access is relatively independent of male socio-economic power, and men from different socio-economic backgrounds are able to have access to sex with multiple women without having to pay for it, without incurring the moral reprobation of their peers, and without being forced into marriage.[67] In Fukuyama's words: "What changed after the 1950s was that many rather ordinary men were allowed to live out the fantasy lives of hedonism and serial polygamy formerly reserved to a tiny group at the very top of society."[68]

There are three possible reasons that could be proffered for sexuality being so closely associated with male status. To the extent that sexuality was associated with the socio-economic status of powerful men, it retained its association with power and status even when the connection was less strong. Serial sexuality is attractive to men of all classes because, if access to women is restricted, it functions as a sign of the man's status – of victory over other men. Male competitiveness, validation, and status were channeled through the realm of sexuality. For men, sexuality was a mark of status in terms of the capacity to compete with other men in securing the attention of the female sex: "Women provide heterosexual men with sexual validation, and men compete with each other for this."[69] Furthermore, men transferred to sex and sexuality the control they had formerly held in the household, and sexuality became the realm within which they could express and display their authority and their autonomy. Detachment in sexuality came to signal and organize the broader trope of autonomy and control, and, thus, of masculinity. Emotional detachment could be viewed as a metaphor for masculine autonomy, which the separation between sex and marriage had encouraged. Finally, through sex, men both competed with and forged bonds with other men by casting women's bodies as the object of male solidarity.[70] In other words, sexual freedom made sexuality a site for the exercise and display of masculinity for men whose status in the three arenas of work, home, and male sociability had been eroded: it transformed sexuality into status. If sex for men was a way to display their status and to bond with other men, the demise of men's control over the household and of their autonomy in the workplace resulted in a sexuality that was *hypertrophied*, in that it merged and expressed at once the three aspects of masculinity as status: authority, autonomy, and solidarity.

The central role of sexuality in this redefinition of masculinity was greatly facilitated and accelerated by the intense sexualization of women and men throughout the twentieth century: that is, by the fact that sexual relationships were no longer regulated by moral frameworks, and by the fact that sexual attractiveness – sexiness – had become an explicit attribute of gender identity, detached from the moral performance of the self.[71] In chapter 2 I argued that sexuality has become a field of struggle. I can now suggest more precisely that this is because sexuality enables the acquisition and maintenance of male social status – an arena where men compete with each other for the affirmation of their sexual status.

One might hypothesize that if, after the 1960s, sex and sexuality had become the prime site for the exercise of women's freedom, this may have been because serial sexuality was closely associated with male power. However, even though the conditions of sexual encounters have become intensely sexualized for both men and women, and even though sexuality has become a status signal for both genders, their sexualization has not followed the same path. Evelyn Blackwood, an anthropologist, points out that "men and women are positioned differently in relation to sexuality," where "differently" refers to "differences in ability to control or name acts, to claim rights to certain practices, to label some practices as permissible and others not."[72] Randall Collins, a sociologist, meanwhile, describes it as "a system of stratification by sex."[73] This difference between the sexes is pronounced in terms of sexual strategies, and it is to an exploration of women's pairing strategies that we now turn.

The Dynamic of Women's Exclusivist Strategies

Undoubtedly, women's greater readiness to commit is a direct outcome of what we may call their exclusivist pairing strategy. One reason for this strategy suggested by Susan Brownmiller is that women are exclusivist as part of a contract between men and women in which the man protects the woman from rape in exchange for her fidelity and dependence.[74] The woman's exclusivist strategy is viewed here as an outcome of women's dependency, gender inequality, and unequal power relations. Alice Rossi, on the other hand, suggests that women have a "dual innate" sexual orientation – "toward men" and "toward their young,"[75] which explains their exclusivist strategy.

I would argue that heterosexual women who follow an exclusivist sexual strategy are actually motivated more by a reproduction orientation than by a natural orientation toward men. That is, exclusivist sexuality is more likely to be found among women who want motherhood in the institutional framework of monogamous domesticity. These women actually subsume their search for a mate under the construction and perception of their reproductive role.[76] In traditional pre-modern patriarchy, men as much as women are normatively and culturally compelled to have children in order to have households to command and names to propagate. Traditional patriarchal masculinity needs a family to assert itself because it needs to rule over children, women, servants and land. In societies of contested patriarchies (like ours), men are far less normatively compelled to biological reproduction because the family is no longer a site of control and domination. The main cultural imperative that shapes masculinity is that of psychological autonomy, upward mobility and economic success in economic organizations. It is thus women who now take on the sociological roles of having *and* wanting children. In that process, the ecology and architecture of the choice within which they operate have changed considerably. In particular, biological time now plays a significant role in shaping women's cultural *perceptions* of their bodies and their pairing strategies. Women who choose to have children and marriage (or heterosexual domesticity) as the framework within which to raise these children are constrained by a perception of their body as a biological unit organized in and by time. Two main factors are responsible for this perception. There is a considerable amount of evidence to suggest that entry to the labor market and higher education are causing women to postpone both marriage and childbearing (while less educated women are postponing marriage but not childbearing).[77] Because contemporary women are deciding to enter the marriage market later than their counterparts in the mid-twentieth century, and because heterosexual women still overwhelmingly opt for motherhood, they operate within a much greater time constraint than did their pre-1960s counterparts.[78] Parodying Heidegger, we can say that modern middle-class women in the marriage market think of time not from the vantage point of death, but from the vantage point of their "fertility." In the realm of love, finitude for women is marked by the horizon for childbearing. For example, Catherine Townsend, the sex columnist for the UK *Independent* newspaper, wrote:

> Now that I've just hit my thirties, I'm ready to confine my wild bedroom antics to one (very lucky) man, and am convinced that my sexual exploration will make me a much better partner, both in and out of the bedroom. I'm more stable, confident, and happier than ever. But dating is harder, because there is more on the line. I'm still undecided about children, but the reality of the biological clock means that I feel I have less time to waste on the wrong person, just in case I do decide to have kids.[79]

The second reason for the sharper perception of time is related to the fact that the beauty industry and the availability of data on the "narrow" reproductive time windows of women serve massively to construct a woman's (more than a man's) body as a unit defined by chronology (and thus threatened by decay). The prevalence of "sexiness" and of increasingly more stringent criteria of beauty have had the effect of increasing the subjective importance of youth and consequently the awareness of aging, especially among women. While until the nineteenth century, an "older" woman (a woman in her late twenties) might have been desirable based on her accumulation of property or money, modern criteria of sexiness, because they are associated with youth and appearance, make women highly conscious of the process of aging and, thus, accentuate the organization of femininity within the cultural category of time (in pre-modern Europe, in 25% of marriages the man was younger than the woman). The contemporary situation puts women at a structural disadvantage: when women operate under the normative constraint of childbearing (mostly within the framework of a heterosexual partnership) and the perception that biology constrains them, they view the choice of a mate as organized in a limited time frame. This perception of time, especially in their thirties and forties, tends to produce a perception of diminished options, which, in turn, may generate a greater willingness to commit to a man earlier and faster. In the words of Bridget Jones, the thirty-something heroine of Helen Fielding's eponymous novel: "As women glide from their twenties to thirties [...] the balance of power subtly shifts. Even the most outrageous minxes lose their nerve, wrestling with the first twinges of existential angst: fear of dying alone and being found three weeks later half-eaten by an Alsatian."[80] Recent research indicates that as fertility declines, women think more about sex, have more frequent and intense sexual fantasies, are more willing to engage in sexual intercourse, and report more frequent sexual intercourse than women in other age groups,[81] thus suggesting a connection between sexual search and the perception of a window closing.[82]

An Internet forum exemplifies how men perceive themselves as operating in a market in which the imbalance in emotional availability is caused by the different perception of time:

> If she is much older and has children, rest assured that her adult children are already too old to care about you. If the woman is only five years your senior, listen for a ticking sound beating in her head, like in "The Tell-Tale Heart". By age 30, if she has invested any time into you, the ultimatums are secretly being loaded like torpedoes. Prepare to issue countermeasures. Hot on the heels of the marriage ultimatum will be the request for children. It will actually be more like a papal decree to Catholics. If you can keep an older woman as a fling and make sure her children are all in college, then enjoy the ride. Otherwise, break it off while you can.[83]

This call to avoid the pitfalls of matrimony, attachment, and responsibility for children is underpinned by the self-evident assumption that women are more interested in matrimony/commitment than men because their time frame is more limited.[84] Biological time – as a culturally salient category of perception constituting an individual's choice – is a fundamental dimension of women's architecture of choice, the cognitive and emotional mechanism through which they make decisions and thus command less bargaining power than men, who are far more oblivious to the temporal dimension and thus are equipped with a broader cognitive time span in which to make a choice.

A second aspect of the ways in which a new ecology of choice shapes the diminished sense of options among middle- and upper-middle-class women is demography. Historically, during the first two hundred years of capitalism, women were doubly segregated: in low-paid jobs and as sexual and gendered actors.[85] This made marriage a crucial venue for their economic and social survival and status. The pipeline to marriage was attachment to one male – love – which made sexuality critical to women's economic and social existence and led to their hypertrophied investment in marriage as an emotional sphere. Also, overall, the female pairing strategy is homogamy or hypergamy: that is, to choose a man with an educational (and, therefore, socio-economic) status that is similar to or higher than their own.[86] Since 1980, the educational level of men has increased more slowly than that of women,[87] and given that men's earning power, on average, has decreased against that of women, there are fewer educated men earning the same as or more than their female counterparts.[88] This implies also that a larger proportion of middle- and upper-middle-class educated women are competing for, and thus creating a shortage in, the same pool of educated and affluent men.[89] However, although there are a larger number of women competing for the same educated men,[90] the prevalence of ageism – discrimination on the basis of age – renders the sample of male partners larger than the sample of women, based on the norm that in relationships women can (and even should) be younger than men. Counterintuitively, between the 1970s and the 1990s, men's odds of marrying younger women *increased* while women's odds of marrying younger men *decreased*.[91] This is because men are now more directly dependent on the market for economic survival and can rely only on themselves to survive economically – thus making them less dependent on women's accumulated property and wealth. If men can choose younger, less affluent, less educated partners, this implies simply that the samples they can choose from are much larger. These facts combined generate a discrepancy in the size of the samples available to both sexes, with the result that educated women have fewer men to choose from.[92]

This in turn suggests that commitment phobia is related to the fundamental transformations in the ecology of choice that allow men to control the terms in the sexual bargain. The greater sexual access to a larger number of women, the shift to serial sexuality to confirm status, the discrepant size of the samples from which men and women can choose owing to different homogamic strategies, and the different cognitive constraints exerted by the category of time indicate that men can choose from a much larger sample than women can, and that men are now making choices in conditions of more abundant choice than are available to women. Another way to say this is to suggest that men are more likely to view the marriage market as a sexual market and tend to stay longer in such a sexual market, whereas women tend to view the sexual market as a marriage market and would tend to stay in it for less time.

I now want to show in more detail how the objective and subjective sizes of samples available to choose from relate to commitment phobia, through an analysis of what I referred to earlier as the architecture of choice: that is, how choice itself is conceived.

Hedonic Commitment Phobia

From a cultural standpoint, there are two ways of experiencing commitment phobia: as *hedonic*, in which commitment is deferred by engaging in a pleasurable accumulation of relationships; and as *aboulic*, in which it is the capacity to want to commit that is at stake: that is, the capacity to want relationships. Another way to describe this divide is that one category includes a series of relationships and an inability to fixate on one partner;[93] and the other is a category of those unable to desire a relationship. The first could be characterized as overflowing with desire, the second as deficient in desire. The first is characterized by the difficulty to settle on one object from an abundance of choice, the second by the problem of not wanting anyone.

One example of the sheer effect of abundance of sexual choice can be found in the essay by Marguerite Fields selected as the winner of the *New York Times* "Modern Love" college contest. As Fields explains about one of her male friends, a fellow college student:

> Steven explained that it's not a question of faithfulness [to his girl-friend] but of expectation. He can't be expected not to want to sleep with other people, so he can't expect her to think differently. They are both young and living in New York, and as everyone in

New York knows, there's the possibility of meeting anyone, every-where, all the time.[94]

In this quote, clearly the difficulty to settle on one object is due to the abundance of choice and to the permanent sense of possibilities.

A 36-year-old man, employed in a high-tech corporation, had numerous relationships, ranging from one-night stands to successive long-term relationships and cohabitation lasting between a few months and a few years. He reported extensive use of the Internet to find a partner. I asked him if there were things in a woman's profile that "put him off."

Interviewer: Are there things in a profile that put you off, that would disqualify an otherwise good-looking woman?

Simon: The truth is that if somebody writes they want a serious relationship, that would be a put-off. I think these women are stupid. Because you know you will be able to manipulate them easily. A woman who wants something "serious" is basically in your pocket. And that is less interesting.

Interviewer: Do you meet many women like that?

Simon: Yes. Plenty.

This answer is extraordinary in the context of the history of men's and women's relationships in the eighteenth and nineteenth centuries. At that time, and in the first half of the twentieth century, "serious-ness" was a precondition for marriage. A woman's sexual "serious-ness" (i.e., the capacity to resist a man) was a way to establish her reputation in the marriage marketplace and thus to signal both her *intention* to marry and her marriageability. Note the contrast with the modern situation, in which we observe a reversal of this state: a woman who is "serious," and who thereby signals her *a priori* inter-est in a stable and committed relationship, is "uninteresting." Simon's answer reflects his perception that women who want to commit display a form of dependence, because such *a priori* desire will make them an easy prey to men's emotional manipulations. In other words, if we accept what he says, if a woman is keen to commit, the man is unerringly able to control her precisely because of her desire to commit. This could be interpreted as the expression of male power over women, but this would ignore the man's dislike of an *excessive power* over the woman. It is this excess of power that in turn prevents his falling in love. This is strangely congruent with the claims of

Shulamith Firestone (and others) that the feeling of love is "obstructed by *an unequal balance of power.*"[95] In Firestone's view, men can fall in love when they manage to neutralize and forget the fact that women belong to an inferior class. Here, "seriousness" marks this woman as belonging to such a class. It prevents this man from being attracted or from falling in love. It obstructs his capacity to bestow value on her because a "serious woman" precisely lacks value; she does not demand that the man performatively executes and proves his sexual status. In this sense, she lacks value because dominating her would not represent a victory in the competition with other men in the sexual field. That is, if sexuality is a field of struggle, status and prestige for men can be attained only if men can demonstrate to themselves and to others a victory over other men. A "serious woman" does not represent a victory over other men and does not demand the performative exercise and display of masculinity. This example from an Internet forum site illustrates this point:

> I think members of both sexes are often attracted to people who are not attracted to them. Someone who doesn't want you is irresistible. Often, when I know a girl is into me, that's a big turnoff. – Tom, 26, NY[96]

Men like Tom and Simon behave as if in a marketplace in which a greater supply of love than demand for it creates an *a priori* disequilibrium, which compels them to find ways to distance themselves. Distance and detachment, as we shall see, are key features of men's emotional styles when interacting with women.

Daniel is 50 years old; he works in an Israeli university, but lived in the US for many years. He holds radical left-wing views on many political issues and is a self-proclaimed feminist. He is wealthy, professionally highly successful, and divorced with two children. By his own admission, he had a good marriage to a woman with whom he still has a strong connection. However, shortly after becoming 40, he felt the urge to leave his wife and children when he fell in love with another woman, whom he subsequently left for yet another woman, whom he also left.

My first question to him was:

> What role does love – by which I mean romantic love – play in your life?

Daniel: All my life revolves around love. All my life revolves around love. Period. This is the very center of my life. The rest of my life all revolves around this issue. In the last few years I even understand better and better that behind my work there always was a Muse, a woman behind it. There is hardly a second in the day in which I don't think about love. I am hopelessly Romantic.... I am always busy with the topic of love.

However, what he means by "romantic" is quite different from how many women describe it. I asked him:

What do you mean you are always busy with love?

Daniel: It means I am always thinking about a woman, of course not always the same. When I think about a woman, I always think about her as *the* woman of my life, whether that relationship is real or simply fantasized. I have strong fantasies.

Interviewer: You refer to several women.

Daniel: Yes, because I like women. But I will always direct my thoughts to one single woman at a given point of time.
        A few months ago I was going out with a woman; we were going to the movies; we came back in her car, and we were talking, and then she calls me Danish, she made up a pet name for my name [Daniel]. At the very same moment, I felt as if she was raping me. Physically. I felt a kind of violation of my being. I had a physical experience of revulsion and rejection. I felt invaded. I felt immediately that with this woman, there is no chance. I don't want – didn't want the love of this woman.

Interviewer: Did you separate from this woman?

Daniel: The day after. I told her immediately that I could not stand being called this way. I told her I could not be with her.

Daniel starts by describing a series of life-enhancing experiences in which love plays a central role. He does not view himself as unable to commit or to love. On the contrary, he is overwhelmingly committed to the experience and sentiment of "Love" and claims to "wilt" like a flower if he does not experience it. But here, love and the exaltation associated with it do not derive from a steadfast commitment to one person, but from what consumer studies scholars dub the "Variety Drive,"[97] a result of choice in a market of possibilities and the emotional excitement of beginning a new relationship. Daniel, like Simon, is in a market where there is huge sexual choice in the economic sense, in that he has numerous options. Here I would hypothesize that both men are expressing a need for distance: one cannot bear a woman's *a priori* commitment; the other cannot bear a manifestation of closeness beyond boundaries known only to him. This is not a fear of intimacy as popular or even not-so popular psychology would have it.[98] Both men express a strategic attempt to establish some distance from their respective women by creating an emotional boundary because women are much more likely to want to commit to a relationship, to want it earlier, and to want exclusivity. Women present themselves as being sexually and emotionally more available than men, which, in turn, makes men – of equal or superior socio-economic status to them – better able to control the emotional terms of the encounter. In economic terms, we can say that in a market that essentially is controlled by men through their command of economic resources, if a woman gives sex freely and signals her *a priori* desire to commit, she is giving away too much. Women's emotionality is dominated by men through an emotional relationship of supply and demand, abundance and scarcity: a good in great supply creates an abundance of choice, which is accompanied by the problem of hierarchizing, building preferences and ascribing value. Abundance makes it difficult to ascribe value. Scarcity, by contrast, enables a quick assignment of value. Abundance is what permits Daniel to experience variety, to leave an otherwise perfectly good marriage, and to redirect his fantasies to a larger number of women. The problem is that the various objects of his desire, by virtue of their accessibility and number, lose value, because value derives from the capacity to order and to hierarchize, which is more difficult if there are too many available options and if these are not significantly different. Scarcity is precisely the social process through which an object or a person is made to acquire value: "Scarcity means that people want more than is available."[99] Conversely, it means also that when the supply of objects outstrips demand, the desire for them decreases.

The quotes above are characterized by the implicit equation these men make between desire and distance. I suggest that the cultural mixture of erotic excitement, boundary creation, and distancing they display constitutes a mechanism for finding a compromise between abundance and scarcity. Although the contrast might be overdrawn, we can say that while the problem of a pre-modern man and woman was to match each other's value as it was more or less objectively established (finding someone of similar family lineage, fortune, status, etc.), in the modern situation, subjective desire in the face of an abundance of choice is plagued by the economic and emotional problem of fixating on an object that has value and on the problem – for oneself – of monitoring and creating such value, thus endowing scarcity with an important role in the constitution of desire. To that extent, desire becomes economic: that is, it bears traces of the economic question of value, and of the quasi-economic mechanisms for creating value. It is the nature of romantic desire that has become economic, in the sense that desire is more closely associated with the dynamic of scarcity, as a way to bestow value. Take another example. This is a man aged 55, highly educated, divorced, and a father of one child. During the interview, he recounted his various relationships.

Interviewer: In your previous relationships did you reach a moment where you wanted to split up?

Steven: Yes. Always. [...] That's the story of my life. Most of the time I wanted to be alone.

Interviewer: So why did you go out with women?

Steven: Partly out of conformity.

Interviewer: If I understand you correctly, you're saying you had girl-friends but it was always "until further notice."

Steven: Yes, correct, beautiful. I felt until now that I could have a partner but it had to be temporary, limited, twice a week and a little on the telephone and that's it. That's enough for me, I don't need any more of it so I don't need partnership. Partnership is a burden. I have tons of people I could go out with but I don't have time. This is interesting and this and this, and I can't do it all. Why do I need a relationship to burden me now?

Interviewer: Do you think that's something true of women too?

Steven: No. At least from what they say, no. Let's say this, I'm speaking about the women I was with, it was never sym-metrical. They always wanted more of it. Why they wanted more of it, I don't know.

Interviewer: What is "it"?

Steven: More of it is more dates with me; more to be in touch; more talk; I hear them say all the time they don't sleep with you to sleep with you, they do it out of love and all that. I don't know, they have that saying, in conversation, in practice, it's true women wanted more of what I could offer, and that's really, that's always why it ended, with the fact that I couldn't offer more.

Interviewer: It always ended with that?

Steven: Yes, always.

Interviewer: Was there any exception to that?

Steven: Yes. There was this one time where this very famous journalist called me up; we met and she fucked me, the way men normally fuck women; which means she took her pleasure where she could and then left, did not call, and did not return my call. I was shocked. This never happened to me. That's the way a man usually behaves to women, but not the reverse.

Interviewer: Let's go back to the issue you raised before, of women who wanted more out of the relationship than you did. You're saying, for example, that they wanted to live with you and you didn't want to?

Steven: Let's say, I really couldn't. All my relationships, maybe I'm mistaken with one, but all my relationships ended with this. Always I let her break up with me, I think. That's the story I tell myself at least. I think it's pretty accurate, I don't know if I let them break up with me, but it always ended because I couldn't offer more... They wanted to live with me, share bank accounts, their bed, their books with me, but I couldn't do that.

Interviewer: So you can say these women wanted you more than you wanted them.

Steven: Absolutely; they always wanted more than I could offer.

Interviewer: Do you like the fact that you were wanted, more than you wanted them?

Steven: It's mixed. Because you have to manage all these demands. But it's true that it gives you a feeling of power. The one who is wanted more has more power.

Interviewer: Is that why you wanted less of them? To have power?

Steven: Maybe. But I don't know if it was very conscious or calculated.

This exchange articulates some of the elements discussed previously. The story told by this man is one of serial relationships, and abundance in two meanings of the word: the supply of women was abundant, and they bestowed their affection and love abundantly, in surplus, so to speak – that is, in a way that exceeded his demand. In fact, as he himself suggests, women always "wanted" more of him than he was willing to give, and his self-perception is that he constantly had to manage women's over-supplying of affection and need.

Desire here is incorporated within an economic view of emotion, where over-supply diminishes value and scarcity creates value. The point here is that sexual freedom creates abundance, which, in turn, generates the problem of assigning value to the object of desire, and only an object of value marks a victory in the competition with other men. That is, the modern situation in which men and women meet each other is one in which sexual choice is highly abundant for both sides; but while women's reproductive role will make them end the search early, men have no clear cultural or economic incentive to end the search. The avoidance strategies of all these men are not the mark of pathological psyches, but constitute a strategic attempt to *create scarcity*, and thus value, in a market where they cannot assign value, because women's sexual and emotional availability is in over-supply and because they control the sexual field. *Bridget Jones's Diary* is an illustration of the inexhaustible supply of clichés applied to the contemporary world of dating:

> Men, [Tom claims] view themselves as permanently on some sort of sexual ladder with all women either above them or below them. If the woman is "below" (i.e., willing to sleep with him, very keen on him) then in a Groucho Marx kind of way he does not want to be a member of her "club".... [T]he way to a man's heart these days is not through beauty, food, sex or alluringness of character, but merely the ability to seem not very interested in him.[100]

In reflecting on consumer culture, Russell Belk and colleagues suggest that what shapes our desires is the "scarcity or inaccessibility of various possible objects of desire."[101] Referring to the classical sociologist Georg Simmel, they argue that "we desire most fervently those objects that transfix us and that we cannot readily have. Objects' distance or resistance to our pursuit intensify our desire."[102] While some portion of human desire might be universally structured by this principle of scarcity, scarcity becomes a salient feature of desire precisely when abundance interferes with the problem of assigning value and when competition structures desire. For example, Gerald is a 46-year-old writer, journalist, and poet. He recounted an intense relationship with a woman who was having several parallel sexual affairs, all of which he knew about:

> It hurt me a great deal that she was having all these sexual affairs, but at the same time, it made her more desirable, because I had to prove myself all the time to her, because nothing was taken for granted, and also because I wanted to believe, no, I believed it actually, that I was the one she liked most, that she was most committed to.

Interviewer: So did you feel in competition with the other men she was seeing?

Gerald: Absolutely; all the time; that was difficult, but at the same time more exciting, it made her more difficult to get, so more worthy in a way, because I felt she never belonged to me entirely.

Or consider, Ronald, a 37-year-old art curator and artist, who told me that he practises polyamory: that is, he is involved simultaneously in many loving relationships with women.

Interviewer: Do you think there is one woman who could have made you prefer monogamy? I mean I am asking because you just said you don't know if there is one woman who could have made you monogamous.

Ronald: That's a tough one; I think if I met a woman like me, who did not want only one relationship, who accumulates men like I accumulate women, then, uhm, I think she would intrigue me enough for me to want to be only with her.

These accounts shed light on the reason why the highly decried and derided manual *The Rules*, published in 1995, had such resounding success and became something of a cultural phenomenon, with sales of more than two million copies. What the manual purports to teach is precisely the art of boundary creation and maintenance in the face of a structural situation in which men control the heterosexual encounter. The manual teaches and preaches that women must now become experts at creating distance in order to acquire scarcity and therefore value. It provides rules such as:

- 02: Don't Talk to a Man First (and Don't Ask Him to Dance)
- 03: Don't Stare at Men or Talk Too Much
- 05: Don't Call Him & Rarely Return His Calls
- 06: Always End Phone Calls and Dates First
- 07: Don't Accept a Saturday Night Date after Wednesday
- 12: Stop Dating Him if He Doesn't Buy You a Romantic Gift for Your Birthday or Valentine's Day
- 15: Don't Rush into Sex & Other Rules for Intimacy.[103]

In the context of a feminist politics of equality and dignity, these rules are both silly and demeaning. But the success of the book is deserving of some attention. It can be explained by the fact that these rules constitute cultural strategies to create scarcity and thus to increase the emotional value of women in a market where men control women's emotionality through women's readiness to commit. While *The Rules* is a very misguided attempt to correct the structural emotional imbalance between men and women, it hits at the core of the emotional imbalance in heterosexual relationships.

Abundance is thus an economic and emotional effect of sexual fields that are structured by hierarchy and competition and transform the nature of desire, activating it through the principle of scarcity, which, in turn, is supposed to reflect value and position in the sexual field. Thus, sexual abundance affects desire and the desire to desire. This is even more apparent in the second category of commitment phobia, which includes men (and, to a lesser, but real, extent, women) who cannot bring themselves to *want* to fixate on a romantic object.[104]

Aboulic Commitment Phobia

Aboulia can be described as a more advanced stage of the culture of abundance, in which the capacity to want and to desire unravels. Here are some examples from the Internet.

Dear Jeff,

I have been dating this girl for a year and a half. But since recently I have been *having doubts* and can't seem to get the thoughts out of my head. I come from a broken home and it seems to me that maybe I have just too many issues and they finally caught up to me.

My problem here is that I have doubts and am scared and don't think I can go on sometimes, but when I am with her I am happier and don't think of those things as much. Through all this I still feel as though I care about her and no matter how my mood changes, whether it be good or bad I know I still really care about her and love her.

I see her with me in the future but at the moment these reoccurring thoughts make it hard to stay positive. If you have seen this before or have any advice that would help me, because I really don't want to break up with her.

Jeff's Answer

I very rarely tell people what to do in these questions and answers, but in this case I just can't resist. STAY WITH THIS WOMAN! Why do I say this? Because your reasons for wanting out are all about fears and issues from the past. [...]

Anyone who agrees to a monogamous long-term relationship, or engagement, or marriage, can't help but question whether or not this is really the best person they will ever meet? *It's only natural to wonder if someone you might meet down the road will be better than your current partner.* (emphasis added)[105]

Below is an email exchange in an advice forum.

Until recently I've always had relatively low self-esteem and would be one to think of myself as more of an outsider looking in, believing that people did not really notice me. This reduces yourself confidence [*sic*] to the point that you feel unattractive. Needless to say I have been single for quite a while which leaves you feeling lonely and occupying your thoughts on meeting someone, thinking it will solve all your problems. Anyhow, I don't really want to get bogged down in too many theories at this stage. The main point in my mind is I believe that you are either with someone one, or not with them (in a relationship sense) as I can't seem to comprehend that whole "in-between" thing. I don't put this down to rushing into things or having high expectations of marriage or anything (my family history of marriage is rather shaky!). More that I just seem to believe that no matter how uncertain the path when you start out together, there is still some form of link that must be cut to return back to going it alone so to speak. *I for one am petrified of initiating that "cut" which is probably at the root of my fear. I'm scared stiff of hurting people's feelings and the moment you step into any form of relationship, you have someone [sic] feelings to think about and I find that responsibility quite overwhelming.* (emphasis added)

Some of the responses to this post:

[…] Maybe what you need to try and do is learn yourself that *you don't have to promise the earth* to people to get them to think lightly of you. And that if things don't always go to plan (as they seldom do) then that is not a reflection on you being a failure or a bad person. What are you like in situations where people ask things of you? Do you find it hard to say no?
[…]
As for the commitment, i think that *it stems from again promising too much* and promising it for the wrong reasons, and worrying that the new person will see through this. Maybe you just have to learn to take less pressure off yourself from the start. Good luck, Geo. (emphasis added)

I am just realizing now that I am also commitment phobic. I realize that this has been a pattern for almost all of my relationships. I realize that a lot of it comes from my parents marriage and divorce, and I immediately associate long term relationships with inevitable pain and suffering.

I love everything about the man I am dating but, as others have said above me, I feel *empty, emotionless and inadequate when I think of him and my feelings towards him.*
Everyone says that acknowledging the problem and talking about it is the first step, but what next?!? The anxiety is taking over my life. I had a panic attack so extreme I actually passed out. I am terrified of this happening again. I have never heard of anyone actually passing out from panic (other than tony from the sopranos, heh). I really really need help, any sort of direction would be appreciated.[106]

These posts revolve around three key themes. The first is the difficulty of developing emotions and thus preferences for an object, and the difficulty of settling on one person, a problem I describe as one of ascribing value to an object. However, and secondly, far from being hedonic, these accounts express a diminished sense of self, a self that doubts itself and has no demonstrable inner resources to actually desire what it wants. And the final theme is related to the difficulty of projecting the self into the future: that is, the oppressive character of promising. We see enacted here a deeply conflicted form of self-hood, in which the actors wish they could will something they cannot bring themselves to desire or in which they anticipate regretting something they have willed. Thus the fear of commitment manifests itself as *a flaw* in the structure of the will and as the incapacity to reconcile the emotions with the volition to commit. While in the previous accounts, the emotions are present and consist of a cycle of excitement and novelty, here the emotion itself seems to be defective. The fear and anxiety experienced by these men (and this woman) emanate from the yawning gap between the cultural ideal of a long-lasting committed relationship and too sparse resources for achieving these ideals. The question then is to understand the mechanism that depletes the cultural resources required for commitment. Although philosophers have tried to understand why we desire things we know are harmful to us, here the problem is that these people cannot bring themselves to will something that will be good for them (it is a problem of *akrasia*). In some ways, what is in question is the structure of love and desire as they relate to the core of the self. Harry Frankfurt suggests that love and care are intrinsically conducive to commitment. Commitment is a component or dimension of the will; it is a cognitive, moral, and affective structure that enables people to bind themselves to a future, and to forgo the possibility of maximizing their choices. Love is binding because

[t]he necessity that is characteristic of love does not constrain the movements of the will through an imperious surge of passion or

compulsion by which the will is defeated and subdued. On the contrary, the *constraint operates from within our own will itself*. It is by
our own will, and not by any external or alien force, that we are constrained. (emphasis added)[107]

It is precisely this type of will that is affected and disorganized in
these accounts which brings me to the last part of my argument: that
commitment phobia is precisely a cultural performance around the
problem of choice. The concept of the will evoked by Frankfurt is
viable only to the extent that it resonates with social institutions and
mechanisms of choice. When these change, the "inner" power of the
will as a constraining force also changes. In chapter 2 I referred to
the ecology and architecture of choice, which are the mechanisms
that shape and constrain the structure of the will. In the following
section I present the cultural repertoires and techniques used in
romantic decision-making, which in turn constitute the new architecture of romantic choice.

The New Architecture of Romantic Choice or the Disorganization of the Will

In pre-modern marriage markets, choice was shaped by the close
interaction of the self with family and the work environment, and,
perhaps because of that, it was binding. Modern marriage markets,
in contrast, seem to operate through the seemingly unconstrained,
free, and unfettered encounters between people whose faculty of
choice is not only exercised, but *ongoingly in demand*. Yet the faculty
of choice, far from being based on pure emotionality, actually entails
a complex affective and cognitive apparatus to evaluate partners, to
consult oneself about one's emotions toward them, and to predict
one's capacity to sustain these emotions. Modern intimacy and pairing
are not acts only of pure volition; they are also the outcome of choice
based on complex sets of evaluations.[108] Of course, it could be claimed
that choice described thus is not particularly modern. Historian Alan
MacFarlane suggests that during the ten years between puberty and
marriage, sixteenth-century English peasants and servants "were
constantly aware of solicitations and invitations, constantly examining their feelings. Starting with mild flirtations, many passed through
a series of affairs before finally settling on a particular partner."[109]

However, modern choice differs considerably in being characterized by three elements whose combination makes it properly contemporary: it is exercised usually through a large number of options, real

or imagined, or real *and* imagined; it is the outcome of a process of introspection in which needs, emotions, and lifestyle preferences are all weighed; and it emanates from individualized will and emotionality, engaged and responding to another's pure will and emotionality, which in principle need to be constantly renewed. That is, because a love choice is never entirely binding, it must be renewed through the ongoing and constant production of sentiments. Modern romantic choice is plagued by the problem of having to navigate between the cognitive monitoring of voluntary choice and the involuntary dynamic of spontaneous sentiment. Precisely because they are characterized by a deregulation of the mechanisms of choice, marriage markets create forms of choice that are increasingly similar to those operating in consumer markets. Consumer choice is a culturally specific category of choice, exercised through a combination of rational deliberation, refinement of taste, and the desire to maximize utilities and well-being. It is this new architecture of choice which, combined with the ecology of choice described in this chapter and chapter 2, inhibits decision and commitment. I next examine the components of this new architecture of romantic choice which affects men and, to a much lesser but definite extent, women.

As already mentioned, the sheer increase in and abundance of real and imagined sexual partners are a major cause of the transformation in the ecology of choice. This transformation has emerged as a result of the collapse of religious, ethnic, racial, and class rules of endogamy, which in principle allows anyone to access the marriage market.[110] It is accentuated by the extraordinary increase in the number of potential partners available through the medium of the Internet. This abundance of choice, real and imagined, induces important cognitive changes in the formation of romantic emotions and the process of settling on one love object. In fact, research on the effect of the abundance of choice on the process of decision-making suggests clearly that the greater availability of options inhibits rather than enables the capacity to commit to a single object or relationship. There are a number of explanations for why the capacity to choose and to commit to a choice has undergone a significant change in modernity. One of the transformations entailed both by the abundance of sexual choice and by the freedom to choose is that individuals are required to engage in an ongoing effort of introspection to establish their preferences, to evaluate their options, and to ascertain their sentiments. This demands a rational form of self-inspection which is accompanied by an essentialist (authentic) regime of emotional decision-making in which the decision to pair with someone has to be made on the basis of emotional self-knowledge and the capacity to project emotions into the future. According to this view, finding the best possible mate consists of choosing the person who corresponds to the essentialized self, the set of preferences and needs that define the self. Crucial to this conception of choice is the idea that through introspection, which entails a hyper-cognized process of decision-making, a rational assessment of our own and another's compatibility and qualities can and must be established. According to this model, introspection is supposed to lead to emotional clarity. In this sense, introspection is a major characteristic of choosing a mate in that it implies that both men and women must establish the strength and depth of their emotions, must envision the future of their relationship and the likelihood of its succeeding or failing. I would suggest that the strong cultural emphasis on introspection through the channels of popular psychological culture constitutes a major cultural attempt to engineer techniques to make choices. There are a number of reasons why we can and should doubt the capacity to make such choices.

(a) There is a great deal of evidence in cognitive psychology to suggest that human beings have built-in cognitive biases that prevent them from adequately evaluating, introspecting, and knowing what they want, and predicting their future feelings. In separate works, the cognitive psychologists Timothy Wilson and Daniel Gilbert (among others) show that people are ill equipped to engage in what Gilbert calls "affective forecasting,"[111] or the capacity to know how we will feel, because of cognitive biases: that is, systematic errors of thought (empathy bias, impact bias).

For example, Eugene is a 54-year-old divorced man who has been involved with 38-year-old Suzanna for two years.

Eugene: It has been difficult, although I love her very much.

Interviewer: Can you say why it has been difficult?

Eugene: Well, she wants children, a family. And I feel I cannot give her that. I've been there, I've seen it. I hesitated for a long time, I thought about this endlessly, I scrutinized myself as long as I could, and the amazing thing is that I just could not see one way or another what I wanted to do. I love her very much, but I don't want a new family, and in the end because I could not decide, I just couldn't decide what I wanted, we broke up. I broke up. Maybe she could have continued this way for a little while, but I felt I did not have the right to hold her back, she needs to have a family with someone else. But until today, I don't know if I did well, until today, I don't know what I really wanted.

This man cannot come to a decision, despite having undertaken a lengthy process of introspection, which has paralyzed his will at the same time as activating his rational capacity to evaluate situations. This is reminiscent of the words by the poet Theodore Roethke, quoted by psychologist Timothy Wilson: "[S]elf-contemplation is a curse/ That makes an old confusion worse."[112] Eugene is waiting for an emotional self-revelation which he cannot achieve through rational introspection because the self is not a "hard," fixed, knowable entity with clear edges, and with content. The social self is in fact a pragmatic entity, ongoingly shaped by circumstances and others' actions. In engaging in introspection, we try to discover fixed needs or wants, but these needs or wants are being shaped in response to situations. For this reason, introspection interferes with the capacity to feel strong and unmitigated emotions, activated through non-rational cognitive circuits.

(b) In the realm of romance and consumer choice, a greater number of available options often entails a very extensive process of information-gathering in order to adjudicate between different options, which may be a form of thought known as "rationality" and may be associated with masculinity. Such highly cognized and rational techniques of information-gathering, far from facilitating the process of decision-making, in fact complicate it, because of the problem that cognitive psychologists call "information overload." Cognitive psychologist Gary Klein has shown how having too many options motivates people to make comparisons, which diminishes the capacity to make quick decisions that rely on intuition. Decisions based on intuition are made faster, require emotions to be mobilized and use tacit knowledge unconsciously accumulated over time, and involve a willingness to take a risk.[113] Weighing and comparing options, by contrast, involves decomposing an object, a person, or a situation into components and trying to evaluate and weigh these attributes through a reasoned comparison between options, whether real or imagined. This form of evaluation relies not on holistic judgments, but on information that is parsed down. This has the result of breaking down the object to be evaluated into separate and discrete components in a process that thus blurs intuitive evaluation, viewed here as a non-formulatable or propositional form of decision-making, and stunts the capacity for strong emotional commitment. Intuition is necessary to make evaluations and decisions that cannot be made rationally because the formal weighing of options does not contribute to the strength or intensity of the individual's emotions. "Giving reasons" and decomposing an object into components diminishes the emotional force of decisions, which allows us to speculate on the very capacity of commitment. Deriving reasons in the process of decision-making may result in a loss of connection with the capacity to act on emotion and intuition because, by introspecting, people decompose a stimulus into different attributes: "There is evidence that evaluating a stimulus on several different dimensions *causes people to moderate* their evaluations" (emphasis added).[114]

(c) Following these insights, there is a very interesting finding that the rational evaluation of a given object (or person) tends to moderate and dampen positive appreciation of it. In other words, the act of cognizing the attributes of persons or objects diminishes their emotional appeal. Timothy Wilson and Jonathan Schooler conduct experiments that show that taste and evaluation, both of which are based on non-cognitive mental operations, are affected by verbal introspective evaluations (the spelling out for oneself of the evaluation criteria), and suggest that these introspective verbal evaluations in turn diminish the individual's overall positive evaluation of a stimulus.[115] This is because two processes could be at work. The first is related to the interference between verbal and non-verbal modes of evaluation. When the former replaces the latter, this tends to diminish the non-verbal capacity of "liking" or "disliking": for example, food tasting or visual appraisal are better achieved when *not* verbalized. The second process at work here is that the possibility of comparing many options tends to moderate one's feelings toward a given option.[116] Wilson and Schooler suggest that the process of rehearsing reasons – that is, the process of verbalizing the reasons for a specific choice – may diminish the capacity to make an intuitive decision. In that sense, a highly verbalized culture of choice may considerably reduce the capacity to be drawn into an emotional bond *for no* reason, and to make a commitment based on intuition. It is the cultural practice of intuition that becomes undermined in this case.

These findings might connect to other findings in the sociology of marriage. Although premarital cohabitation rates have increased dramatically, 40% of these relationships last less than five years, and most last for only two years. And while 55% of cohabitations culminate in marriage, these marriages are more likely than others to end in divorce.[117] Cohabitation is often viewed by both men and women as being motivated by a desire to resolve the decision related to marriage or life-long commitment. However, creating the reflexive conditions on which to base this decision may be incompatible with or at least not necessarily connected to commitment, which derives from a different cognitive and emotional structure than that promoted by introspective self-knowledge. There is some research that shows that pre-engagement/premarital cohabitation tends asymmetrically to reduce men's commitment to their partners,[118] to be associated with lower marital satisfaction quality, and to increase the risk of divorce.[119]

(d) The most significant impact of abundance on choice is that the greater number of options leads to what economist Herbert Simon calls a shift from satisficing to maximizing. Satisficers are people who are happy to settle for the first available, "good enough" option;[120] maximizers look for the best possible option. Several experiments show that greater abundance of choice, rather than simplifying choice, makes it more difficult, for this latter reason. Barry Schwartz suggests that one of the central mechanisms of a "maximizing" mindset is the anticipation of regret and the feeling of missing out on what economists call "opportunity costs." Greater choice creates apathy because the desire to maximize one's options and anticipation of regret over lost opportunities[121] affect the energy of the will and the capacity to choose.

For example, consider Philippe, a 48-year-old mathematician who has lived in New York City for the last twenty-five years:

Interviewer: What were the significant love stories of your life?

Philippe: Well it depends what you mean by that. I could say the five women with whom I have lived, but I could say also none, because with each and every one of them it was always the same problem, that I could never bring myself to feel "she was the *one*," the one and only, you know what I mean?

Interviewer: No, what do you mean by that?

Philippe: Well, for example, I lived with a woman for two years, we had a great relationship, interesting discussions, we laughed, we traveled together, we cooked, it was very comfortable. But when she started saying that she wanted to have children, then I had to ask myself what I really felt for her, and I just couldn't feel that kind of "Wow!" feeling, the kind of feeling I imagine you must have to make such a decision.

Interviewer: What do you mean?

Philippe: Like I must feel this is the woman of my life. I've got to be with her, otherwise I would be miserable, that she is the most stunning woman I could have, and I just couldn't feel this. I always felt that if it was not this one, it would be another one [*laughs*], maybe I am deluding myself but I feel that there are plenty of beautiful, smart women out there who will always want me. But the sad side of this maybe is that I also don't think there will be this stunning, outstanding woman out there that will make me lose my head.

This man's comments show how multiple options dampened his capacity to feel strong emotions for a woman. In a market of good choices, it is difficult to find one solution that outdoes any others because the capacity to be swayed in one's choice by strong sentiments derives from a sense of limited options or having identified the best deal.

Another example of the role of perception of choice and real increase in choice and the ensuing desire to maximize gains in the process of looking for a life partner appeared in the sociologically highly informative *New York Times* piece on "Modern Love" written by Diane Spechler. It recounts the adventures of one of her students (also her lover) in searching for a mate through a TV matchmaking program: "[T]he casting directors had begun analyzing my student's answers on questionnaires, sifting through hundreds of applications from women, and e-mailing him pictures of potential mates."[122] Although the man is involved in a very satisfying relationship with the narrator, he enrolls in this process and sifts through hundreds of profiles of women, selecting them on the basis of their physical appearance (some being "not attractive enough") and psychological compatibility. The TV show reflects the contemporary situation of choice based on information prior to the meeting. This man was eventually ejected from the program on the basis that he was too "picky," an attribute reinforced by the very conditions of choice. Pickiness, which seems to plague the entire field of romantic choice, is not a psychological trait, but rather is an effect of the ecology and architecture of choice: that is, it is fundamentally motivated by the desire to maximize choice in conditions where the range of choice has become almost unmanageable.

Commitment has instrumental and affective components.[123] Choosers in the marriage market clearly are trying to combine the rational and emotional dimensions of choice-making. However, research suggests that the affective dimension of commitment ultimately is the strongest because commitment cannot be a rational choice. The process in which the architecture of romantic choice is faced with ever-larger numbers of potential partners diminishes the capacity to make a strong affective commitment because it mobilizes cognitive processes that increasingly interfere with and undermine emotionality and intuition.

The features of choice described above are the cognitive and sociological conditions that set up the psychological state known as *ambivalence*. While ambiguity refers to a property of cognition (uncertainty about whether an object is this or that), ambivalence refers to emotions. For Freud, ambivalence was a universal property of the psyche and consisted of a mixture of love and hate. The philosopher David Pugmire defines ambivalence more generally as the simultaneous existence of two conflicting affects toward the same object.[124] However, I would argue that contemporary romantic ambivalence is different again: it refers to dampened feelings. "Cool ambivalence" might better describe this state, since it implies one of the main emotional tonalities referred to earlier, namely aboulia. Modern ambivalence takes a number of forms: not knowing what one feels for someone else (Is it true love? Do I really want to spend my life with him?); feeling conflicting emotions (the desire to explore new relationships while continuing in the current relationship); saying something but not feeling the emotions that should accompany the words (I love being with you, but I cannot bring myself to commit completely). Ambivalence is not intrinsic to the psyche but is a property of the institutions that organize our lives. Institutional arrangements are often responsible for people wanting conflicting goods: love and autonomy, and care and self-reliance, as expressed in the different institutions of family and market. Also, culture does not provide a clear sense of hierarchy among competing goods. As Andrew Weigert suggests, "If the conceptual labels used to interpret primary emotive experiences contradict each other, the result is blunted emotions. Neither dominates experience."[125] Ambivalence has a direct impact on emotions and feelings: "Without firm feelings toward who we are, action is hesitant, halting, and truncated."[126] Robert Merton, one of the first sociologists to analyze ambivalence, suggested that it may result from conflicting normative expectations within a role, but that such contradictions do not necessarily undermine this role. On the contrary, Merton reasoned that ambivalence can be functional to the social order. I would argue that it is functional to a situation where choice has become abundant and not limited by clear time frames. But while ambivalence may not be a problem, Merton posited that "it is the indecision that may follow and block action. The problem is abulia, although the pain is ambivalence."[127] Because desire cannot fixate on a single object and cannot desire what it in fact craves for, it becomes divided against itself.

Promise-Keeping and the Architecture of Modern Choice

The features described above explain, at least in part, why commitment and keeping promises have become problematic aspects of personhood. This is not to say that these aspects were unproblematic in the past, or that they affect all domains of social life. Promise-keeping, for example, can be viewed as one of the great institutional and psychological achievements of modernity, especially in the realm of economic transactions. I would suggest, however, that the nature of romantic will has changed and that its characteristic feature is its disconnect between emotional/sexual experience and commitment. Commitment, writes economist Amartya Sen, is defined by the "fact that it drives a wedge between personal choice and personal welfare."[128] In other words, to commit oneself means to make a choice in which one forgoes the possibility that one may increase one's welfare. Commitment implies a specific capacity to project the self into the future, the capacity to stop the process of searching and decision-making by forgoing the possibility of better prospects. Commitment occurs when a current choice seems the best possible one, and/or when one settles for a "good enough" choice. In a sense, then, commitment and love are deeply intertwined – at least subjectively. As philosopher Jean-Luc Marion puts it: "[T]o say, 'I love you for a moment, provisionally' means 'I don't love you at all' and accomplishes only a performative contradiction."[129] To love, Marion says, is to want to love always. This raises the question: when and why do choices no longer include the emotional force that binds one to the future?

Commitment is oriented toward the future, but it is a future in which one assumes that one will be and will want what one is and one wants in the present time. This is the temporal structure of promises:

> Verbal promises are no less unstable than other utterances in this regard; in fact, they are more so because promises are further characterized by a temporal disjunction. The locutionary moment of promising is in the present, but its illocutionary force is "future oriented and prospective" [....]. [E]very promise assumes a date at which the promise is made and without which it would have no validity.

As a result, "the present of the promise is always a past with regard to its realization."[130] This imaginary temporal disjunction is precisely what is in question in the cultural structure of the self in modernity. This is because the narrative of selfhood, shaped by psychological culture, has disposed of or at least eroded the performative and ritual ways of engineering emotions.

Ritual can be defined as follows:

> The presentation of ritual's "as if" universe, the subjunctive, requires neither a prior act of understanding nor a clearing away of conceptual ambiguity. Performance simply and elegantly sidetracks the problem of understanding to allow for the existence of order without requiring understanding. In this way, it is similar to kinds of decision we must make to take any concrete action, where we accept that we have as much understanding as we are likely to get and even though it is incomplete (as it always must be) action must be taken. This is true for a medical intervention, a financial investment, a marriage commitment, a declaration of war, or the planting of a highway – for virtually all forms of human endeavour.[131]

In other words, choice regulated by ritual is opposed to choice that is grounded in a regime of authenticity, introspectiveness, and emotional ontology. The first views commitment as a performative achievement generated by an act of will and a series of socially conventionalized rituals, the second as the outcome of introspection based on "real" emotions. Promise-keeping becomes a burden for the self because, in a regime of authenticity, decisions must reflect the "deep underlying" emotional essence of the self, and must follow the dynamic of "self-realization." As self-realization must be in a progression of self-development and change, it is more difficult to picture what the future self might be. Self-realization in this sense presupposes the potential discontinuity of the self: tomorrow I may be something that I am not today. The cultural ideal of self-realization demands that one's options should be kept open for ever. The ideal of self-realization entails a fundamentally unstable monitoring of the self, in which to develop and to grow imply that tomorrow's self must be different from today's. In the ideal of self-realization, one does not know what one may want tomorrow because, by definition, one does not know what will be one's multiple and higher selves. In the words of sociologist Robert Bellah and his colleagues, "[T]he love that must hold us together is rooted in the vicissitudes of our subjectivity."[132] The ideal of self-realization is a very powerful institution and cultural force: it is what makes people leave unsatisfying jobs and loveless marriages, attend meditation workshops, take long and expensive vacations, consult a psychologist, and so on. It fundamentally posits the self as a perpetually moving target, as something in need of discovery and accomplishment.[133] A single man wrote in a column for the *New York Times* about his choice not to enter marriage and domesticity: "One of the hardest things to look at in this life is the lives we didn't lead, the path not taken, the potential left unfulfilled."[134] The ideal of self-realization disrupts and opposes the idea of the self and of the will as something constant and fixed, and as praiseworthy precisely *because* of its constancy and fixity. To self-realize means not committing to any fixed identity and especially not committing to a single project of the self. In other words, the ideal of self-realization affects the very capacity and desire to project the self along a continuous straight line.[135]

Perhaps echoing this ethos, Derrida suggests that

> [a] promise is always excessive. Without this essential excess, it would return to a description of knowledge of the future. Its act would have a constative structure and not a performative one. [...][I]t is within the very structure of the act of promising that the success comes to inscribe a kind of irremediable disturbance or perversion. [...] Whence the unbelievable, and comical, aspect of every promise, and this passionate attempt to come to terms with the law, the contract, the oath, the declared affirmation of fidelity.[136]

I take Derrida's comment about promise-keeping to be somewhat symptomatic of the profound change to the structure of commitment in modernity, a change tightly intertwined with the modern ecology and architecture of choosing a mate. While, in Jane Austen's world, promises demonstrated the character's morality, in the testimonies above, promises are overwhelmingly oppressive. Promises have become a burden on the self. While promise-keeping locks the future in the present and the present in the future, now the future is open-ended and radically inalienable. It cannot be given to someone else. The difficulty related to articulating promises is in turn related to the profound changes in the ways that the future is incorporated in the emotional structure of modern love. The main characteristic of modern intimacy, which Anthony Giddens celebrates as ushering democracy,[137] is that it can be interrupted at any moment if it ceases to correspond to emotions, tastes, and volitions.[138] It is in this cultural context that promises can become "comical." Commitment is exercised in the framework of choice as the paramount organizing metaphor of selfhood. Promises – at least in the romantic context – become comical if relationships are based on the permanent exercise of choice and if choice leans on an essentialist emotional regime: that is, the view that relationships must be formed and based on sincere emotions, which must precede and ongoingly constitute the relationship.

The transformation of the structures of will and commitment has given rise to new forms of relationships, such as "hooking up" and BTP, or "Boyfriendy Type Person," which institutionalize ambivalence and the difficulty involved in making a choice:

> BTP: Acronym for Boyfriendy Type Person. The BTP is not quite your boyfriend yet, but is more important to you than a casual fling. This term is used during that in-between stage before you reach "official" boyfriend and girlfriend status. The BTP is someone you don't feel right calling your boyfriend yet, but you have been seeing quite a bit of each other, talking on the phone etc. and have strong feelings for each other but have not yet made the final leap into coupledom. You don't neccessarily have to be sleeping together, and you can be seeing other people (and not consider it "cheating"), though you may be feeling a bit guilty about this/get pissed off if you find out he is doing it, because the relationship is getting more serious. This term is used frequently by commitment-phobes. GTP is the female equivalent.[139]

However facetious, these expressions indicate a transformation in the patterns of connectedness between men and women, in which the cores of will and commitment have been transformed by the situation of choice in which the self is faced with a large number of possibilities and cannot project itself along a continuous line linking the present to the future.

To capture the modern cultural specificity of such commitment phobia, we can compare it to Kierkegaard's decision to break off his engagement to Regine Olsen. Debate has continued about his motivation: some think it was his deep, religious streak, others that it was his chronic melancholy and depression, or his concern that he would not be able to make her happy. Kierkegaard seems to have been committed to an uncompromising ethic of religious authenticity: he feared his marriage would be based on a lie because he would be unable to share many aspects of his inner life.[140] The motive of choice does not emerge in his decision to break off the engagement: whether this was the best choice he could make, whether she was the right person, whether it was "too early to settle down." In Kierkegaard's case, his ending of the engagement was a way of affirming the strength, not the weakness, of his will. This example illustrates how the cultural content of "commitment phobia" can differ in the sense that it may not contain the motive of "choice."

Sexual Abundance and Emotional Inequalities

Although both men and women have embraced freedom as the most fundamental value and institutional practice of their subjectivity in modern intimacy, they have followed different paths, which have provided different forms of this status. In addition, the new ecology and architecture of sexual choice affect the balance between the two genders. Numerous studies converge in finding that men engage more frequently in casual sex than do women and that, therefore, their attitude to casual sex is more positive.[141] Some studies report men paying more attention to physical attractiveness,[142] while others show that women need more emotional involvement than men to engage in sex.[143] Men are much more motivated by sex "than women, who tend to value more significantly intimacy, love, and affection," a view which resonates with Maureen Dowd's quote in the epigraph to this chapter.[144]

These findings are usually interpreted as pointing to different biological drives dividing men and women. However, I suspect that evolutionary biologists are looking to "nature" for some justification for the current social organization. If my analysis in this chapter is correct, sexuality is channeled differently for men and women, according to different strategies for gaining status: for men, sexuality has become the prime arena in which they can exercise their status of masculinity (authority, autonomy, and solidarity with men); for women, sexuality remains subordinate to reproduction and marriage. Men's and women's sexualities provide a crucial connection to social power, but the strategies they adopt are different. A deregulated sexuality in the context of an eroded and contested, but still present patriarchal organization of family and economy divides the paths to sexual encounter into serial sexuality and emotional exclusiveness. These two sexual strategies are not simply "different"; they give considerable advantage to the group of men who dominate the sexual field (owing to their occupation, economic power, sexual competence, etc.) because in the context of a deregulated sexuality, seriality provides greater emotional strategic advantage and power than the exclusivist strategy.

Women's sexual exclusiveness entails emotional attachment. The desire for exclusiveness makes women more likely than men to feel and express their emotions earlier and in a more intense way. Because women's sexual choice is linked to the fact that a woman's socioeconomic status is more directly dependent on a single man when mothering is at stake, women are more likely to be sexual and emotional exclusivists.[145]

Serial sexuality, by contrast, is accompanied by emotional detachment, and for a number of reasons: if sexuality is serial, detachment is more adaptive (serial emotional attachment would be very costly); chronological or simultaneous accumulation of partners tends to dampen the feelings for a single partner by virtue of the exposure to a large number of partners; and detachment is a form of ostentatious display of sexual capital to other men. In other words, serial sexuality – as an index of masculinity as status – is accompanied by male emotional detachment, which, in turn, plays an important role in commitment phobia, which expresses men's ecology and architecture of choice, and the resultant control over the heterosexual encounter with which it provides them. In more than one way, then, serial sexuality entails emotional detachment.

A telling example is to be found in the *New York Times* "Modern Love" essay quoted earlier by Marguerite Fields, in which she declares: "Sometimes I don't like them [men], or am scared of them, and a lot of times I'm just bored by them. But my fear or dislike or boredom never seems to diminish my underlying desire for a guy to stay, or at least to say he is going to stay, for a very long time."[146] This essay provides a powerful illustration for the asymmetry between men and women, precisely in terms of women's desire to commit and to see men commit to them.

These characteristics of women's and men's sexual strategies set up the conditions for what I call *emotional inequality*: serial sexuality provides men with the structural advantage of withholding their emotions, being more reluctant than women to commit to one relationship because they have a larger sample to choose from (in terms of time span and demographic characteristics). The following vignette is an example of emotional inequality. An Internet column user advises another woman:

I think you are right to be hesitant to force commitment with a "'commitment-phobe." My husband was terrified of commitment, would break up or leave me each time a new stage of commitment was introduced (when I wanted to start a more steady relationship, when I wanted to move in together, when I wanted to marry, and even after we married, when I wanted a child). He finally did settle into commitment after our son's birth, but then after a while I started to have issues – because I had been so pro-active in our relationship, I finally doubted that he loved me. It's an issue that he does need to solve in therapy – if he really wants to, which isn't certain. I am in therapy now trying to figure out mine. And there can be lots of pain involved (and in my case, the exacerbation of self-doubt) when trying to found a committed relationship with such a man. That's my experience, at any rate. unhappily committed.[147]

This woman's account and her pseudonym describe a state of emotional imbalance and inequality between men and women, and her attempts to address these emotional inequalities through therapy. These emotional inequalities are shaped in the context of the deregulation of heterosexual relations, of the fact that the conditions for choice for men and women have changed, and of the fact that those actors who have greater choice command a stronger position in the sexual field, whether because of their sexual attractiveness, youth, education, income, or a combination of any of these.

The terms of the bargain between men and women are shaped by their emotional positions in the romantic transaction. While in the nineteenth century, masculinity was expressed by emotional steadfastness and by the almost ostentatious display of men's capacity to make and keep promises, modern masculinity is more often expressed by a withholding rather than a demonstration of sentiment. Conversely, in the nineteenth century, women were more likely than men to be emotionally reserved, while today they are more likely to be emotionally expressive. As Vera, a supervising psychologist, puts it: "The main problem I have seen in my consultation for the last twenty years and in the consultation of the psychologists I train is that women want more love, more emotions, more sex, more commitment, and men evade all of them. Men even want less sex, by which I mean they want a less demanding form of sex."

Bourdieu coined the term "symbolic domination" to designate the ways in which some groups come to define reality and worthiness. Echoing this, I would suggest the term "emotional domination," which is exerted when one side has a greater capacity to control the emotional interaction through greater detachment, and greater capacity to exert choice and to constrain the choice of the other. The emergence of free-market conditions for pairing hides the fact that they have been accompanied by a new form of *emotional domination* of women by men, expressed in women's emotional availability and men's reluctance to commit to women, because the conditions of choice have changed.

As in the realm of economic relations, asymmetric relations caused by a lack of social regulation are obscured by the appearance of spontaneity and individuality. I suggest thus that we should describe commitment phobia as a specific emotional and relational pattern binding two people otherwise free to make choices in an environment where both exercise their choice in a different ecology and architecture of choice.

However, many would contest my analysis on the grounds that since the 1970s, seriality has increasingly characterized women's sexuality, thus making their sexuality and emotionality far less monolithic than is described above. Serial sexuality has been espoused by some women as an emancipated lifestyle, as the result of new injunctions to experience pleasure and equality. This is obviously true, but I would suggest that women adopted serial sexuality as a response to and imitation of men's power by this means. In light of the theory of symbolic and emotional domination, this is not surprising: if serial sexuality is an attribute of male status, it is likely to generate both imitation (of power attributes) and strategic responses (the only appropriate response to detachment is greater detachment). For women, serial sexuality has always coexisted with exclusivity and, thus, has been fraught with contradictions. Women tend to mix sexual strategies: serial and exclusive. More precisely, for women, seriality is a way to achieve exclusiveness, and is not an end in itself. Women opt for both the serial and exclusivist strategies, with the serial ultimately being subordinated to the exclusivist. In a nationwide best-seller, *Unhooked*, Laura Sessions Stepp writes about college girls who display new sexual habits, exemplified in the practice of "hooking up": "These young women chatted about their numbers [boys with whom they hook up] as if there were compiling data in a brokerage firm. They kept count in planners stowed away in bedside tables and typed names on Excel spreadsheets along with details and grades for performance."[148] This is in line with my analysis in chapter 2 of cumulative sexuality as a form of capital. As Stepp explains:

> [Y]oung people have virtually abandoned dating and replaced it with group get-togethers and sexual behaviors that are detached from love and commitment – and sometimes even from liking. Relationships have been replaced by the casual sexual encounters known as hookups. Love […] is being put on hold or seen as impossible; sex is becoming the primary currency of social interaction.[149]

But as Stepp's research and anecdotal evidence suggest, girls are more likely to feel love in a relationship if it involves sex. Stepp suggests that this creates a great deal of confusion, characterized by the fact that girls want to be attached and yet try to deny their need for attachment. The most consistent pattern she observes is that of girls fighting their need to be loved, and play-acting their indifference to and detachment from boys. In a British best-seller, *Breaking the Rules*, Catherine Townsend, recounts an autobiographical tale of multiple sexual adventures, foregrounding an emancipated, polymorphous, and highly active sexuality.[150] However, the narrative of her sexual adventures is entirely subordinated to her search for a single mate, whom she finds but who is not willing to commit to her. Her sexual adventures are experienced in the context of the search for a life partner. Another example is the TV series *Sex and the City*, together with its film spin-offs, which depicts women's free serial sexuality, but, as many have observed (and decried), this is subordinated to their search for a single partner. Finally, at the end of her "Modern Love" essay, Marguerite Fields – quoted earlier – suggests that: "I tried to think about my conversation with Steven [about his resistance to monogamy, see above], I tried to remember that I was actively seeking to practice some Zenlike form of nonattachment. I tried to remember that no one is my property and neither am I theirs."[151] These examples are illustrative that female serial sexuality is ultimately dominated by exclusivist sexuality. Women's emotions and desire for commitment are often *a priori* inscribed in their strategy of pairing and, as a result, women are more likely to experience conflicting desires, employ confused emotional strategies, and be dominated by men's greater capacity to withhold commitment through serial sexuality.

Conclusion

Freedom is not an abstract value, but an institutionalized cultural practice shaping such categories as the will, choice, desire, and emotions. The will is influenced by a structure of objective and subjective constraints, one of the most significant of which, in modernity, is freedom of choice. The modern architecture of choice presupposes a large number of possible partners for both men and women, and the freedom to choose freely one's partner, based on volition and emotion. But the pairing strategies and the architecture of choice attached to them entail different strategies to withhold and monitor detachment. Precisely because the sexual arena has become a competitive arena which bestows status and erotic capital, and because the trajectories for this erotic capital take different routes for men and women, men's commitment phobia becomes a cultural problem. That commitment phobia is the expression of a particular, culturally specific architecture of choice can be illustrated by comparing it with this cultural fantasy in which commitment is also withheld: Isadora Wing, the heroine in Erica Jong's novel *Fear of Flying* (1974), talks about the "zipless fuck," which has very different cultural meanings:

> Zipless, you see, not because European men have button-flies rather than zipper-flies, and not because the participants are so devastatingly attractive, but because the incident has all the swift compression of a dream and is seemingly free of guilt; because there is no talk at all. The zipless fuck is absolutely pure. It is free of ulterior motives. There is no power game. The man is not "taking" and the woman is not "giving". [...] No one is trying to prove anything or get anything out of anyone. The zipless fuck is the purest thing there is.[152]

This fantasy is underpinned by a different architecture of choice than the commitment phobia described in this chapter. In this fantasy, pure pleasure, sovereignty, and the equality of both parties are enacted. What makes this pleasure pure is precisely that the question of choice does not emerge; there is no ambivalence or anxiety about abandoning or being abandoned. It is a form of pure pleasure shared by both parties, where emotional detachment has no painful meaning – for that matter, no meaning at all – and is shared symmetrically. Such pure hedonism is made possible by the fact that neither of the people involved is called on to choose. It is precisely this pure intensity that is absent in the many accounts of men and women that revolve around the idea of commitment phobia, because this is predicated on the difficulties, ambivalence, and anxieties created by choice and by the abundance of choice, by the difficulty to create the emotional conditions for commitment, and by emotional inequality.

Emotional inequalities occur through the transformation of the (romantic) will: how a person loves and chooses to bind his or her life to that of another, itself the outcome of a transformation of the ecology and architecture of choice. As in the case of the market, the effects of freedom of choice are made all the more invisible in that pleasure is procured through the twin cultural ideals of autonomy and abundance, the two cardinal cultural vectors of the idea of freedom. Autonomy, freedom, and reason are the overarching goods of modernity, enabling each other and being a condition for the other. The very conditions of the institutionalization of freedom – in the transformation of the ecology and architecture of choice – have affected and transformed the will, as the core notion of personhood on which these ideals are based. It could be suggested also that much of therapy, self-help, and coaching culture can be reduced to cultural techniques to monitor choice and make decisions in an increasingly volatile market of possibilities. In this process, therefore, freedom becomes aporetic, for in its realized form, it leads to the incapacity or lack of desire to exercise choice. If there is a history of freedom, then we can say that we have moved from the struggle for freedom to the difficulty to choose, and even to the right not to choose.

4

The Demand for Recognition
Love and the Vulnerability of the Self

My Worthiness is all my Doubt –
His Merit – all my fear –
Contrasting which, my quality
Do lowlier – appear –

Lest I should insufficient prove
For his beloved Need –
The Chiefest Apprehension
Upon my thronging Mind –

'Tis True that Deity to stoop
Inherently incline –
For nothing higher than Itself
Itself can rest opon

So I – the Undivine Abode
Of His Elect Content –
Conform my soul as 'twere a Church
Unto Her Sacrament –

Emily Dickinson, "No. 791"[1]

[Achilles to Penthesilea]
True, by the power of love I am your slave, And I shall wear these
    bonds forevermore;
By luck of arms, though, you belong to me;
For it was you, my precious friend, who sank
At *my* feet when we fought, not I at yours.
        Achilles to Penthesilea, in Heinrich von Kleist, *Penthesilea*[2]

In his *Meditations*, Descartes draws the contours of a defining moment in modernity: a consciousness that grasps itself in doubt, and which in that very same action attempts to establish the certainty of what it knows. In his third Meditation, Descartes writes:

> I am a thinking (conscious) thing, that is, a being who doubts, affirms, denies, knows a few objects, and is ignorant of many, – [who loves, hates], wills, refuses, who imagines likewise, and perceives; for, as I before remarked, although the things which I perceive or imagine are perhaps nothing at all apart from me [and in themselves], I am nevertheless assured that those modes of consciousness which I call perceptions and imaginations, in as far only as they are modes of consciousness, exist in me.[3]

Descartes's intellectual acrobatics consist of claiming that the method to reach certainty lies in the exercise of doubt and that the ego is the only instance which can both doubt and certify knowledge, doubt being the way to establish certainty.

Much has been written about the will to control contained in the Cartesian attempt to establish the certainty of knowledge from within the walls of one's consciousness.[4] Less attention has been paid to the definite pleasure the ego takes in being able to constitute itself as the object of certainty.[5] In Descartes's text, the experience of doubt has a jubilatory character in the Lacanian sense of the pleasure that a baby takes in anticipating control over its body. Cartesian doubt is jubilant and jubilatory because it anticipates certainty.

Contemporary philosopher Jean-Luc Marion pursues Descartes's reflection and affirms that his metaphysics of objects – that is, a metaphysics whose purpose is to establish the certainty of objects – cannot help establish the certainty that is more important, namely the certainty of the *moi*, self or ego. The ego needs not only and not primarily an epistemic or ontological certainty, but an erotic one, which is perhaps the only certainty that can respond to the question of what certainty is worth. Marion suggests that the lover is opposed to the "cogitans" because where the latter looks for certainty, the former looks for *assurance* (or "reassurance") and replaces the question "Do I exist?" with the question "Does anybody love me?"[6]

Marion's reframing of Descartes's attempt to establish certainty is not fortuitous. It is symptomatic of the fact that ontological security and a sense of worth are now at stake in the romantic and erotic bond. To say that sexual encounters have become organized in social fields is precisely to say that they can produce social status and a sense of worth. Even a casual glance at modern sexual and romantic relations reveals that sexuality and love have become important components of the individual's sense of self-worth. I would claim that in the conditions of late modernity, it is the erotic question that best articulates the problem of reassurance, and that this has replaced the epistemic question in a shift that is fraught with the aporias of the self in modernity.

Why Love Feels Good

Love has been viewed by philosophers as a form of madness;[7] yet, it is a peculiar form of madness for its power derives from the fact that it enhances the ego and provides it with an accrued perception of its power. Romantic love enhances the self-image through the mediation of another's gaze. To quote one of the classics on the matter, Werther, "She loves me. And how precious I have become to myself, how I – I can say this to you, who have understanding for such emotions – how I worship at my own altar since I know that she loves me!"[8] When in love, the other becomes the object of one's uncritical attention. David Hume makes the point with apt irony: "One who is inflamed with lust, feels at least a momentary kindness towards the object of it, and at the same time fancies her more beautiful than ordinary."[9] Simon Blackburn comments that "[l]overs are not literally blind. They do see each other's cellulite, warts, and squints but the strange thing is that they do not mind them and might even find them enchanting."[10] Such forgiveness is intrinsic to love and has the result of making the object of love (temporarily) value him/herself more markedly. Freud also was struck by the fact that the erotic phenomenon is characterized by a peculiar mode of evaluation: "[W]e have always been struck by the phenomenon of sexual over-evaluation – the fact that the love object enjoys a certain amount of freedom from criticism, and that all its characteristics are valued more highly than those of people who are not loved, or than its own were at a time it itself was not loved."[11]

For Nietzsche, it is not the fact that one is the object of another's uncritical attention that increases one's sense of worth, but rather the very act of loving increases one's vital energy: "One seems to oneself transfigured, stronger, richer, more complete. [...] [I]t is not merely that it changes the feeling of values; the lover *is* worth more."[12] As Simon Blackburn puts it:

[T]he lover not only makes up the object of his desire, but also makes himself or herself up in their own imagination, in something of the same way that people are said to brace themselves when they look at flying buttresses, and to rock to and fro when they imagine being at sea. The poetry or feigning can take over the self, and for the moment at least we are what we imagine ourselves to be.[13]

Whether the emphasis is on the absence of criticism or on the vitality of the act of loving, there seems to be agreement that to be in love is to overcome a sense of ordinary invisibility, and entails a sense of uniqueness and an increased sense of self-worth.

That love enhances one's sense of self – in being uncritically loved and in loving – would seem thus to be a central component of the feeling of love, across a wide variety of socio-historical contexts. Yet, I claim that the sense of self-worth provided by love in modern relationships is of particular and acute importance, precisely because at stake in contemporary individualism is the difficulty to establish one's self-worth and because the pressure for self-differentiation and developing a sense of uniqueness has considerably increased with modernity. In other words, whatever subjective validation love may have provided in the past, this validation did not play a *social* role and did not substitute for social recognition (except in cases of social mobility, when a person of higher class married someone of a lower class). Romantic recognition had a less marked sociological character. I argue that it is the very structure of recognition that has been transformed in modern romantic relationships, and that this recognition goes deeper and wider than ever before.

From Class Recognition to Recognition of the Self

In 1897, two books of advice on courtship were published, both written by Mrs Humphry: *Manners for Men* and *Manners for Women*. The advice consisted of guidance about class and gender codes in middle-class courtships: men were counseled about their deportment and manners, how to walk in the street beside a woman, whether to introduce a woman before introducing a man, whether to offer an umbrella to an unknown lady, whether to refrain from smoking in the presence of ladies, which hand (right or left) to offer a lady stepping into a carriage, and how to extricate oneself from the problem of not having enough money to pay at a restaurant. The advice to women consisted of exhortations about remaining self-possessed, and sprinkling one's conversation with laughter (albeit not too loud), about how to ride a bicycle elegantly, which food and wine to serve when entertaining, which flowers to put on the table, and when to curtsey.

Many – if not most – of the advice books of the period were concerned with codifying gender and class within the realm of romance because they were aimed primarily at successful courtship, which generally depended on the ability to adopt the codes of the well-bred middle class. These books offered rituals of recognition, but a recognition which could be bestowed only if a person was able to show and display a list of *behavioral* do's and don'ts, which principally confirmed one's own and others' class membership and gender identity. Conversely, to honor another person's self was to produce signs which acknowledged and confirmed one's own and the other's social class and gender. To offend the other would amount to what sociologist Luc Boltanski called offending their *grandeur*, their relative importance and ranking on the social scale.[14]

Contemporary self-help books on dating are vastly different in content. The first chapter in *Dating for Dummies*[15] is titled "Who am I?" and has subheadings such as "Being Self-Confident" and "Finding Out What Makes You Tick"; *Mars and Venus on a Date*[16] includes sections entitled "The Dynamics of Male and Female Desire," "Acknowledge Men and Adore Women," and "Uncertainty"; while *Date…or Soul Mate?*[17] includes the chapters "Know Yourself" and "The Powerful Impact of Emotional Health." In these contemporary advice manuals, the center of gravity in the advice on courtship has shifted: it no longer refers to (middle-class) propriety, nor even to strongly coded sex and gender conduct, but focuses on the self, disconnected from rank and defined by interiority and emotions. More precisely, what is at stake, for both men and women, in these modern discussions of courtship is a view of one's worth as bestowed by others through proper rituals of recognition.

In a characteristic example, we read in *Mars and Venus on a Date*:

> The man's *confidence*, which allows him to risk possible *rejection* to ask a woman for her number, generates in a woman the *reassuring* feeling that she is *desirable*. When she considers his request and gives him her number, *his confidence is increased. Just as his active interest made her feel special, her receptive interest generated increased confidence in him.* (emphasis added)[18]

Here, class and gender boundaries have obviously disappeared. Instead, it is one's self that must be properly taken care of, and this self is now "essentialized," it exists beyond one's social class. The sense of worth now inheres in the self. As the author of the popular *Date...or Soul Mate?* further puts it: "The fact is, all of us are dying to feel good about ourselves, and when we feel especially good around a certain person, we will be amazed at how important and attractive that person becomes for us and vice versa."[19] The rituals of recognition must here acknowledge the "essence" of the self, not one's membership of the right class, and "feeling good about oneself" has become both the cause and purpose of falling in love. A wide variety of psychologists and psychoanalysts echo the view that the self needs to be reconfirmed. Psychoanalyst Ethel Spector Person puts the point succinctly: the experience of love is one in which the other is invested with a very high value and where the value of the self is always in question and demands to be confirmed.[20] Person's terminology and analysis point to an important transformation in the meaning of love in modernity. She writes:

> In mutual love, the lovers *validate* one another's uniqueness and worth. They literally confirm the existence and worth of each other's subjectivity. In love, there is a chance for the lovers to be fully known, accepted without judgment, and loved despite all shortcoming. [...] *Our insecurities* are healed, *our importance guaranteed*, only when we become the object of love. (emphasis added)[21]

The notions of "validation" and "insecurity" do not appear in the vocabulary of eighteenth- or nineteenth-century accounts of romantic love and constitute a new terminology and a decisively new way to conceive of the love experience. In fact, the notion of "insecurity" has become so central to contemporary notions of love (and of much contemporary advice on love and dating) that it compels us to inquire about its meaning.

Such psychological description contains and addresses features of our social world. What in common psychological language is called "insecurity" points to two sociological facts: (a) that our worth and value are not prior to interactions and are not *a priori* established, but are in need of being ongoingly shaped and affirmed; and (b) that it is our performance in a relationship that will establish this worth. To be insecure means to feel uncertain about one's worth, to be unable to secure it on one's own, and to have to depend on others in order to secure it. One of the fundamental changes in modernity has to do with the fact that social worth is performatively established in social relationships. Another way to say this is to suggest that social interactions – the ways in which the self performs in them – are a chief vector to accrue value and worth to the self, thus making the self crucially depend on others and on its interactions with others. While until the middle or late nineteenth century the romantic bond was organized on the basis of an already and almost objectively established sense of social worth, in late modernity the romantic bond is responsible for generating a large portion of what we may call the sense of self-worth. That is, precisely because much of marriage and romance was solidly based on social and economic considerations, romantic love did little to add to one's sense of social place. It is precisely the dis-embedding of love from social frameworks that has made romantic love become the site for negotiating one's self-worth.

To be able to appreciate what is so distinctive about the contemporary situation, we can briefly compare it to nineteenth-century courtship rituals. Although it may be a risky task to evaluate the content of people's emotional lives in the past, these rituals offer some interesting points of comparison and alternative ways of thinking about how the self was organized and taken care of in courtship. A frequent feature of nineteenth-century courtship was that men engaged in praising the woman they were courting while the woman's response frequently was to diminish her own value.

On April 9, 1801, Frances Sedgwick wrote to her father concerning her husband-to-be, Ebenezer Watson (whose marriage proposal she had originally rejected): "I wish I thought my own merits proportional in any fit measure to his. [...] As for me insignificant as I am, I can hope to cause little happiness anywhere but through countless time you will be remunerated for all your goodness to me."[22] Women openly expressed their sense of inferiority to their suitors. Far from being an isolated case, Sedgwick's feelings reverberated throughout the century. For example, in her study of nineteenth-century courtship, Ellen Rothman suggests that, "as the more idealized sex, women were more likely than men to fear that their lovers pictured them too highly. A Long Island teacher pleaded with her fiancé: 'While you think of me, so far superior to what I am, I would have you know me, just as I am; weak, frail, impetuous & wayward.'"[23] After her engagement to Albert Bledsoe, Harriett Coxe had similar feelings, but she confined them to a "private" letter, in which she wrote: "The depth and fervour of his affection for me, should not excite my vanity for I know that he greatly overrates me in every way." A New York woman, Persis Sibley, hoped her suitor would not make that mistake, writing to her admirer: "[D]o not look upon me as without faults for no doubt you will find many. I should not wish you to be disappointed by thinking me faultless." Sibley believed she had failed to convince her fiancé that she was "not faultless." She imagined the "severe trial" she would face when, after marriage, she would "see the scales falling from *his* eyes who has been blindly worshiping me as perfection. [...] 'Tis injurious to anyone to be overrated."[24] And Mary Pearson "considered herself unworthy of the affection [her suitor] Ephraim offered her and undeserving of his praise."[25] "[W]here Ephraim saw 'all that [his] imagination ever suggested as contributing to constitute a woman who could make [him] happy,' *she* saw only an ordinary woman full of self-doubt and insecurity."[26] And in a later example, Samuel Clemens (Mark Twain), in his courtship of Olivia Langdon, wrote:

> Now please *don't* feel hurt when I praise you, Livy, for I know that in doing so I speak only the truth. At last I grant you one fault – & it is *self-depreciation*. [...] And yet, after all, your self-depreciation is a virtue & a merit, for it comes of the absence of egotism, which is one of the gravest faults.[27]

In England – which had so many cultural affinities with the US – we observe similar presentations of the self, in the correspondence between Elizabeth Barrett and Robert Browning, for example. To the modern observer, it is striking that a not insignificant part of the Barrett–Browning correspondence is devoted to Robert's claims about Elizabeth's uniqueness and exceptional character, and Elizabeth's rejections of these declarations. In a letter written in September 1845, Elizabeth claims: "That *you* should care at all for *me* has been a matter of unaffected wonders to me from the first hour till now – and I cannot help the pain I feel sometimes, in thinking that it would have been better for you if you had never known me" (emphasis added).[28] In February 1846, when their courtship was already very advanced, Elizabeth wrote: "[N]othing has humbled me as much as your love."[29] And in March 1846: "[I]f you do not keep lifting me up quite off the ground by the strong faculty of love in you, I shall not help falling short of the hope you have placed in me."[30] Each of such claims in turn elicited strong protests from Robert and an intensification of his declarations of love and commitment. In a different example, Jane Clairmont, Lord Byron's lover for a short while, strayed from the passive role that should have been hers, yet respected the conventions of love letters when she wrote to him: "I do not expect you to love me, I am not worthy of your love. I feel you are superior, yet much to my surprise, more to my happiness, you betrayed passions I had believed no longer alive in your bosom."[31]

In these declarations, women stage their inferiority, but an inferiority not vis-à-vis the men who love them specifically, but rather vis-à-vis moral ideals of character (with the exception perhaps of the last example). This is bolstered by the observation that men also express self-doubts, albeit less frequently and less characteristically. Harry Sedgwick, a member of the Boston elite, was engaged to Jane Minot. During a period of separation of seventeen months they exchanged numerous letters: "One constant theme throughout this exchange was Harry's (un)worthiness – intellectually, spiritually, and professionally – as Jane's partner. [...] Toward the end of winter Harry experienced a brief crisis of confidence: 'I wish I could look into destiny,' he wrote, 'merely to know one thing – whether I shall ever become unworthy of you and forfeit your esteem.'"[32] We can infer certain things from these forms of self-depreciation. First, they presuppose that actors have "objective" ways of evaluating themselves. What is staged here is one's capacity to look at oneself through outside eyes and to hold oneself accountable to objective criteria of worth: that is, criteria that are common to and shared by both men and women. Moreover, it is quite possible that what is staged here is simultaneously one's capacity to criticize oneself (and therefore to display one's character) and one's capacity to build intimacy by revealing to another one's flaws and faults. In displaying their capacity to uphold an ideal of character, and to criticize their own self in the name of that ideal, these women and men stage a self that is not in need of what contemporaries would call "emotional support" or "validation." This is a self that can perform its own self-evaluation, and which derives a sense of worth not from "being validated" by another but from being held accountable to moral standards and from being improved in order to reach these moral standards. Undoubtedly such rituals of self-depreciation invite ritual protests from the other side; but rather than requests for "validation," they functioned as "tests" of the man's resilience and commitment. Here again, it is not the woman's "self" or need for validation that is at stake, but rather the man's capacity to display and prove his steadfastness.

These rituals of self-depreciation differ importantly from the danger that looms over contemporary romantic relationships, namely that they fail to generate validation. Let me explain with examples gleaned from popular culture and my interviews. Susan Shapiro wrote a memoir about "five men who broke [her] heart." She makes us privy to a conversation with her husband, Aaron, in which she refers to an ex-boyfriend of hers, Brad.

Brad's email said "I still love your brain." Why don't you ever say that? It was the first compliment in years that made me feel good.

"He still loves to fuck with your brain." Aaron stood up, taking his bag into the Bat Cave [i.e., his den].

I followed, moving the scripts on his faded gray couch so there was room to sit down. I knew he was out of it, but we'd barely spoken in the week. He expected to find me waiting in the exact same place, as if he'd left a bookmark.

"You never call me smart," I said.

"I compliment you all the time." He was annoyed. "I just called you beautiful."

He didn't get it, I always had to explain. "I grew up the only girl with three brothers everyone called brilliant. I was cute or pretty or adorable. That doesn't do it for me. Don't you know me at all?" I pleaded. "Why do I need ten thousand books and clips everywhere? To overcompensate. To convince everyone I'm smart 'cause nobody ever said it...to convince myself," I said. "I become what's missing."

"Now that's smart," Aaron said, patting my forehead. "You ugly pig."[33]

This woman's complaint and request are motivated by her need to see her self validated, in both a personal and a social way. She demands from her husband confirmation of her social worth. To take another example, a 56-year-old woman talking about her marital difficulties says:

> You know I have a very sweet husband; he is loyal and devoted. But he just does not know to do those small things that make you feel good.

Interviewer: Like what?

Christine: You know buying little presents, surprising me, telling me how wonderful I am. Even though I know he loves me, he does not know how to make me feel wonderful and special.

Interviewer: Even though he loves you?

Christine: Yes. [*Silence*] You know loving is all about the how, not the what. Even though I know he loves me. But that something that makes you feel special and unique has always been missing.

In the nineteenth century, loyalty and commitment would have been considered crucial testimonies of love. But here they are deemed insufficient precisely because love must imply an ongoing, interminable process of "validation": that is, a reconfirmation of one's own individuality and value.

If, as Sartre suggests, the lover *demands* to be loved,[34] it is because in this demand lies first and foremost a social demand for recognition. The compliments the two women quoted above want from their husbands point not to a defective "narcissistic" personality or to a "lack of self-esteem," but rather to a general demand that romantic relationships provide social recognition. Social worth is no longer a straightforward outcome of one's economic or social status, but has to be derived from one's self, defined as a unique, private, personal, and non-institutional entity. The erotic/romantic bond must constitute a sense of worth,[35] and modern social worth is chiefly performative: that is, it is to be achieved in the course of and through one's interactions with others. If "the lover, preparing to meet the beloved, worries about his smell, his clothes, his hair, his plans for the evening, and *ultimately his worthiness*" (emphasis added),[36] it is because, in modernity, love has become central to the constitution of worth.

Although he did not theorize his sociology as a sociology of modernity, Erving Goffman paid a great deal of attention to the performative dimension of social interactions: that is, to the ways in which they produce or fail to produce a sense of worth (when they "save face," pay due deference to another, etc.). Goffman appears to take for granted that interactions, if successful, ought to produce a sense of worth, and seems to presume that interactions are universally structured in this way. But this is a result of a long process of transformation of social structure and of sociability in Western Europe. From the seventeenth century onward, in salons, courts, and manuals of conversations and etiquette, both aristocracy and the middle classes endlessly codified new forms of behavior which aimed at properly recognizing and paying deference to others as persons through facial expressions, bodily comportment, and speech. This process differs from the deference given to others in order to preserve their sense of honor, because social worth became progressively disentangled from *a priori* ascribed status. In other words, recognition, as the implicit imperative that we bestow value on another person *as a person, regardless of his or her status, in* and *through* social interaction, is part and parcel of the formation of modernity. At the level of theory, it was Axel Honneth who established in a definitive way the importance of recognition in interpersonal relations. (His use of "recognition," however, is broader than mine.) As he defines it, recognition is an ongoing social process which consists of backing up "the positive understanding [that people have] of themselves." Because "self-image [...] is dependent on the possibility of being continually backed up by others,"[37] recognition entails an acknowledgment and reinforcement of another's claims and positions, at both the cognitive and emotional levels. Recognition is the process by which one's social worth and value are ongoingly established in and through one's relationships with others.

Thus, in contradistinction to the vast amount of scholarship which explains the power of romantic love in modernity through the ideology of individualism,[38] I argue that this power derives from the more primary fact that love provides a strong anchor for recognition, the perception and constitution of one's worth, in an era where social worth is both uncertain and ongoingly negotiated. But why is this so? Why can love do what other sentiments are less able to do? I can offer a possible explanation for this.

Combining the insights of Émile Durkheim and Erving Goffman, Randall Collins[39] claims that social interactions function as rituals which create emotional energies that bind or separate actors. These emotional energies are exchanged in a market based on emotional (rather than purely cognitive) negotiations. The goal of this social exchange is to maximize emotional energies. The accumulation of successful interaction rituals creates emotional energy that becomes a kind of resource we can capitalize on, a way of dominating others, and of building further social capital. Emotions – emotional energy specifically – are thus the source of positive interaction ritual chains, which in turn can be capitalized in other, not strictly emotional domains. Emotional energy accumulated in purely "social" domains (friends or family) can be transported, carried over, so to speak, into other domains, such as the economic realm. Thus, what Collins calls emotional energy is actually an effect of recognition properly carried on; recognition accumulated in one realm is carried over in other realms. While he does not ask whether some interaction rituals are more important than others, or carry "more" energy, I claim that love is a central link – for some, perhaps *the* central link – in the long chain of interaction rituals. That is, romantic love is central to the recognition order by which in modernity social worth is accrued to a person through interaction ritual chains. This is because it is the most intense and total way of producing emotional energy, an effect of the ego-enhancement induced by love. Two examples can be offered: Talia is a 42-year-old academic, with two children; she works at a large American university on the West Coast. After telling me the story of her break-up with a man with whom she had an extramarital affair, she adds:

You know it hurt, I agonized over it, but I feel that I also took away very important things from that story.

Interviewer: Which things?

Talia: He was, well he is a very famous academic. Everyone is in awe of him. Before I met him, I felt I was this invisible, insignificant thing, that no one paid attention to me. I always felt the more stupid one in the room. But when he chose me, when we were having this affair, I felt I had become a very special person, I literally felt smarter, and I could go up to people I would have never dared to talk to, I could talk to them and feel their equal. Even now that it is over, I feel I learned something important about myself, because if he could think I was special, then I felt I was special. I became less afraid of people.

Interviewer: By having been loved by him?

Talia: Yes, by having been loved by him.
Wait a minute, well, I don't know if he even loved me; sometimes I felt loved, sometimes I wasn't so sure, but I felt desired, I am sure he desired me tremendously. So yes, by having been desired by him.

In an autobiographical article on love published in the *New York Times* in 2010, the writer Laura Fraser recounts the end of an encounter with a man in Italy after her husband had left her. "We parted on the fourth day at the train station in Naples, with me memorizing his face, feeling bereft and hopeful. I was sure I would never see him again but I was happy that he had managed to make me feel *desired*" (emphasis added).[40] Here, feeling desirable trumps her feeling of bereavement from her "failed marriage," precisely because love is at the heart of the problematic of worth and recognition.

Love and desire here are nodes in a social chain in which one form of emotional energy can be converted into another. Because the experience of love anchors the question of worth, love in modernity has the capacity to produce and stabilize *social* value. As Honneth argues, love is the paradigm for the establishment of "recognition," a simultaneously psychological and sociological process.[41] Never really either private or public, the modern self establishes its value through processes that are at once psychological and sociological, private and public, emotional and ritualistic. Clearly, then, in modern erotic/romantic relationships what is at stake are the self, its emotions, interiority, and, mostly, the way these are recognized (or fail to be recognized) by others.

Recognition and Ontological Insecurity in Modernity

Yet, it is also the role played by recognition that creates ontological insecurity. The need for what Marion calls "assurance"[42] takes on a particular poignancy and acuteness when the conditions to secure recognition are both uncertain and fragile. Indeed, the modern cultural obsession with "self-esteem" is nothing but an expression of the difficulty experienced by the self to find anchors of ontological security and recognition.

The move from pre-modern to modern courtship is the move from publicly shared meanings and rituals – the man and woman belonged to a common social world – to private interactions in which another's self is evaluated according to multiple and volatile criteria such as physical attractiveness, emotional chemistry, "compatibility" of tastes, and psychological makeup. In other words, the changes undergone by love in modernity have to do with the transformation of the very tools of evaluation on which recognition depends: that is, with their refinement (how elaborate they are) and their individualization. Social class and even "character" belong to a world where the criteria to establish value are known, publicly performed, and there for everyone to judge. Rank, value, and character are publicly – that is, objectively – established and shared. Because social worth has become performative – that is, because worth must be negotiated in and through individualized tastes, and because of the individualization of the criteria for worth – the self is faced with new forms of uncertainty. Individualization is a source of uncertainty because the criteria for evaluating others cease to be objective: that is, cease to be submitted to the examination of several social agents who share the same social codes. Instead, they become the result of a private and subjective dynamics of taste.

For example, "sexiness" and "desirability" – although they follow canons of public images of beauty – are entirely subjected to an individualized, and hence relatively unpredictable, dynamics of taste. "Desirability" as the paramount criterion for choosing a mate greatly complicates the dynamics of recognition. It creates uncertainty related to the fact that, in becoming individualized, desirability implies that men and women have little ability to predict whether they will attract a potential mate and/or sustain his or her desire. Although there are cultural models and prototypes for desirability, to be "desirable" depends on a highly *individualized dynamic of taste* and psychological compatibility, and is thus ultimately unpredictable. These criteria for desirability are all the more unclear in that they are more refined (i.e., they have a much higher degree of specificity), and more subjective (made to depend on the idiosyncratic psychological makeup of the person who chooses).

In modern romantic relations, recognition is both crucial and complex because worth is performatively established, because this process has become highly individualized, and because of the ensuing multiplication, and thus unpredictability, of criteria for choosing a mate. This in turn makes love the terrain par excellence of ontological insecurity and uncertainty *at the very same time* that it becomes one of the main sites for the experience of (and the demand for) recognition.

For example, consider Daniel, the highly successful 50-year-old man whom we met in chapter 3. Despite exuding a great deal of self-confidence, he claims:

> Love is great, but also difficult. But the difficulty is not one of suffering, but one of magic. What is difficult also is that there is no certainty. You are never certain. Relationships are not like a contract. [What is difficult] on a day-to-day basis is when I lose confidence that I am getting the love I want.

Interviewer: What can make you feel this way?

Daniel: Not to get the right signals. The signals that indicate I am loved. For example, she sent me an SMS expressing concern about me. That made me very happy. Then, I sent her an SMS asking she updates me about her day. She said OK, and then at night I get this email; "I have guests. Will talk tomorrow. Sleep well." And that throws me off. Then I analyzed every single word, and tried to scrutinize them. [....] These things can make me cry, not feel blasé.

Despite this man's attractiveness and professional success, his sense of self is threatened when not appropriately recognized by his partner because, as he himself presents it, love is an uninterrupted flow of signs and signals that must back the self's worth. The capacity to produce and reproduce recognition in love must be periodically staged. In other words, recognition is not something that is given once for all, but rather a complex symbolic work that must be maintained through repeated rituals and which can threaten and engulf the self when not properly executed.

In a book on shy singles, the author, a psychologist, describes in psychological terms an experience which is in fact sociological:

> In my experience as a New York City psychologist, dating is the
> common denominator that triggers shyness among single men and
> women of all ages. In their quest to find someone with whom to share
> their lives, many of my clients tell me they are often plagued with *such
> intense feelings of fear, rejection, and unworthiness that they grasp at
> any excuse to stay home.* [...] About a decade ago, I began to notice
> that client after client reported feeling socially incompetent, invisible
> to others, and fearful – especially in dates and in social situations.
> (emphasis added)[43]

Precisely because worth is not known in advance and because it is
performatively generated – that is, bestowed by and in the romantic
interaction – these romantic interactions elicit acute anxiety: what is
at stake in them is the performance of the self and hence its worth.
These clients' sense of invisibility or, to use a more common term,
their "fear of rejection" is thus first and foremost a fear of what
Honneth dubs "social invisibility," a state where one is made to feel
socially unworthy. As Honneth suggests, social invisibility can be
produced through subtle, not overt, forms of humiliations. Expressive
responses of the face, the eyes, and smiles constitute the elementary
mechanism of social visibility and an elementary form of social recognition.[44] It is this social invisibility that threatens the self in romantic relationships precisely because signs of validation hold the promise
of providing full social existence. "During this first stage [of court-
ship], shy singles feel overwhelmed [...] by the fear of rejection and
uncertainty. They simply can't make the first move – to say hello,
make eye contact, ask someone out for a drink, or initiate intimacy."[45] The widely discussed "fear of rejection" is thus a social fear,
caused by the fact that social worth is established almost only and
exclusively by the recognition granted by others. Shy singles more
than others embody the threats over the social definition of one's
existence. "[A] Shy obsessively criticizes himself for blunders – real
or imagined. This kind of punishment unintentionally weakens the
self and depletes self-esteem."[46] This self-critique is substantially different from the nineteenth-century self-depreciatory strategies discussed above: it does not consist in a display of character, itself based
on the (approximate) knowledge of self-worth and of the ideal one
should aspire to. Rather, it reflects what we may call "conceptual
self-uncertainty," or the uncertainty about one's self-image and about
the criteria for establishing such a self-image. Conceptual uncertainty
is chiefly tied to the fact that the criteria of personhood and character
ideal have become unclear, and to the fact that social relationships
are plagued by uncertainty about one's social worth and about the
criteria against which one will be judged to establish worth.

Conceptual uncertainty stands on the opposite side to the self-depreciation evoked above: such self-depreciation was explicitly stated and ritually performed rather than hidden; it does not threaten the self ideal and even embodies it, it calls for another's ritual reassurance and thus creates a bond, and finally it presupposes an implicit reference to moral ideals known to both parties.

The "fear of rejection" is a danger ever-looming in relationships, because it threatens the entire edifice of self-worth. Let me offer some examples. Writing to his brother Theo, Van Gogh describes the ways in which his love was rejected by Kee, his cousin.

> Life has become very dear to me, and I am very glad that I love. My life and my love are one. "But you are faced with a 'no, never never'" is your reply. My answer to that is, "Old boy, for the present I look upon that 'no, never never' as a block of ice which I press to my heart to thaw."[47]

Here, being rejected clearly is not translated as a threat to one's status or sense of worth. It is yet another opportunity for a man to show and prove his capacity to thaw the ice of someone's rejection. Compare this with a 40-year-old lesbian woman in a new relationship, who said in an interview:

> We had an amazing weekend where I met her friends and family, and also we had amazing sex, and after that weekend she tells me, maybe you should come only for two hours tonight, or maybe we should wait till tomorrow to see each other. I felt such anger and rage at her. And you know, now, as I am talking to you, I feel overwhelmed with anxiety. I feel paralyzed. How could she do that to me?

This woman is engulfed by acute feelings of anxiety because her lover's request to meet for "only" two hours boils down to a feeling of "social annihilation." In her autobiographical memoirs, Catherine Townsend, the sex columnist for the *Independent*, recounts her break-up with her boyfriend. The break-up brings her to such levels of agony that she attends a Sex and Love Addicts Anonymous Meeting. At the meeting, she presents herself in the following way:

> My name is Catherine, and I'm a love addict [...]. Until today, I couldn't figure out why it couldn't get over my last relationship. But I think it's because I wanted to be good enough to be the One for him. I think *I wanted to prove, on some unconscious level, that I was good enough to get someone to marry me*. So I was desperate to keep my ex no matter what. (emphasis added)[48]

Clearly, her suffering is about her sense of self-worth, which can be constituted or annihilated by love. Or, to quote another contemporary testimony by Jonathan Franzen:

> The big risk here [in love], of course, is rejection. We can all handle being disliked now and then, because there's such an infinitely big pool of potential likers. But to expose your whole self, not just the likable surface, and to have it rejected, can be catastrophically painful. The prospect of pain generally, the pain of loss, of breakup, of death, is what makes it so tempting to avoid love and stay safely in the world of liking.[49]

And in a *Glamour* blog on the Internet, a woman recounts that when she separated from her boyfriend, her "heart was in a blender," and that "it took months (if not years) to get fully over him." Her friends helped her overcome her distress by telling her she "*was awesome*, fed [her] lots of chocolate and watched [with her] endless cheesy movies."[50] The reaction of these friends is typical of the widespread intuition that a romantic break-up threatens one's basic sense of worth and the foundations of one's ontological security. These findings are confirmed in research conducted by two sociologists quoted in the "Modern Love" column in the *New York Times*: "For women, whether they're in a relationship at all – no matter how awful – is what counts. 'It's a little bit pathetic,' Ms Simon [the researcher] allowed. 'Even though there's been so much social change in this area, women's self-worth is still so much tied up with having a boyfriend. It's unfortunate.'"[51]

The caveat to this last claim is that if women's self-worth is *still* tied to having a boyfriend, this is not because they have not managed to rid themselves of an unwelcome vestige of the past, but precisely because women are modern in their dependence on love for their sense of self-worth. Advice literature on dating, sex, and love has become uncannily profitable precisely because the stakes of love, dating, and sex have become very high in terms of their capacity to establish social and self-worth.

But some will retort that surely the self has always been implicated in romantic affairs in which love was uncertain and unreciprocated. Surely pain and suffering are among the oldest tropes in world literature on love. That is obviously true, but for sociologists, the question of *how* the self is implicated, praised, or devalued is of crucial importance. My claim is that not only is the self differently implied in romantic interactions, but the very experience of psychic suffering in modernity differs from the ways in which it was experienced in the past. I would argue that although pain is one of the most ancient motifs of love, it was experienced in four different and/or overlapping cultural frameworks, which have become foreign to our sensibility. These four pre-modern cultural framings of romantic suffering are: the aristocratic, the Christian, the Romantic, and the medical.

In the history of Western Europe, perhaps the first widespread cultural model which put suffering at the center of the experience of love was courtly love.[52] In the literature of the troubadours of Provence, the sufferings provoked by unrequited love purified the soul of the lover. This suffering in fact is the very source of the troubadour's poetic inspiration. Owing to Platonic influences, courtly love was intensely idealistic, and thus was able to transmute love and its suffering into a noble experience. More than that: love and its suffering ennobled both lover and beloved; in this scheme, then, love would "make people better, finer, more likely to realize their human nature."[53] A clear example of this is the following account:

> I find the pain of love so pleasing that, though I know it intends to kill me, I neither wish nor dare to live without *Midons* [My Lady] nor to turn elsewhere; for she is such that I will derive honour simply from dying as her faithful lover or, if she should keep me, a hundred times greater honour; therefore I must not be slow to serve her.[54]

Suffering does not annihilate the self; on the contrary, it magnifies and exalts it. Clearly, suffering is integrated in an overall narrative of selfhood extolling masculine valor, loyalty, strength, and dedication to a woman. Suffering is thus an expression of aristocratic values.

The aristocratic ideal of suffering was intertwined with Christian values: it did not make reciprocity the condition for love, and it viewed suffering as a purification of the soul. Christianity provided a narrative framework to organize the experience of suffering, and even viewed it as the theological mark of salvation. Christianity, as a cultural frame, made sense of suffering, made it into a positive and even necessary experience, one that elevated the soul and allowed one to achieve a godlike state. In this cultural matrix, then, suffering does not undermine the self; it helps constitute and exalt it. With the dwindling of Christianity, romantic suffering became yet another source of self-worth in artistic expression, and especially in the Romantic movement. As in Christianity, suffering was thought to be an unavoidable, necessary, and superior dimension of existence.[55] Lord Byron, one of the most representative figures of the Romantic movement, praised self-destruction and the destruction of others in love. He could thus write: "My embrace was fatal. [...] I loved her, and destroy'd her."[56] Byron, like other Romantics, was a sensualist who viewed pain as the manifestation of a greater existence. "The great object of life is sensation," he wrote to his future wife, "to feel that we exist, even though in pain."[57] Thus, the lack of reciprocity was not experienced as an annihilation of the self, because recognition and self-worth were not based on the experience of love and because the self was thought to express its vital energies in a variety of experiences, ranging from loving to agonizing. Romantic expressions of romantic suffering were culturally framed and constructed under the organizing experience of melancholia. What characterizes melancholia is that it *aestheticizes* the feeling of love and, as in courtly love, ennobles the person experiencing it. Romantic melancholia was mostly male and was integrated into a model of the self in which suffering bestowed heroism on the afflicted man, who thus proved the depth of his soul through his capacity to endure. In melancholia, suffering does not affect or undermine the self's sense of value, but helps express a form of delicacy and sophistication of the soul. One may go even further and claim that for those affected it accrued a kind of symbolic/emotional capital. Moreover, as these ideas of love and suffering were often, though not exclusively, a male prerogative, this may also indicate that they functioned to enhance the image of masculinity as a vital energy, as a form of prowess.

Women, especially in the higher intellectual echelons, were, however, no strangers to this sensibility. Margaret Fuller, a contemporary of Ralph Waldo Emerson in the first half of the nineteenth century and a woman of formidable character and intelligence, had what we can describe as an unhappy love life: she frequently loved people who did not or could not reciprocate her passionate feelings. Cristina Nehring summarizes the ways in which Fuller made sense of her experience:

> Fuller believed in suffering. She believed in its purifying force and in her own capacity to bear it. Sometimes she wondered whether or not her sex was especially suited to face suffering. She pointed out that where the men in the life of Christ regularly fled in his hours of need, the "women could no more stay from the foot of the cross than from the Transfiguration."

The women who loved Christ would not be "exiled from the dark hour." "They demanded to learn from it. They demanded to be deepened by it – as Fuller was deepened by her tragedies."[58] In the previous examples, the aristocratic aestheticization of suffering combined with religious transfiguration to render it an order of experience that lent meaning and even greatness to the self. These examples constitute more than anecdotal evidence. They point to a cultural pattern in which love sufferings were incorporated and recycled into an ideal of character, and did not constitute a threat to the self's sense of self-worth.

The only tradition that did not idealize love sufferings and make them an aspect of the ideal of selfhood was medical discourse. In the sixteenth and seventeenth centuries, the disease known as "love-sickness" was viewed as a disorganization of the body, which, although it affected the soul, did not point to the self's sense of worth. In the sixteenth century, Robert Burton viewed the victims of love as "slaves, drudges for the time, madmen, fools, dizzards, *atrabilarii*, besides themselves, and blind as beetles."[59] The sufferings of love were the result of bodily disturbances, and thus on the same level as organic diseases. Similarly, Jacques Ferrand, a French doctor, born in the late sixteenth century, wrote:

> In May 1604, when I was just beginning my practice in Agen (where I was born), I diagnosed, by presence of most of these symptoms, the love madness of a young scholar, a native of Le Mas d'Agenais. [...] I saw before me a young man, sad without any reason who was jovial only a short time before; I saw his pale, lemon-yellow and wan face, his hollow-set eyes, noting that the rest of his body was in rather good condition.[60]

The disorder was understood as a bodily disorder, or even as a temporary disorder of the mind, but again not as a disorder that threatened one's sense of self-worth. In seventeenth-century England, a doctor/astrologer called Richard Napier addressed and cured a wide variety of ailments. The historian Michael MacDonald analyzed the notes Napier left and describes the nature of some of these ailments as follows:

> Almost 40% of the men and women who described their anxieties and dilemmas to Napier complained about the frustrations of courtship and married life. [...] Passionate attachments were very common among the astrologer's clients. Lovers' quarrels, unrequited love, and double-dealing accounted for the emotional turmoil of 141 persons, about two-thirds of whom were young women.'[61]

Most women's marital complaints heard by Napier had to do chiefly with "appalling failures to be financially responsible, generally loyal, sober, and kind."[62] Obviously, there is no dearth of contemporary men who are failing in their duty to support their families, but modern complaints against men are more likely to be framed in terms of their incapacity to care for the *self* of the women. Moreover, the pangs of love suffering were described and experienced as bodily sensations, not as experiences pointing to flawed psyches. The medical discourse did not exalt suffering for its own sake, but rather aimed to remove it, as one might a physical disease.

Modern romantic suffering is also to be excised, but with radically different models of the self: it is to be excised in the name of a utilitarian and hedonist model of the healthy psyche in which suffering marks either a flawed psychological development or a fundamental threat to one's sense of social worth and self-respect. That is, in contemporary culture, a well-developed character is expressed through one's capacity to overcome one's experience of suffering or, even better, to avoid it altogether. Romantic suffering has stopped being part of a psychic and social economy of character formation and even threatens it.

More than that: what is properly modern about romantic suffering is the fact that the object of love is intricately intertwined with the self's value and worth, and that suffering has become the mark of a flawed self. The result is that the defection of the object of love undermines the self. The ontological insecurity of the self and the need for inter-subjective recognition are thus made more acute by the fact that there are no further cultural/spiritual frameworks, as it were, to recycle it and make it play a role in character formation.

Recognition vs Autonomy

Exploring the paradoxes of desire, Alexander Kojève, perhaps Hegel's most interesting commentator, suggests that desire can be satisfied at once with the "development of individuality" and with the "universalization of reciprocal recognition,"[63] obtainable in an egalitarian social order. Kojève had in mind the universalization of class recognition, but this can easily and equally be applied to the realm of gender relationships, in which one would expect greater gender equality to have brought about both greater individuality and reciprocal recognition. In fact, a particular interpretative strand of the Hegelian struggle for recognition views increasing autonomy as the condition for increasing recognition. The freer the slave becomes, the more recognition he or she can claim and receive.

Yet, if this position can be defended in the realm of politics, it is far more complex in the realm of erotic relations, as it is oblivious to the contradictions that divide erotic desire against itself. In fact, I would even claim that it is precisely the development of individuality and autonomy that makes modern erotic desire fraught with aporias. As Judith Butler claims: "Desire thus founders on contradiction, and becomes a passion divided against itself. Striving to become coextensive with the world, an autonomous being that finds itself everywhere reflected in the world, self-consciousness discovers that implicit in its own identity as a desiring being is the necessity of being claimed by another."[64] Such a claim by another person is beset with contradictions, because "we have to choose between ecstatic and self-determining existence."[65]

In loving and longing for another, one always runs the risk of being ignored and of seeing one's love unfulfilled. The dread of seeing one's desire thwarted transforms the experience of love into a (potentially) eminently reflexive one. And such reflexivity is produced by the way in which recognition conflicts and interacts with another ritual which determines the sense of self-worth, namely autonomy. My claim is thus that recognition is constrained by cultural definitions of personhood in which the autonomy of the performer and of the object of recognition rituals must be simultaneously affirmed.

In his analysis of young people's romance, Ori Schwarz gives the following examples of when people choose (or not) to take pictures of the person they are involved with: "A woman in her late twenties, currently not in a relationship, described herself as an 'obsessive documenter': 'whenever I begin to have feelings [for someone], the wish to document awakes.'" Yet, she "wouldn't photograph anyone until [she] was confident in the relationship, so [she] wouldn't panic him": she "doesn't want to make him run away, to put pressure, to look too much in love."[66]

This short account describes a very common experience in love, namely the need to monitor the expression of feelings (bestowal of recognition on another) in order not to weaken one's own position in a relationship. For recognition is always contained in a dynamic in which one must display one's autonomy. Autonomy is established by a very careful monitoring and even withholding of recognition. Romantic relationships contain an intrinsic demand for recognition, but to be performatively successful, the demand and the performance of recognition must be carefully monitored so as not to threaten the autonomy of the self, in both the person giving and the person receiving recognition. Another example from Schwarz is as follows:

An urban lesbian in her late twenties who wanted to take photos "was a bit worried that it might be misinterpreted as showing too much

interest on my side/too advanced a stage/over-intimacy etc. etc. I
ignored [it] and did photograph when I wanted to, but I made it very
clear that there were no hidden intentions and no reason to worry."[67]

Here, the "worry" derives (absurdly so) from the fear that her
partner may receive more love, care, or attention than she would
be able to reciprocate. The possibility of showing more care than
wanted by the other side is so threatening that she takes great pains
to correct the possible semiotics of her act in order to guarantee her
status in the relationship, in turn signaled and established by a
display of autonomy. Far from being contained in an unlimited
process of reciprocity, recognition functions as a limited good because
of the ways in which it is constrained by the interactional imperative
of autonomy, which consists in the implicit affirmation of one's own
autonomy and acknowledgment of another's autonomy. Thus, many
of the difficulties at the beginning of relationships derive from negotiation over autonomy and recognition: how much autonomy and
recognition one should display and receive constitutes the crux of
the emotional negotiation in an early relationship.

The tension between recognition and autonomy becomes complicated by the fact that in most romantic relationships recognition
cannot remain static. Because of the institutional and narrative
entanglement of love with marriage, commitment is the narrative
telos of the process of recognition, that which binds the emotional
to the institutional.[68] Many, if not most, romantic relationships must
either end or lead to "commitment." Yet, because of the structure of
autonomy, commitment is that which cannot be asked. For example,
in a website on relationship dilemmas:

> I've done some googling on the issue [of her boyfriend's still using his
> profile at Match.com] and it's making me worried. He and I haven't
> had a formal "defining the relationship talk" (quite frankly, I'd rather
> just wait to see how things iron themselves out), so I can't help but
> wonder: is he dating other women? Am I just a fling for him? I don't
> want to bring this issue up with him because things have been so easy-
> going and drama-free.[69]

If asking a man about his loyalty and commitment can be viewed as
"drama" and "being difficult," it is because, for this woman, autonomy must trump the demand for recognition. In the absence of ritual
codes of conduct, the tension between recognition and autonomy
explains why the question of who makes the first move has become
fraught with difficulties. "The frightened or self-protective lover
attempts to persuade the beloved to love him *first*, before he risks

opening up. He may be motivated by fear, usually stemming from feelings of worthlessness and inferiority."[70] A lover is frightened because autonomy and recognition are in tension. I can offer another such example. We can unravel the reasons why the ultimate demand for recognition – commitment – is withheld in the case of Irene, a 38-year-old public relationships manager from New York City.

Irene: I met Andy five years ago. When I met him, I was involved with someone else, but things were not going so well with him, and Andy seemed very eager to have me. So I started dating him, and at first I cannot say I was crazy about him. But he did all the right things: he wrote love notes, took me by surprise to places, bought me little presents, cooked dinner for me. After one year, he got a promotion as a general sales manager, and he was asked to move to Europe, to London. He asked me to join him. I thought about it, and quickly decided to accept. My contract at my firm required me to give a three-months resignation notice, so I could not join him immediately. I arrived there two months later. When I arrived there, on the day I arrived actually, I sensed he had cooled down. Just inexplicably cooled down. I kept asking him questions, if something had happened, why he was less loving. But he was evasive, and said he didn't know if he could commit himself. I left three months later, back to NYC, feeling completely devastated.

Interviewer: Completely devastated.

Irene: But you know what? I still loved him. It's not like he behaved horribly to me. He wasn't horrible. He was more sorry. You know what I mean? He simply stopped loving me. And it's not like he had promised to marry me. He hadn't. But he stopped loving me. What can you say to that? Love me, because I'm wonderful? Of course, I couldn't say that. That would be stupid. And although I had left my job for him, given up my rent-controlled apartment, took out my savings, given up my life basically, I was not angry, just hurt. That's why I kept loving him. Maybe a part of me loved him more.

Interviewer: So you gave up your life as you just said, without a promise of marriage. Was that easy?

Irene: It's not that I did not mind that. I did mind. But there is this thing with me, where I am always afraid to look like I am putting pressure.

Interviewer: What do you mean "putting pressure"?

Irene: Like looking desperate. Giving ultimatums. Behaving as if the single most important thing is to get married. Pressuring a guy is not good for the relationship, it is not good for your self-image. So I did not pressure. But maybe it was a mistake. Maybe I should have been assertive and made more demands on him. I should not have left without a promise of marriage. But I was young and afraid to scare the guy off.

Interviewer: Why is it not good for your self-image?

Irene: Uhmm...If you put pressure, you come across as needy. Not your own person somehow. You don't want to look needy. And also, there's this view that if you put pressure, the guy's going to run away. Because you're needy.

Interviewer: So to say to a guy you want a serious, committed relationship is needy?

Irene: Absolutely. I would love to say freely "I love you," "I want to spend my life with you," but if I did it I would feel like the inferior party. You want to remain cool.

Interviewer: Can you say why?

Irene: I don't know why. I think men – not all, but many – just aren't into marriage and commitment. They feel they have all the time in the world to make up their minds. And if you want them too much, they will pull away, it's just one of these things all the girls I know believe. You have to do it slowly, smartly and not be pushy.

Many elements make this story typical of a certain pattern in the relationships between men and women. The woman here is swayed by the man: that is, she is *persuaded* to enter the relationship. What persuades her to enter the relationship is not a mystery; it is the fact that it endows her with abundant recognition, which suggests that recognition can precede and generate love. This pattern is particularly relevant for women, who are less likely than men to have access to public channels to affirm their worth; thus their sense of worth is tied particularly to romantic recognition. Also, even if this woman did not formulate a clear request, the fact she "gave up" everything was (probably rightly) interpreted by her boyfriend as a desire to commit everything to him. Finally, the fact that she could not bring herself formally to request from him a reciprocal act of commitment suggests that autonomy trumps the need for recognition, that she herself acted in an entirely committed way, yet could not secure a reciprocal and similar pledge from her boyfriend.

Contrast this with the situation in the nineteenth century, where among the English upper and upper-middle classes a young girl found a mate by formally "coming out": that is, by having a ball organized for her to declare herself eligible for marriage and desirous of meeting possible life mates. In this cultural and social order, the declaration of commitment is intrinsically embedded in the structure of the meeting: a woman (or man) does not have to hide or contain the intention to commit, because that is the very definition and raison d'être for the debutante's "coming out." This openness – looking for a prospective spouse – did not constitute a threat to the woman's own self-image or autonomy. Whatever coquetry or playfulness were contained in actual romantic interactions, it did not bracket, suspend, delay, or hide the intention to commit oneself and to marry. In fact, "lack of seriousness" jeopardized men's and women's reputations on the marriage market and constituted an emotional disadvantage. Modern romantic relationships, by contrast, are caught within curious paradoxes which derive from the fact that both men and women must act *as if* commitment were not *a priori* embedded in the relationship. The intention to commit must be the accomplishment, not the precondition, of a relationship. Hence, the very question of commitment becomes *a priori* disentangled from romantic relationships at the very same time that these relationships are required to provide an ongoing work of recognition. Finally, Irene, the interviewee quoted above, suggests that, in contradistinction to the nineteenth century, in which promise-keeping was a central component of the moral edifice of commitment, requesting a promise has become illegitimate, and this despite the obviously high personal price to the woman. In *Girls Gone Mild*,[71] Wendy Shalit, a conservative critic of sexual relationships, also observes women's reluctance to make demands on men, but, in conformity with the reigning therapeutic ethos, she attributes this to a lack of self-esteem and the over-sexualization of women. Like many conservative thinkers, Shalit correctly identifies an area beset with problems yet fails to understand their causes.

Confusion is a psychological trait, but its etiology often has a sociological basis. I suggest it is caused frequently by the presence of two structural principles that are in conflict. In Irene's story, the desire to preserve a certain image of her self trumps the defense of her self-interest. This is because her self-image does not precede the romantic interaction, but rather has become something to be crucially negotiated and established *in* it. Self-image depends on worth that must be established inter-subjectively. In other words, it must be negotiated in particular interactions in which the display of one's autonomy and one's capacity to respect another's autonomy – i.e., *not* to make demands on another – are constantly at stake. Note that "putting pressure" is perceived as a threat to the autonomy both of the person being pressured *and* of the one doing the pressuring. The cultural motif that defines and constitutes worth here is autonomy, which in turn explains why requesting promises is conceived as exerting "pressure" (an idea which might have seemed strange to, say, Victorians in England). This idea makes sense only in the context of a view of the self in which promises are viewed as posing limits on one's freedom: that is, the freedom to feel differently tomorrow from the way I feel today. Given that a limit on one's freedom is viewed as illegitimate, requesting commitment is interpreted as an alienation of one's own freedom. This freedom in turn is connected to the definition of relationships in purely emotional terms: if a relationship is the result of one's freely felt and freely bestowed emotions, it cannot emanate from the moral structure of commitment. Because emotions are constructed as being independent of reason, and even of volition, because they are viewed as changing, but, more fundamentally, because they are seen as emanating from one's unique subjectivity and free will, demanding that one commits one's emotions to the future becomes illegitimate, because it is perceived to be threatening to the freedom that is intrinsic to pure emotionality. In commitment, there is thus the risk of forcing the hand of someone to make a choice that is not based on pure emotions and emotionality, in turn alienating one's freedom.

I would suggest that, to the extent that in modernity men have internalized and most forcefully practiced the discourse of autonomy, autonomy has the effect of exerting a form of symbolic violence that is all the more naturalized and difficult to perceive. Consequently, autonomy is (and must remain) at the center of the project of women's emancipation. In interview, Amanda, a 25-year-old woman, said the following:

> I stayed with Ron for two years and in these two years, I never told him "I love you." He never told me "I love you" either.

Interviewer: Why was that, do you think?

Amanda: I did not want to be the first to say it.

Interviewer: Why?

Amanda: Because if you say it, and if the other person does not feel this way toward you, you become the weaker one; or they will resent you for that; or they will take advantage of it; or they will become distant as a result.

Interviewer: Do you think he told himself the same thing? That he did not want to say it?

Amanda: I don't know. Maybe. Although, you know, I think men,
              for some reason, have more freedom to say it. My feeling
              is that both men and women know that the man can say
              it first, the woman doesn't have that freedom. A woman
              will not pull away from a man if he tells her he loves her,
              whereas a man will freak out and will think she wants
              the ring and the white dress.

We can also take an example from *Sex and the City*, which many
regard as the bible on modern dysfunctional relationships. "Carrie
said: 'How come you never say "I love you"? 'Because I'm afraid,'
Mr Big said. 'I'm afraid that if I say "I love you" you're going to
think that we're going to get married.'"[72]

Clearly, men dominate the rules of recognition and commitment.
Male domination takes the form of an ideal of autonomy to which
women, through the mediation of the struggle for equality in the
public sphere, have themselves subscribed. But when transposed to
the private sphere, autonomy stifles women's need for recognition.
For, it is indeed a characteristic of symbolic violence that one cannot
oppose a definition of reality that is to one's own detriment. My point
is not that women do not want autonomy. Rather, it is that they are
in a position fraught with tension because they carry simultaneous
ideals of care and autonomy, and, more critically, because often they
view themselves as having to worry about their own *and* the man's
autonomy. For example, Shira, a 27-year-old graduate, relates that
when she was together with her boyfriend,

> I would say, for example, that I preferred to go home;
> and then he would say he wanted to go to Sammy [a
> friend]; then I would start crying, just crying, with him I
> never dared to tell him really what I thought of him; I
> was kind of scared; maybe I was scared to lose him; that's
> why I didn't say anything; but I would cry.

Interviewer: Did you cry a lot?

Shira: I cried very much.

Interviewer: Can you say why?

Shira: Well all these years, I think I was just afraid to tell him
              what I really thought.

Interviewer: Can you give me an example of something you are afraid
              of telling him?

Shira: It could be anything and everything really. For example,
              on Saturday, I wanted to lay around at home and just be

together and eat together, but he just wanted to go and be with his friends.

Interviewer: Did you cry when he was around or when he was gone?

Shira: When he was around.

Interviewer: Did it make him stay?

Shira: No, unfortunately not.

Interviewer: Do you have other examples like that?

Shira: Frankly, there are too many. Mostly, it was about me wanting something and things happening in such a way that my desire would be ignored or thwarted. Or, for example, I loved staying home and cooking good food. And then I put a lot of attention to making the food look nice. I expected him to say something about it, to take notice, but he usually wouldn't. And I would feel hurt, and I would cry.

The distress experienced by this interviewee derives from the fact that she is caught in a contradiction which she cannot name: her tears are a direct expression of her dependency and need for recognition. Yet, despite her difficult emotions, she cannot formulate a formal demand in order to preserve his and her autonomy (or at least the image of it). In that sense, one could say that the imperative for autonomy trumps the imperative for recognition, and even makes it unintelligible. Other examples of the ways in which autonomy stifles women's emotions are easy to find. Catherine Townsend – the *Independent*'s sex columnist referred to earlier – can be described as a remarkable exemplar of sexual emancipation. Yet, this is how she describes what she calls "the very female position": "[S]o I found myself in that very female position of pretending that I didn't have a care in the world, while secretly wanting to throw myself on his lap and scream, 'Please love me!'"[73] And Lisa Rene Reynolds, a psychologist, musing about Internet dating, says: "You think people won't respond to your profile if you say you want marriage and kids, so you don't take a chance and go after what you really want."[74] To repeat then: my point here is not that women have no drive for autonomy, or that they should not have it. On the contrary: I would contend that men can follow the imperative for autonomy more consistently and for a longer part of their lives and, as a result, they can exert emotional domination over women's desire for attachment, compelling them to mute their longing for attachment and to imitate men's detachment and drive for autonomy. It follows that women who are not interested in heterosexual domesticity, children, and a man's commitment will find themselves more likely to be the emotional equals of men.

In the absence of clear sequences and rituals to conduct courtship, in order to maintain one's own and another's claim to autonomy and emotional freedom, the self struggles to get recognition from another without being in a position to demand it. That is, because the self's value is not established in advance, it becomes an object of inter-subjective negotiation. One's value is constantly threatened by the possibility that one may not display enough autonomy. The tension between these two imperatives – maintaining autonomy and getting recognition – produces an economic view of the self and the psyche: that is, a view in which recognition must always be balanced by autonomy and in which recognition is not over-supplied. In its struggle to establish its value or to bestow it on another, the self leans on a model of exchange in which unavailability functions as an economic signal of value, and vice versa, in which "loving" can become "loving too much." It is this very economic logic that overwhelmingly underlies psychological advice to women. For example, in her aptly named best-selling *Women Who Love Too Much*, Robin Norwood, a psychologist, tells the stories of some of her clients/patients. One of them, whom she names Jill, met a man Randy and was having "a great time with him. [...] He let me cook for him and really enjoyed being looked after. [...] We got along beautifully." Norwood continues her story as follows:

> But [...] it became clear that Jill had almost immediately become completely obsessed with Randy. When he returned to his San Diego apartment, the phone was ringing. Jill warmly informed him that she had been worried about his long drive and was relieved to know he was safely home. When she thought he sounded a little bemused at her call, she apologized for bothering him and hung up, but a gnawing discomfort began to grow in her, fueled by the awareness that once again she cared far more than the man in her life did. "Randy told me once not to pressure him or he would just disappear. I got so scared. It was all up to me. *I was supposed to love him and leave him alone at the same time.* I couldn't do it, so I just got more and more scared. The more I panicked, the more I chased him." (emphasis added)[75]

The author obviously presents Jill as behaving pathologically, because a healthy psyche is able to balance autonomy and recognition, that is, two psychologically conflicting principles. A healthy psyche, moreover, must be economically well behaved: that is, it must make demand adequate to supply, and supply adequate to demand. Clearly, this story suggests that one of the functions of advice literature is precisely to help the reader monitor the flow of emotional supply and demand contained in the dynamic of recognition. Because the self's value is negotiated in and by interactions, because signs of autonomy function as signs of value, the self becomes the site of an economic calculus, whereby it can depreciate itself by, as it were, recognizing ("loving") another "too much." As discussed in chapter 3, recognition is constrained by and organized within an economic view of emotions in which an over-supply of recognition can jeopardize and stifle demand for it. It is this imperative that structures many of the uncertainties contained in romantic relationships. This economic view of supply and demand is expressed by the divorced, 46-year-old woman in the autobiographical story below:

Anne: You know, what I find impossible in relationships is all these power games: do I call him, don't I call him? Do I tell him I like him very much or do I play it indifferent? To be hard to get or to be sweet and loving? I find it maddening.

Interviewer: Explain to me. What do you mean?

Anne: What do I mean? Look, in most cases – I mean I am not talking about great love like you meet once or twice in a lifetime – in most cases, you meet someone and you kind of like him, but you are not sure where it might lead to. Now if you find out you don't like him so much, that's great, because you don't feel you are in his hands, you don't feel anxious. But if you like him more than he does at the beginning, that's when troubles start. Because if you like him, then you must become careful about what you say, how you say it. If you show you like him too much, typically the man will run away. If you are too reserved, he will think you are cold.

Interviewer: Why do you think the man will run away? Did it happen to you?

Anne: Oh yes.

Interviewer: Can you give me an example?

Anne: Well I think I can give you a few. I was with a man, and at first I was ambivalent, unsure if I wanted to be with him. Mostly, because I thought he was a kind of cold fish. After two weeks, I said I did not want to pursue the connection. He begged me to give him another chance. So I did. Then he started to be warmer, and I started to really like him. But every time I would speak about the future, he would pull back. The more ambivalent he was, the more I put pressure. In the end, he became so ambivalent, that we broke it off.

Or there was that time when I was having this intense, torrid affair with a man fifteen years older than me. The man was acting very much in love. He would call me every day. He wanted to make plans for the weekend ahead of time. He suggested we take together all kinds of vacation. Then one day after I called him, it took him two days to get back to me on the phone. I told him I was hurt by this. He became upset, and actually turned cold to me. He said he did not understand what the fuss was about.

With another guy, we had been six months together and he would turn his cell phone off a lot because he was a musician. I commented about that and asked if he could turn it on more often so that I could reach him. And he went on and on about how I wanted to restrict his freedom.

Interviewer: And what did you say to that? Do you remember?

Anne: I said something like to be in a relationship is to restrict one's freedom, that you could not have it both ways. And from that conversation, things went downhill.

Interviewer: Can you say why?

Anne: I think it is every time the same story. At first men like me very much. Then I become insecure, for one reason or another. I need to know whether they love me or how much they love me. I just can't ignore this question. So I ask questions, I make demands, maybe you could even say I start nagging, I don't know [*laughter*]. That's basically the dynamic: something in the relationship will elicit my anxiety. I will express it, I will want to be reassured, and the man will start pulling away.

Interviewer: Do you have an idea of why that is the case?

Anne: I think there are these power games men and women play. I have thought about it a lot. I think men and women's relationships are fucked up to the core, because it is as if men can be truly interested in a woman only if she is distant from them, or withdraws something from them, or something like that. If a woman expresses neediness, anxieties, desire for closeness, then forget it, the man will just not be there. It is as if the man needs to prove to himself he can win her over and over again.

Interviewer: Can you say why or when you feel anxiety?

Anne: Uhmm…I think that deep down it comes from a feeling of being worthless, and asking the other person to show that I am worth something. Something in the relationship will trigger it. I will feel the man is not loving, or not loving enough. Then I will ask him to reassure me. Usually, they won't.

Psychological conventional wisdom undoubtedly would indict this woman with "insecurity" and look for causes of this anxiety in a thwarted childhood. In psychological theory, anxiety is seen either as the memory trace of a traumatic event, or as a signal that the foundations of the ego are about to collapse because it is trapped between the contradictory demands of the super-ego and the id. According to Freud and subsequent psychological theories, what makes anxiety neurotic is the fact that it is diffuse, free-floating, and with no clear object. But if we interpret this woman's speech literally, her anxiety has a very definite and defined object and an entirely social character: she needs recognition, but she struggles with the opposite imperative to maintain her boyfriend's and her own autonomy, because failing to do so would in fact jeopardize her status in a relationship. While both recognition and autonomy have become crucial features of social interactions, they pull actors in opposite directions. Thus anxiety can be viewed here as the result of a tension between the demand for recognition and the threat that such a demand seems to pose to autonomy; between an economic view of the self in which the self must be the strategic winner of an interaction, on the one hand, and a desire to give oneself away in an agapic fashion, on the other, with no economic calculus regulating the exchange. The women who "love too much" are fundamentally guilty of misunderstanding the economic calculus which ought to govern relationships, and of mismanaging the imperative of autonomy by subsuming it under an imperative of care and recognition. I would suggest that this tension – between autonomy and recognition – is responsible for creating a new structure of self-doubt.

From Self-Love to Self-Blame

In Jane Austen's *Sense and Sensibility* (1818), Elinor comes to understand that Willoughby, her sister Marianne's assiduous suitor, does not intend to marry her sister and she later learns that he was engaged to someone else at the time Marianne thought him to be hers.

That some kind of engagement had subsisted between Willoughby and Marianne, she could not doubt; and that Willoughby was weary of it, seemed equally clear; for, however Marianne might still feed her own wishes, *she* could not attribute such behaviour to mistake or misapprehension of any kind. Nothing but a thorough change of sentiment could account for it. Her indignation would have been still stronger than it was, had she not witnessed that embarrassment which seemed to speak a consciousness of his own misconduct, and prevented her from believing him so unprincipled as to have been sporting with the affections of her sister from the first, without any design that would bear investigation.[76]

Willoughby is guilty of a grave moral fault. And the nature of this fault is very clear: he has misled Marianne into thinking he is committed to her; although he made no explicit promises, he behaved in such a way as to indicate he would do so. Both his social circle and Willoughby himself *know* that active courtship is almost equivalent to commitment, and that failing to follow up on one's commitment constitutes an infringement of one's sense of honor. Both emotional and real damage can be done by failing to follow through on a promise since it affects the woman's prospects of finding another suitor. Even more interesting is that Willoughby commits this dishonorable act and is also in love with Marianne. Clearly, then, sentiments are not necessarily the source of matrimonial decisions. In fact, it is precisely against such an unfeeling and calculated conception of marriage that Austen was writing. Moreover, when Willoughby publicly refuses to talk to Marianne and thereby to acknowledge their romantic connection, her distress comes from his change of heart as well as from her public display of lack of reserve and lack of decorum, the cardinal virtues preached by Elinor. It is as much Marianne's unrequited love for Willoughby as her outward failure to follow the proper rules of behavior that puts her in a state of distress. Private distress provides a normative peg on which Marianne can "hang" her suffering and thereby explain it. Her deficiencies are not internal, but external – they are related to her behavior and not her essence, who she is. However crushing her disappointment, it does not put into question her sense of self. Finally, her social environment morally condemns Willoughby so vehemently that her pain is never entirely private; it is visible to and shared by others. In taking on with her the burden of her pain, they partake with her in a clear moral and social fabric. In that sense, her suffering has what philosopher Susan Neiman dubs "moral clarity."[77]

In *Northanger Abbey* (1818), Isabella Thorpe breaks off her engagement to James Morland for a better financial prospect in the person of Captain Frederick Tilney. In recounting the sad story, Morland writes a letter to his sister Catherine and expresses neither dejection nor rage, only relief: "Thank God! I am undeceived in time!" And he goes so far as to feel genuinely sorry for what Isabella's brother – John Thorpe – will feel upon learning about his sister's behavior. "Poor Thorpe is in town: I dread the sight of him; his honest heart would feel so much."[78] Morland's reaction is clearly one without deep pain and agony. In fact, the only clearly expressed feelings he has are those of empathy and sympathy for Isabella's brother. Such sympathy comes from the knowledge that Isabella has infringed a code of honor known and shared by himself, by her brother, and by their whole social milieu. Breaking up a marriage promise for a better financial prospect is a *public* act, accountable to a multitude of others, an infringement of moral codes of honor. Morland's sympathy also comes from the knowledge that adhering to such codes is as important to one's status as one's personal preferences. Because Isabella's act dishonors her and her brother's name, Morland can empathize with Thorpe for his sister has caused him *real*, not imaginary, harm. As in Willoughby's case, the infamy here therefore clearly attaches to the person who breaks his or her promises, not to the person who was abandoned, Marianne or Morland. On the contrary, the text lets us suppose that Morland is reinforced and bolstered in his sense of moral impeccability, while Thorpe even becomes the (curious) victim of his sister's breach of promise. To quote McIntyre in his discussion of Homeric society, questions about "what to do and how to judge" are not

> difficult to answer, except in exceptional cases. For the given rules which assign men their place in the social order and with it their identity also prescribe what they owe and what is owed to them and how they are to be treated and regarded if they fail and how they are to treat and regard others if those others fail.[79]

In this order, if disappointed romantic relationships generate psychic suffering, it is one that is always mixed with moral outrage and a sense of social inappropriateness, thus suggesting that blame and responsibility are clearly allocated and that they are allocated outside the self.

Honoré de Balzac's *La Femme Abandonnée* (The Deserted Woman) (1833) offers another interesting illustration of the way in which, in the nineteenth century, blame was allocated in cases of abandonment. The Vicomtesse de Bauseant, a married woman, took a lover, who abandoned her. Her husband, upon learning about the affair, repudiates her, but, divorce not being an option, she exiles herself to a French province. This novel offers perhaps one of the richest and most detailed descriptions of what it meant for a nineteenth-century French upper-middle-class woman to be abandoned. But what is interesting for our discussion is the fact that the story frames her disgrace in social terms, not in terms that hinge on her sense of self. On the contrary, the point of the novel is precisely to show that despite society's ostracism, this woman displays an immaculate and superior character: it is the norms of her environment that are responsible for a destitution that is essentially social but that does not concern her sense of worth. The heroes and heroines of eighteenth- and nineteenth-century novels may suffer a great deal after being abandoned, but that suffering is always organized in a moral framework in which blame is clearly allocated. This is how Balzac describes the Vicomtesse de Bauseant's most ardent wishes in her state of "abandonment": "The world's absolution, the heartfelt sympathy, the social esteem so longed for, and so harshly refused."[80] What she strove for was to be rehabilitated in the eyes of her social milieu. Clearly here it is the arbitrary and stifling norms of her social milieu which are held responsible for this woman's destitution.

In Alexandre Dumas's *La Dame aux Camélias* (1848), Marguerite, a "kept woman" for the upper echelons of French society, suffers agony when she leaves her lover Armand under the pressure of his father. But again it is the norms of which she and her lover are victims that are viewed as responsible for her being abandoned by him. Even though Marguerite is a "kept woman," the novel clearly points to the cruelty of social norms which prevent her from being loved by Armand, not to her inner self, presented, on the contrary, as superior and noble. Throughout she shows herself to be an admirable woman, and it is precisely her capacity to suffer because of her lover's departure that reveals to the reader and the protagonists of the novel her depth and strength of character. The capacity of heroes to suffer in the face of unrequited, unreciprocated, or impossible love points to the strength and depth of their character, precisely because the source of their suffering derives from the fact they cannot change their social fate, station, and status.

We can observe an astonishing reversal in contemporary affairs: that is, in stories of people who have been abandoned. Indeed, contemporary stories of betrayal or abandonment entirely lack "moral clarity" and point instead to a significant transformation of the moral structure of blame and of the sentiments that follow this structure.

Examples gleaned from Internet sites devoted to breaking up directly bear this out. On a medical/psychological site, the first story posted reads:

> I just recently broke up with my boyfriend of 3 years. I found out he
> had been lying and stealing. He went as far as to steal my mother's
> boyfriend's engagement ring and then I found it and he gave it to me
> and proposed. When I found out it was a stolen ring I got extremely
> upset and hurt that he lied to me and my *family* like that. [...] Is it
> worth getting *back* into this relationship if he gets the help he needs?
> I don't want to be alone but I know jumping to a different relationship
> will just make it worse.[81]

This story is obviously shaped by a clear sense that stealing, lying,
and cheating are morally wrongful acts. Yet, no less clear in this
account is the fact that the moral significance of their relationship is
uncertain, for his moral failings do not entail any clear course of
action, or, for that matter, any clear condemnation. This is borne out
by the fact this woman medicalizes her boyfriend's moral misbehav-
ior, which in turn obfuscates the proper reaction to him. Not only
does she not proffer any moral condemnation toward the person who
has betrayed her, but she uses the Internet primarily as a way to ask
for moral guidance from others, not knowing herself how to weigh
the moral significance of her story.

Such self-doubt – and the attendant need to be advised by an
anonymous community of Internet users – stems from the structure
and position of the self in contemporary relationships, a position in
which the self has difficulty in assigning a moral weight to another's
behavior, and, more critically, in which the self is called upon to feel
implicated in another's failings.

The difficulty of articulating a moral point of view in weighing
the story becomes more poignant and clear when no legal norm
(such as stealing) is infringed. In fact, it is as if the onus of moral
responsibility veers toward the person who is abused. Shira, the articulate and attractive 27-year-old graduate whom we met above, relates
the following:

> When I separated from my former boyfriend I felt that
> something was wrong with me; I still feel it today; but
> then it was much stronger; then I felt I was a terrible
> person; I did not believe in myself at all. But I did a lot
> of work on myself during this past year and I'm very
> proud of myself. It was a whole process.

Interviewer: Can you explain to me what it means not to believe in
           yourself?

Shira: It's a shocking experience; when it happened, I felt it was
           naturally the end of my world, the end of my life; I don't
           think I've thought about committing suicide but I felt I

had nothing to live for; I felt as if my only reason for living had disappeared.

Interviewer: How long did this feeling last for?

Shira: It was about seven months; it lasted until I traveled to India; yeah it was about seven months that this horrible nightmare lasted.

Interviewer: Horrible nightmare.

Shira: Horrible nightmare. *It feels as if you are nothing and you are expecting just to hear one word from him to feel good with yourself again just for one moment, I felt I simply needed to hear that he still loved me, that I was not this horrible person.* During that period I was asking him a thousand times what happened; I was obsessed by the question of what happened and why it happened; I'm the kind of person who needs to understand things and I couldn't accept the fact that I would not understand really why something like that just ended. (emphasis added).

In *The Curse of the Singles Table*, a memoir on being a single woman, Suzanne Schlosberg recounts a three-year relationship with a man. When it becomes obvious that he has no intention to marry her, live with her, or have children with her, she decides to break up with him.

Soon, I'd find myself slipping into some light self-flagellation: [...] Sure, he had his weak moments, but who said I was perfect? Maybe all we needed was a little more time. Maybe I could have figured out a way to make it work. Maybe *if I hadn't been so demanding, so impatient, so narrow-minded.* Maybe...maybe everything was my fault![82]

Perhaps one of the best examples of such self-incrimination comes from the *New York Times* column "Modern Love," on the difficulties of moving and resettling in San Francisco. The author, a single woman, muses: "I couldn't stop coming back to the same question, no matter how much I hated myself for asking it: If I were worth loving, wouldn't there be a man standing there with me?"[83] A classic representation of this discussion is contained in the international best-seller *Bridget Jones's Diary*, in which the single thirtysomething Bridget claims:

When someone leaves you, apart from missing them, apart from the fact that the whole little world you've created together collapses, and that everything you see or do reminds you of them, the worst is the

thought that they tried you out and, in the end, the whole sum of parts
which adds up to you got stamped REJECT by the one you love.[84]

If we compare these contemporary stories with Jane Austen's, the
differences are obvious and striking: it is the person left in the former
who feels defective and even guilty. In these modern accounts, the
abandoned person's basic sense of self is severely threatened. In lieu
of moral condemnation, these women draw a straight line from their
boyfriend's departure to their selves and their sense of worth. It is
Shira's very sense of self that becomes the main site of the drama of
break-up and abandonment. Being left is experienced by her as pointing to an essential, if incomprehensible, deficiency of her self. But
such an experience, lived as psychological and private, is primarily a
social one because her sense of unworthiness is related chiefly to the
repertoires of reasons with which she explains to herself his departure,[85] in turn chiefly related to the fact she does not use any moral
language to make sense of or to condemn the man's behavior.

At face value, the reason for this lack of moral language might
seem deceptively obvious: modern intimate relationships are based
on contractual freedom, and such freedom precludes the possibility
of holding one morally responsible for bailing out. But this explanation cannot satisfactorily explain Shira's or Bridget's accounts, because
the nub of their stories is that they feel responsible for being abandoned, and hence unworthy. It is this implicit chain of cause and
effect that structures these stories and that demands clarification.
Such a chain is a clear example of what Marx and Engels call "false
consciousness," which we can characterize by the fact that the subject
is unable to know and to formulate the nature and causes of his/her
(social) distress, and that when trying to come to terms with it, s/he
uses someone else's – in our examples, the man's – point of view, to
their own detriment. (In our stories the woman accuses herself of the
sin of being abandoned.) But, in the accounts above, that the man's
point of view so easily overwhelms the woman's requires some explanation. It is tautological to assume simply that this is what ideology
does. False consciousness cannot in itself be the explanation, but
rather is the explanandum, that which must be explained. What is
the mechanism by which we come to adopt another's point of view
and defend another's interest? To understand the power and efficiency
of false consciousness, we must expose its mechanics, its nuts and
bolts, the ways in which it connects the psychic to the social. I argue
that such false consciousness – feeling responsible for being left – is
explained by the ways in which several features of our moral universe
intertwine with the power of men, i.e. the structure of recognition in

romantic relationships (and probably in modernity in general); by the fact that the ideal of autonomy interferes with recognition and operates within a fundamentally unequal structure of the distribution of autonomy; and by the fact that psychological modes of explanation frame notions of self and responsibility. I would propose the counterintuitive claim that it is not a *lack* of morality in romantic relations, but rather the *very moral* properties of modern love, as shaped by the tension between the imperative of autonomy and recognition, that explain how and why the structure of moral blame has become radically transformed.

The Moral Structure of Self-Blame

The main cause for the transformation of the moral structure of blame is related to the fact that the tension between recognition and autonomy has been solved, by and large, by an increasingly greater emphasis on autonomy through therapeutic modes of self-control. In therapy culture, autonomy is acquired when the subject is able to understand the role of his or her past in determining his/her present condition. This in turn implies an explanatory model in which one's failures must be viewed as manifestations and even irruptions of past traumatic or unresolved events which the subject is called on to be aware of and to master. A significant portion of psychological advice claims quite simply that if abandonment and neglectful or detached lovers (or the threat of them) hurt so much, it is because the anxious person has had a traumatic childhood experience in which s/he has experienced (real or imagined) abandonment, neglect, or distance. Thus, even if therapy does not intend to make subjects bear the responsibility for their failures, in practice it demands that they locate the reasons for their failed lives in their private histories, and in their refusal to resolve their problems through introspection and self-knowledge. In claiming that we are always the willing but blind accomplices of our destiny, therapy makes the self somewhat responsible for its failures and for rejecting any and all forms of dependence. While for sociologists dependence is the unavoidable outcome of the fact that we are social creatures, and thus is not a pathological condition, for psychologists, dependence should be excised, and choosing "emotionally unavailable" partners always points back to a deficiency in the chooser. For example:

> Just over two and a half years ago I stumbled across the realisation that not only did I love Mr Unavailables (emotionally unavailable men)

but that I was a commitment-phobe that was *sabotaging all of my relationships, unbeknowst to me.* I started sharing my insights here and at Baggage Reclaim, and I am still astounded by the number of women that are just like me. (emphasis added)[86]

Or:

It took "centuries" for me to stop blaming the men and start *taking responsibility for my low self worth* and how it played out in my choices of men. (emphasis added)[87]

In a similar vein, Irene, the woman quoted earlier, who had withdrawn her savings to join her boyfriend, only to find out he had cooled down, explains why she felt in love with him even after they had broken up.

Interviewer: Can you explain it?

Irene: [*Long silence*] I know it's irrational but I think that deep down I felt it was my fault. That I must have done something to make him run away from me.

Interviewer: Like what?

Irene: Like maybe being too loving, too available for him. I don't know. You know, having my fucked-up childhood mess up with my life [*laughter*].

These women are culturally compelled to take the blame (euphemistically known as "responsibility") for the fact they forge relationships with unavailable men, and even more spectacularly blame themselves for "loving too much." What is activated here is the implicit psychological view that the self is responsible for making the wrong choices and for actually needing the inherently social basis of recognition and worth. Here again consider this interview with Olga, a 31-year-old who works in advertising:

Interviewer: Can you say what you have found difficult in your relationships with men?

Olga: Yes, I can say this very easily! It's that I never know how to behave. If you are too nice, you are afraid to look like you're desperate; if you're cool, then you tell yourself, I did not encourage him enough. But you know, my natural tendency is to be nice, to show the guy I want him, and, somehow, I always feel that drives them away from me.

In some strands of psychoanalytical theory, the ideal self should be able to combine autonomy and attachment, but the popular version of therapy – the one that has counseled "women who love too much" to love less and that has promised the power of "self-esteem" and "self-assertiveness" – has placed autonomy at the center of the self and of interpersonal relations. The therapeutic persuasion addresses the main difficulty of modernity – to have a grounded sense of self-worth – by calling on actors – especially women – to generate self-love and, even worse, to feel inadequate for loving the way women are taught to love: that is, by overt displays of care. Worth is viewed basically as a problem of the self with itself, not as a problem of recognition, which by definition cannot be self-generated. Thus, the theme of "self-love" fundamentally plays up the theme of autonomy and further entraps the self in making it carry the burden for the failures of love. It is this moral and cultural structure that explains the fundamental transformation of the structure of blame, of responsibility and accountability in modern relationships. In addressing the question of how to cope with the anxiety and uncertainty inherent in the search process, much pop psychology advice is thus strangely similar to the advice provided by the highly popular *The Rules*: "Take care of yourself, take a bubble bath and build up your soul with positive slogans like 'I am a beautiful woman. I am enough.'"[88] Or, from an Internet column:

> The common denominator for all these types of obsessive love or love addiction is [...] lack of self-value. Once we realise we're always "safe," whether we're alone or in a couple, *there would be no need to look to others for validation*. We can praise ourselves, love ourselves and value ourselves, thus sharing a complete human being with those we interact with and care for. Emotional hunger can never be fed by others. Romantic illusion is a dream of the perfect person and this of course does not exist, except in fairy tales. Love is not actually something we get from outside ourselves. (emphasis added)[89]

Such advice – substitute love for self-love – denies the fundamentally and essentially social nature of self-value. It demands from actors that they create what they cannot create on their own. The modern obsession and injunction to "love oneself" is an attempt to solve through autonomy the actual need for recognition, which can be bestowed only by an acknowledgment of one's dependence on others. The psychological modes of explanation, ultimately, encourage self-incrimination:

Some people want to understand why: Why do they doubt themselves? Why is their self-esteem eroded? Why does it hurt so much to be abandoned? To not be accepted? To feel slighted by a friend? How did this vulnerability set in? What caused it? What keeps it going?

The simple answer is "unresolved abandonment," but to really understand the whys and wherefores, we have to go back – all the way back to the primal fear of abandonment. [...]

When, as adults, we feel someone's love or acceptance slipping away, our most primitive self-doubts erupt. Our deepest fear explodes in our faces – that someone could leave us and never come back. And this fear is complicated by the fact that it's tied to our sense of self-worth. As the person breaks away from us, we feel a loss of our ability to compel him or her to want to be with us.

We feel as if we are living our worst nightmare – that of being left because we are unworthy. Hence, these episodes of being slighted by a friend, ignored by a teacher, overlooked by a boss, and especially rejected by a lover – have the capacity to erode self-esteem and implant self-doubt.

Repairing the damaged sense of self-worth from cumulative abandonment wounds which have been festering since childhood, *begins with understanding the dynamics of what has happened. But that is only the beginning and there are tools (which are the subject of my books) to rebuild a sense of self which is invincible and which can never again be taken away from you by someone else.* (emphasis added)[90]

This psychologist correctly perceives that self-worth is central to the experience of breaking up, but she also quickly explains it by making the thwarted development of the self the main culprit both for the need for others' bestowal of worth, and for the failure to obtain it. Indeed, the need for others always boils down to a lack of self-esteem, thus obfuscating the necessity of recognition, and making the self bear responsibility for its failures to manage the tension between autonomy and recognition. The shift from blame to self-blame is such that even the absence of a relationship is interpreted backward as the sign of an immature or fundamentally flawed psyche. On an Israeli Internet site, a single woman writes:

Deep down in my heart I know it is my fault. The problem is that I still don't know what I have done. Sometimes it seems to me that maybe I didn't do enough. Other times I fear I did too much. Whatever the case, there must be something deeply wrong with me. And whatever is wrong must be wrong with me. That's at least what the world seems to be alluding to. Not out loud of course, and not in an explicit way. But when you are 31 years old and still single, then a silent consensus gets formed around you suggesting that it must be you. And you know what? I'm starting to believe that maybe it's true.

So let's agree upfront that I am guilty. I agree to the verdict. I bow my head and claim that I am ready and willing to change my ways – if only somebody, dammit, will tell me just what it is that needs to be changed and how. Because if you ask me I've already tried all the techniques known to modern people. I have eaten too many bad cakes on dates, I've drunk too many glasses of whiskey pickup bars, I've had too many witty conversations on the Internet, I have held too many wet hands in new age circles and still not been came out of all this. So please. You are invited to give me your suggestions because the truth is that I have run out of ideas.

Yes, I am angry. And I have good reasons for that. I have borne my loneliness with fortitude and nobility for quite a long time. I kept being optimistic and carried my head high with dignity and patience. I showed I was capable of self-love. Of love for the world and love in general. I learned how to be freer, how to be more restrained, and how to be freer again, and now I am at a loss. I want – no, I demand – love. Let me go back home with a man not as another notch to my ego but as a consolation for a heart that has been forgotten in deep freeze for many years. Just give me that love already, for God's sake, because I've been waiting in a long line for too long and now is the time to say in an unambiguous way: now it's my turn.[91]

The structure of this self-blame has to do with how the prerogative on autonomy is distributed in both genders. Because women's self-worth is the most closely tied to love, because they have been the prime target of psychological advice, and because the use of psychological advice is an extension of their activity of monitoring themselves and their relationships, they are also the most likely to have absorbed the structure of that advice, namely being left or simply being single points back to a deficiency in the self that plots its own defeat. I would suggest that the intensity of self-blame differs for men and women – or, in other words, that the tension between recognition and autonomy is managed culturally by the language of therapy, which is differently inscribed in men and women's positions and relationships.

Doubt that leads to certainty might have been a male trope for a male taking possession of himself, but the self-doubt I have described is a female trope, pointing at a subjectivity caught in the tension between autonomy and recognition and which lacks clear and strong social anchors for the creation of self-value. This is apparent in one of the most striking findings of my study that women, and only to a much lesser degree men, often hold themselves responsible for their romantic difficulties and failures. That the man has the upper hand in the process of monitoring recognition – initiating it and controlling its flow – is also manifest in that he holds himself far less responsible for the successes or failures of the relationship. For example, Sye is 52 years old, a successful professional and divorced, who has had a long series of monogamous relationships:

Interviewer: I have a question that's slightly different from what we've been discussing now: has it ever happened to you, does it happen to you to doubt yourself? In everything dealing with romance, am I attractive/appealing enough? Am I good enough? Something…have you ever had doubts like that?

Sye: No, never.

Interviewer: Never.

Sye: Never.

Interviewer: You mean you always felt desired?

Sye: Yes.

Interviewer: You always felt you were successful?

Sye: Yes.

Interviewer: With women, that is.

Sye: Yes, yes.

Interviewer: And you always felt women wanted you more than you wanted them?

Sye: Yes. Absolutely. Maybe once or twice I had more negative experiences where I wanted women who didn't want me. I can remember two times like that but that's not the dominant experience.

Interviewer: In other words, the dominant experience for you is one where you call the shots.

Sye: At least for the last twenty-two years.

Interviewer: So, let's say if you want someone, your experience is that with a great probability, you can have her.

Sye: No, that's not accurate, I wouldn't say that, but they always wanted me more than I wanted them. What I mean is they wanted me more, women wanted me more than I wanted them, and specific women that I wanted wanted me more. One time, a woman interviewed me and I, when she asked to interview me, I thought about her, I paid attention to her, she was intelligent. And after she interviewed me I called her and asked her if she was available, "because I really like you." She said she also wanted it but she was currently unavailable. That happened to me once but I didn't feel it was a rejection.

Obviously, I do not claim this interview illustrates the experience of all men; it does, however, describe what it means to control the sexual field, a situation shared by some men and by some women, but undoubtedly by more men than women. The process of recognition is not only divided by gender but in fact may express the fundamental social divisions between men and women. For, in contradistinction to Hegel's dialectic of the master and the slave – in which the master can be properly recognized only by an autonomous slave – men need women's recognition less than women need men's recognition. This is because, even in a contested patriarchy, men and women both need other men's recognition.

Conclusion

Reflecting on the consequences of Cartesian doubt for modernity, Hannah Arendt suggests that "what was lost in the modern age, of course, was not the capacity or reality or faith nor the concomitant inevitable acceptance of the testimony of the senses and of reason, but the *certainty* that formerly went with it" (emphasis added).[92] In the same way, we may suggest that what was has been lost in the modern experience of romantic suffering is the ontological security which derives from the organization of courtship in a moral ecology of choice, commitment, and ritual and from the embeddedness of self-value in the social fabric of one's community. The ontological insecurity that accompanies romantic suffering is unequally distributed. Because the imperative of autonomy trumps the imperative of recognition, women live hyper-modernity in the mode of a very un-Cartesian self-doubt, with few or no moral frameworks to organize certainty. That is, while a male Cartesian self-doubt is one that ultimately leads to the assertion of one's position, knowledge, and sentiments in the world, the kind of self-doubt that has been shaped by a therapeutic culture of autonomy and self-love undermines the ontological ground of the self.

5

Love, Reason, Irony*

"[I]n my experience poetry speaks to you either at first sight or not at all. A flash of revelation and a flash of response. Like lightning. Like falling in love."

Like falling in love. Do the young still fall in love, or is that mechanism obsolete by now, unnecessary, quaint, like steam locomotion? [...] Falling in love could have fallen out of fashion and come back again half a dozen times, for all he knows.

J.M. Coetzee, *Disgrace*[1]

Stuart tells me to take a fifty from his wallet, a photo falls out, I look at it, I say, "Stuart, who's this?" He goes, "Oh, that's Gillian." The first wife [...]. In the wallet, two, three years into our marriage. [...]

"Stuart, is there anything you'd like to tell me about this?" I ask.

"No," he says.

"Sure?" I say.

"No," he says. "I mean that's Gillian." He takes the photo and puts it back in his wallet.

I book the marriage therapist, naturally.

We last about eighteen minutes. I explain that basically my problem with Stuart is getting him to talk about our problems. Stuart says, "That's because we don't have any problems." I say, "You see the problem?"

Julian Barnes, *Love, etc.*[2]

---

* The section of this chapter concerning the Internet is based on my article with Shoshannah Finkelman, "An Odd and Inescapable Couple: Emotion and Rationality in Partner Selection," *Theory & Society*, 38(4) (2009), 401–22.

Reflecting and writing on the impact of the French Revolution on social mores, Edmund Burke mused on what was in store for humanity:

> All the pleasing illusions that made power gentle, and obedience liberal, which harmonized the different shades of life [...] are to be dissolved by this new conquering empire of light and reason. All the decent drapery of life is to be rudely torn off. All the super-added ideas, which the heart owns, and the understanding ratifies, as necessary to cover the defects of our weak and shivering nature, and to raise it to a dignity in our own estimation, are to be exploded as a ridiculous, absurd and antiquated fashion.[3]

Burke was anticipating what would become one of the chief sources of the dynamism and discontent of modernity, namely the fact that beliefs – in transcendence and authority – must become accountable to reason. But for Burke, far from auguring a progress in our condition, "the empire of light and reason" exposes us to truths we cannot bear. For, Burke says, as power withers away, our illusions will also fade, and this new nakedness will leave us immensely vulnerable, exposing and revealing both to ourselves and to others the true ugliness of our condition. The scrutinizing of social relations by the implacable gaze of reason can only tear away the harmonious blanket of meanings on which traditional power, obedience, and fealty rest. To be tolerable, human existence requires a modicum of myth, illusion, and lying. Only lies and illusions can make the violence of social relationships bearable. Put differently, reason's indefatigable attempts to unmask and track down the fallacies of our beliefs will leave us shivering in the cold, for only beautiful stories – not truth – can console us. Burke is right: whether reason can give meaning to our lives is *the* fundamental question of modernity.

Marx, the overriding heir and defender of Enlightenment, curiously concurs with Burke's ultra-conservative views in his famous dictum: "All that is solid melts into air, all that is holy is profane, and men at last are forced to face with sober senses the real conditions of their lives and their relations with their fellow men."[4] Marx, like Burke, views modernity as a violent arousal from a pleasant if numbing slumber and a confrontation with the naked, bare, and barren conditions of social relationships. This sobering realization may make us more alert and less likely to be lulled by the fanciful and vain promises of Church and aristocracy, but also empties our lives of charm, mystery, and a sense of the sacred. Knowledge and reason come at the price of desecrating that which we once revered. Thus Marx, like Burke, seems to think that cultural fantasies – not

truth – make our lives meaningfully connected to others and committed to a higher good. Although Marx neither rejected the new
empire of light nor longed to return to the defunct rituals of the past,
we can detect in him the same Burkean dread of what lies ahead of
a humanity in which nothing is holy and everything is profane.

What makes Marx distinctly and profoundly modernist was not
his endorsement of modernity (progress, technology, reason, economic abundance), but precisely his ambivalence toward it. From the
start, modernity involved the uneasy and simultaneous acknowledgment
of the extraordinary energies unleashed by reason and of the desic-
cating danger the exercise of reason could entail. Reason made the
world more predictable and safer, but it also made it emptier. At the
same time as moderns declared themselves free of the opiates that
had fogged the mind and consciousness, they yearned for that which
reason had proudly claimed to release them from – a sense of the
sacred, and the very capacity to believe. The triumphant call of reason
to dissect myths and beliefs became properly modern when it was
intertwined with the mournful longing for transcendent objects to
believe in and to be swayed by. Modernity is defined by its ambivalence toward its legitimating cultural core, by a sense of dread of the
powers it may unleash. Max Weber famously lent this ambivalence
its most poignant sociological pathos with his view of modernity as
characterized by "disenchantment." Disenchantment does not mean
simply that the world is no longer filled with angels and demons,
witches and fairies, but that the very category of "mystery" becomes
disparaged and meaningless. For, in their impulse to control the
natural and social world, the various modern institutions of science,
technology, and the market, which aim at solving human problems,
relieving suffering, and increasing well-being, also dissolve our rever-
ence toward nature, our capacity to believe and to keep a sense of
mystery. The vocation of scientific work is to solve and conquer
mysteries, not to be under their spell. Similarly, capitalists, whose
principal wish is to maximize their gains, often disregard and undermine the religious or aesthetic spheres – which limit, ignore, or altogether subvert economic activity. Precisely because science and economics have considerably expanded the limits of our material world,
helping us resolve the problem of scarcity, the gods have deserted us.
What in an earlier age was governed by faith, personal fealty, and
charismatic heroes becomes a matter of knowledge, control, and
calculable means.

This process toward rationalization does not, however, eliminate
all manifestations of passion; rather, for Weber, it generates attempts
to restore orders of experience dominated by fervor and passion, only

vicariously and thinly.[5] The twentieth-century cult of emotions might be interpreted in this light. But where Weber and others understood rationalization to be opposed to and countered by emotions, I suggest that the challenge for sociological analysis is to understand rationality and rationalization not as a cultural logic opposed to emotional life, but rather as working precisely in conjunction with it.[6] Rationality is an institutionalized cultural force of its own which has come to restructure emotional life from within: that is, it has changed the basic cultural scripts through which emotions are understood and negotiated. While romantic love retains a uniquely strong emotional and cultural hold on our desires and fantasies, the cultural scripts and tools available to fashion it have become increasingly at odds with and are even undermining the sphere of the erotic. There are thus at least two cultural structures at work in the emotion of love: one based on the powerful fantasy of erotic self-abandonment and emotional fusion; the other based on rational models of emotional self-regulation and optimal choice. These rational models of conduct have profoundly transformed the structure of romantic desire in undermining the cultural resources through which, historically, passion and eroticism have been experienced.

Enchanted Love

Weber was not entirely clear about what defined an "enchanted" experience, but we may deduce it, *a contrario*, from what defines disenchantment. An enchanted experience is mediated by powerful collective symbols which key one to a sense of the sacred. It is based on beliefs and feelings that involve and mobilize the totality of the self; these beliefs and feelings are not processed in second-order cognitive systems and are not rationally justifiable. These symbols constitute and overwhelm the experiential reality of the believer. In enchanted experiences, there is no strong distinction between subject and object. Thus, the object of the belief and the belief itself have an ontological status for the believer that is not called into question. The elementary forms of "enchanted" love as a cultural prototype and a phenomenological experience can be said to resemble the following model:

1 *The object of love is sacred.* Guillaume de Lorris (fl. 1230), the French scholar and poet and author of the first section of the *Roman de la Rose*, the medieval poem which intended to teach about the art of love, presents the Lady, the beloved, as on a

pedestal, a quasi-divinity to be worshiped. Such rhetoric of devotion to a sacred object emerged in twelfth-century courtly love, but could be found as late as the nineteenth century. Writing to his lover, Evelina Hanska, Balzac expresses his wishes to adore her in a way that would not suit modern sensibilities: "How I should have liked to remain half a day kneeling at your feet with my head on your lap."[7]

2 *Love is impossible to justify or explain.* Cupid's arrow is the oldest symbol of love as as an arbitrary and unjustifiable emotion. Guillaume de Lorris recounts that once the arrow penetrated his body and flesh, he could no more take it out than he could stop loving the Lady. He cannot not love. Love is a force of its own, compelling obedience. For example, consider Humbert Humbert seeing Lolita for the first time: "I find it most difficult to express with adequate force that flash, that shiver, that impact of passionate recognition."[8] The love is here immediate, irresistible, because it is construed as an act of physical recognition that bypasses the will.

3 *Such an experience overwhelms the experiential reality of the lover.* Writing to his wife Josephine in 1796, when he was the commander of the French army in Italy, Napoleon states, "I have not spent a day without loving you; I have not spent a night without embracing you; I have not so much as drunk one cup of tea without cursing the pride and ambition which force me to remain apart from the moving spirit of my life."[9] Love is here an emotion which invades the entire existential reality of the lover.

4 *In enchanted love, there is no distinction between subject and object of love.* The object of love cannot be separated from the subject loving as such experience involves and mobilizes the totality of the self. Beethoven writing to his lover in 1812, put it succinctly: "My angel, my all, my own self."[10]

5 *The object of love is unique and incommensurable.* Romeo, upon seeing Juliet, declares, "Did my heart love till now?"[11] by which he means that she is the only one he has loved and will ever love. Uniqueness entails the fact that the beloved cannot be substituted for others. It also means his/her virtues or flaws cannot be measured or compared to that of another.

6 *The person in love is oblivious to his or her own self-interest as a criterion for loving another person.* In fact, pain is an essential ingredient of the experience of absoluteness and aggrandizement. In the words of Felix, Balzac's hero in "Le Lys dans la Vallée" ("The Lily of the Valley") (1835): "To love desperately is still happiness."[12]

The model of love at first sight is a slight variation of such an "enchanted" prototype of love. "Love at first sight" is experienced as an event unexpectedly erupting in one's life; it is inexplicable and irrational; it occurs upon the first encounter and therefore is not based on cognitive and cumulative knowledge of the other. Rather, it derives from a holistic and intuitive form of experience. It disturbs one's daily life and provokes a deep commotion of the soul. The metaphors used to describe that state of mind often indicate a force that is overwhelming and overpowering (heat, magnetism, thunder, electricity). Such a version of "enchanted" love is simultaneously spontaneous and unconditional, overwhelming and eternal, unique and total. This ideal-type of romantic love affirms the radical unique-ness of the object of love, the impossibility to substitute one object of love for another, the incommensurability of its object, the refusal (or impossibility) to submit feelings to calculation and to rational knowledge, the total surrender of the self to the loved person, and the possibility (at least the potentiality) of self-destruction and self-sacrifice for the sake of another.[13] This quasi-religious view of love has had several secular cultural variants and, perhaps for that reason, has persisted throughout history.[14] It has known several variations but its basic components – sacredness, uniqueness, experiential force, irrationality, giving up one's self-interest, lack of autonomy – have remained in the literary models that took over with the spread of literacy and of the romance novel.

Modernity, however, marked a profound change in the history of enchanted love in the form of a suspicion for and dismissal of the experience of it. The following quip from Candace Bushnell – the celebrated author of the column which inspired the US TV series *Sex and the City* – is only one of numerous possible illustrations of this state of affairs:

> When was the last time you heard someone say, "I love you!" without tagging on the inevitable (if unspoken) "as a friend." When was the last time you saw two people gazing into each other's eyes without thinking, Yeah right? When was the last time you heard someone announce, "I am truly, madly in love," without thinking, Just wait until Monday morning?"[15]

Bushnell expresses here a thoroughly self-conscious, supremely ironic, and disenchanted approach to love. Lamenting this state of affairs, Maureen Dowd, one of the most prominent commentators of the *New York Times*, wrote: "[C]ulturally, emotionally, the whole idea of romance is gone, gone, gone."[16] What she meant, I think, is that the "enchanted" experience of love and romance has become difficult to subscribe to. That is, although love may remain a very meaningful experience for most people, it does not engage and mobilize the totality of the self. This in turn raises the question: Why has love lost its capacity to be experienced as "enchantment," a surrender of reason and the self? I argue here that the loss of power of love to generate romantic beliefs is the result of the rationalization of such beliefs in the three arenas of science, technology, and politics.

Disenchantment is a fundamental cultural, cognitive, and institutional process of modernity, by which belief becomes organized by knowledge systems, conduct becomes determined by systematic and abstract rules, and, as Weber postulated, faith becomes difficult to sustain. According to Weber, the greatest cultural force shaping disenchantment is the rationalization of life conduct: the fact that it is increasingly "methodical," systematic and controlled by the intellect.[17] Rational action is consciously regulated, not random, habitual, or impulsive; the cultural source of such self-conscious regulation can be religious, scientific, political, or economic. A rational attitude undermines enchantment because in order to know and approach an object, it uses systematic rules, independent of the subject and object of knowledge, thus creating a separation between the subject and object of knowledge and de-legitimizing knowledge gained in an epiphanic, traditional, or intuitive mode. The rational attitude undermines the basis of all beliefs (except perhaps of the belief in reason). It tends also to undermine transcendence by defining action as a means–end relationship. Rationalizing belief entails an undermining of the emotional intensity of and belief in love. Following this definition of rationalization, a number of massively powerful cultural forces – science, political contractualism, and technologies of choice – can be said to have refashioned the sentiment and experience of love, and to have contributed to its rationalization and thus to a profound change in the way in which it is experienced by the subject. It is the convergence and confluence of these three forces which I would argue have been responsible for the demise of the belief in the romantic experience and which have given rise to two structures of feeling, uncertainty and irony, which have profoundly transformed the self's capacity to experience self-abandonment and ecstasy.

Making Love into a Science

The first factor contributing to disenchantment as a cultural process is the prevalence of scientific modes of explanation of love, which

have been disseminated widely through the institutions of the university and the mass media. Throughout the twentieth century, first
psychoanalysis and psychology, and later biology, evolutionary psychology, and neuroscience, deployed their scientific infrastructure by
subsuming "love" under some of their key scientific concepts, as "the
unconscious," "the sex drive," "hormones," "species survival," or
"brain chemistry." Under the aegis of scientific modes of explanation,
these frameworks undermined the view of love as an ineffable, unique,
quasi-mystical experience and selfless sentiment.

Precisely because psychoanalysis and dynamic psychology put love
at the center of the constitution of the self, they eroded its cultural
status as a mystical force by viewing it as the result of psychological
processes such as "psychic trauma," "Oedipal conflict," or "repetition compulsion." The Freudian popular culture in which most
modern polities has become steeped makes the forceful claim that
love is a re-enactment of early childhood conflicts and is often nothing
but the repetition of a drama with other early protagonists who are
the true origin and cause of the present love object. Psychoanalysis
claims that love is caused by the ways in which we formed attachments to early parental figures, and our psyche faced and processed
the Oedipus complex. Love thus became the expression of a universal
psychic structure, and its object is viewed as a prolongation of early
childhood dramas. In creating a straight narrative line between
childhood and adult romantic experiences, psychological culture
makes the love experience into a re-enactment of non-amorous
sequences *per se*, and thus undermines its ineffability and mystery.
Love becomes the object of endless investigation, self-knowledge, and
self-scrutiny.

The self becomes the object of an ongoing process of self-
understanding and careful self-monitoring of the psyche, which leads
to an intellectualization of romantic relationships through the systematic labeling of emotions and through their monitoring by techniques of self-awareness and self-transformation. In making the
human subject the object and target of scientific knowledge, psychology has devised the crucial concept of "personality." Personality is a
set of stable attributes supposed to characterize a person over time,
and a successful love is the result of the compatibility between the
psychological makeup and the attributes of two people. It follows
that romantic compatibility can be evaluated, measured, and predicted using the appropriate psychological tools. Love could thus
become the object of (psychological) metrics, the purpose of which
would be to help establish and monitor the twin ideals of autonomy
and connectedness.

As autonomy progressively stood at the center of the ideal of self-hood advocated by psychology, emotional fusion was deemed as a threat for the autonomy of the self, and was replaced by an ideal of negotiation between two autonomous mature selves. To merge one's self with that of another or to subdue oneself to another came to be viewed as a negation of one's basic claim to autonomy, in turn a sign of emotional pathology. Deploying models of intimacy based on negotiation, communication, and reciprocity, the psy sciences regarded intimate relationships as the ideal relationship emerging from the reflexive monitoring of two autonomous wills, to be tailored to the needs and psychological makeup of the individual, thus liquidating the old association of love with transcendence, a force above the individual's particular needs and will. Love became "intimacy," and intimacy meant that emotional life could be submitted to rules of conduct, the purpose of which was to preserve and carve maximum individual autonomy within the romantic bond.

A third way that psychology has contributed to rationalizing the experience of love is that it deems romantic suffering an unacceptable and unjustifiable symptom, emanating from insufficiently mature psyches. Whereas "pain was an absolutely normal part of the nineteenth-century emotional response to sharing an identity with another human being,"[18] in contemporary psychological culture, suffering no longer signals an emotional experience stretching above and beyond the boundaries of the self: that is, it is no longer the sign of selfless devotion or of an elevated soul. Such love – based on self-sacrifice, fusion, and longing for absoluteness – came to be viewed as the symptom of an incomplete emotional development. The cultural equation of love with suffering is similar to the equation of love with an experience of both transcendence and consummation in which love is affirmed in an ostentatious display of self-loss.[19] Utilitarian models of the polity were transposed to the psyche, and in this new therapeutic culture, ideals of self-sacrifice and self-abandonment were held to be the illegitimate sign of an unhealthy psyche (or a sign that one "suffered" to get some hidden psychic benefit), and hence deeply suspect since autonomy and the capacity to preserve one's self-interest have become synonymous with mental health.

The model of mental health which massively penetrated intimate relationships demanded that love be aligned to definitions of well-being and happiness, which ultimately rejected suffering, and commanded one to maximize one's utilities. This model of health puts knowledge and defense of one's self-interest squarely at the center of the emotionally mature self. To love well means to love according to one's self-interest. The emotional experience of love increasingly contains and displays a utilitarian project of the self, in which one has to secure maximum pleasure and well-being. Suffering is progressively foreign to this new cultural idiom of love. This in turn meant that if love was a source of suffering, it was a "mistake," a wrong evaluation of the compatibility of two personalities, the sign that one needed further self-knowledge which could correct one's suffering and lead to a more mature choice. Reciprocity and the preservation of self-interest have become invisibly embedded in the ordinary experience of love, which can be illustrated through a few contrasting examples.

In *A Midsummer Night's Dream* (1600), this is how Helena, who has *not* been subjected to Puck's spell and tricks, speaks to Demetrius, who, under the influence of Puck, has rejected her love:

DEMETRIUS

Do I entice you? do I speak you fair?

Or, rather, do I not in plainest truth

Tell you, I do not, nor I cannot love you?

HELENA

And even for that do I love you the more.

I am your spaniel; and, Demetrius,

The more you beat me, I will fawn on you:

Use me but as your spaniel, spurn me, strike me,

Neglect me, lose me; only give me leave,

Unworthy as I am, to follow you.

What worser place can I beg in your love, –

And yet a place of high respect with me, –

Than to be used as you use your dog?[20]

Helena naturally expresses her love to her beloved in a way that would be interpreted today not only as a form of self-abasement but as a pathology. Shakespeare's world, by contrast, is likely to have viewed this more benignly, as an ordinary manifestation of the "madness of love." Consider also Julie de Lespinasse, a highly acclaimed and admired eighteenth-century French woman of letters, whose love for the capricious and unfaithful Comte de Guibert was not reciprocated. Though he married another woman, still Julie stood firm in her demonstration of unmitigated passion and in her affirmation of love unchecked by mechanisms of exchange and reciprocity. She declared in a letter to Guibert:

> I love too well to impose a restraint upon myself; I prefer to have to ask your pardon rather than commit no faults. I *have no self-love* with you; I detest prudence, I even hate those "duties of friendship" which substitute propriety for interest, and circumspection for feeling. How shall I say it? I love abandonment to impulse, I act *from impulse only*, and I love to madness that others do the same by me. (emphasis added)[21]

Julie de Lespinasse stands for an ethic of self-abandonment governed by impulsive emotionality, not a calculation of costs and benefits. Far from signaling immaturity or low self-esteem, this capacity to love regardless of reciprocation could have been (and probably was) interpreted as the sign of a great character.

Another example was discussed in chapter 2. Anne Elliot's vow to remain faithful all her life to Captain Wentworth despite the evidence of their separation jars with contemporary sensibility because she subscribes to the view of love as absolute and incommensurable and seems to ignore the commands of her self-interest. The commitment to another here is a total thrust of the self, regardless of its outcome for her well-being. Giving her love once compels her to forgo better prospects, and thus to dismiss what modern society would see as the mark of a mature psyche, namely her self-interest. Today she would be compelled to see a psychoanalyst, lie on the couch, and account for her steadfast determination to sacrifice all her life in a disinterested way, with no expectation of return. Finally, Edith Wharton, writing in 1908 to her lover Morton Fullerton, used an explicitly anti-utilitarian terminology:

> There would have been the making of an accomplished flirt in me, because my lucidity shows me each move of the game – but that, in the same instant, a reaction of contempt makes me sweep all the counters off the board and cry out: – "Take them all – I don't want to win – I want to lose everything to you!"[22]

Helena's, Julie de Lespinasse's, Anne Elliott's, and Edith Wharton's disregard for what would seem to us to be the norm of reciprocity flouts contemporary common sense. It flouts the accepted premise that the choice of a love object should not trump one's well-being, should in fact contribute to it in the expression of emotional reciprocity. The moral and psychological norm of emotional reciprocity that has come to govern our models of romance and relationships in general is based on a utilitarian model of mental health and well-being and is one of the chief sources of the cultural rationalization of love. This model of emotional reciprocity and utilitarianism is ultimately based on a strong program of reason: the choice of a love object had to be taken away from the whims and clutches of the unconscious; if healthy, it had to be grasped by reason and be an object of self-knowledge; it could produce pleasure and well-being, and, most of all, it could and should preserve and affirm one's self-interest.

Biology has had a slightly different impact on the cultural frames through which love has come to be understood. Biologists typically explain love through chemical processes which, even more than psychology, reduce love to factors that are entirely extraneous to the sentiment of love itself. Studies in neuroscience suggest that there is a presence in the brain of a consistent number of chemicals when people profess to feeling love.[23] These include testosterone, oestrogen, dopamine, norepinephrine, serotonin, oxytocin, and vasopressin. For example, a dramatic increase in the amount of dopamine and norepinephrine is said to occur in the brain when one is infatuated with another person. More specifically, higher levels of testosterone and oestrogen are present during the lustful phase of a relationship. Dopamine, norepinephrine, and serotonin are said to be more commonly present during the attraction phase of a relationship.[24] The serotonin effects of being in love have a chemical appearance similar to obsessive-compulsive disorder,[25] which would explain why we seem not to be able to think of anyone else when we are in love. Serotonin levels are also significantly higher in the brains of people who have recently fallen in love than in the brains of others.[26] Oxytocin and vasopressin seemed to be more closely linked to long-term bonding and relationships characterized by strong attachments.[27] In the February 2006 issue of *National Geographic*, Lauren Slater's cover-page article, "Love: The Chemical Reaction," describes attraction and attachment as being triggered by different chemical components. The implication is that the euphoria or exaltation we may feel as a result of being in love is nothing but a chemical and involuntary reaction in the brain. Research by socio-biologist Helen Fisher, for example, also claims that we are biologically programmed to feel intense love for a maximum of two years on average, after which the passion and intensity recede.[28] The result of this reduction of love to brain chemistry is to dispose of a mystical and spiritual view of love and to substitute for it a new form of biological materialism. For example, Catherine Townsend reflects on her need to feel loved. She writes: "According to *Psychology Today*, '... phenylethylamine – the chemical in the brain involved in the euphoria that comes with falling in love – rise(s) with feelings of infatuation, boosting euphoria and excitement.' That sounds like me. Then again, that also sounds like lots of women I know. Are we all dysfunctional love addicts?"[29] Clearly, the mixture of psychological and biological terminology in ordinary conceptions of love is deflationary, reducing emotions to mere chemical involuntary reactions and the experience of love to a physiological experience, devoid of higher meaning.

While offering a different view, evolutionary psychologists similarly attribute the feeling of love to an extraneous factor that serves the human species. According to Dylan Evans,[30] in evolutionary terms, emotions such as love (or guilt, or jealousy) are thought to have helped resolve the "problem of commitment." Given that people must cooperate with each other, how will they commit themselves to another and/or ensure another's commitment? The answer, evolutionary psychologists say, is through emotions. Romantic love in particular may have served the purpose of instilling a desire to reproduce and to ensure that men and women will not walk out on each other on a whim. Here, again, the interpretive shift operated by evolutionary psychology has had the effect of deflating the felt uniqueness and transcendent character of love, making it a mere functional necessity to ensure cooperativeness, articulated at the level of the species. Love here is nothing but the blind necessity of nature and of the social group, expressed through particular stories and individuals.

By their nature, scientific modes of explanation – psychological, biological, and evolutionary – tend to be abstract and extraneous to the categories of felt and lived experience. This contrasts with, say, pre-modern religious explanations, which, when they viewed intense love as the manifestation of spirit possessions, or as a temporary loss of reason, still resonated with the felt experience of the subject. Scientific explanations reduce love to an epiphenomenon, a mere effect of prior causes which are unseen and unfelt by the subject, and which are neither mystical nor singular but provoked by involuntary and almost mechanical – psychic, chemical, or biological – processes. With the prevalence of scientific modes of explanation, it is difficult to hold on to the view of love as a unique, mystical, and ineffable feeling. In that sense, love has undergone the same process of disenchantment as nature: it is viewed no longer as inspired by mysterious and grand forces but rather as a phenomenon in need of explanation and control, as a reaction determined by psychological, evolutionary, and biological laws.[31]

Scientific knowledge is widely promoted through media channels which periodically must provide interpretations of reality. These interpretive frames do not replace traditional romantic conceptions of love, but rather compete with them, and ultimately undermine them. Science tends to subsume particular experiences under general and abstract categories, thus doing away with their particularity. Because, by definition, scientific frameworks aim to explain and find causes, they naturally diminish any experience based on the sense of the unique, the ineffable, and the irrational. The overall effect of scientific interpretive frameworks on the experience of love is dual: *reflexive* and *deflationary*. Actors are made to attend explicitly to the underlying mechanisms motivating their love, and love is made the result of a universal psychological or chemical force, working beyond and beneath the concrete particular desires of specific individuals. Desire thus becomes, in a way, understood as detached from the concrete person to whom it is geared, and, as an involuntary mechanism, is a blind force whose object ends up being eminently interchangeable. To that extent, we may say that romantic desire becomes emptied of its mythological content.

Weber's cultural pessimism consisted in the fact that he did not think that an increase in scientific understanding brought about a greater understanding of the concrete conditions of our lives. As he wrote:

> When we spend money today I bet that even if they are colleagues of political economy here in the hall, almost every one of them would hold a different answer in readiness to the question: How does it happen that one can buy something for money – sometimes more and sometimes less? The savage knows what he does in order to get his daily food and which institutions serve him in this pursuit. The increasing intellectualization and rationalization do not, therefore, indicate an increased and general knowledge of the conditions under which one lives.[32]

As one of Weber's commentators suggests, non-scientific explanations might be superior to scientific ones because they are holistic and more organically connected to the totality of our lived experience.[33] Scientific explanations of our experience, by contrast, distance us from that experience, both cognitively and emotionally. More than that, says Weber, science makes our experience less intelligible, for there is an incompatibility between existential frames of meaning and abstract, systematic ones. Scientific explanations thus undermine the meaningful connection between romantic experience and views of love as mystical and irrational. In making love into an outcome of prior unconscious, chemical, and evolutionary mechanisms, science reduces the capacity to turn love into a mythology, a transcendent force of its own.

Political Emancipation as Rationalization

As the examples provided above suggest, self-sacrifice, self-abandonment, and the capacity to love with no expectation of reciprocity were seen as mostly (although not exclusively) female attributes. One of the main changes in the motif of self-sacrifice was brought about by feminism, understood as a broad cultural persuasion which extended human rights to women and debunked the social and ideological mechanisms that made the disenfranchisement of women possible, invisible, and widely desired. Other sources of the cultural rationalization of love are the norms of equality, consensuality, and reciprocity – contractualism – that have come to dominate the moral vocabulary of our polities and transformed the terms within which heterosexual relationships are negotiated. In his *Politics of Authenticity*, Marshall Berman suggests that "it is only in modern times that men [*sic*] have come to think of the self as a distinctly *political* problem."[34] Given the gender used by Berman, it is ironic that this sentence is particularly and spectacularly applicable to women in the twentieth century. Indeed, feminism has exerted perhaps the single most significant influence on women's subjectivity and on the relations between the sexes. Second-wave feminism profoundly transformed the understanding and practice of the emotion of love.[35] More than any other political and cultural formation, the feminist persuasion has importantly influenced the cultural history of love because it has torn away the veils of male chivalry and feminine mystique. Precisely because it has had such a decisive influence, I want to take stock of the impact of the feminist movement on romantic relations and ask what may have been the cultural impact of feminist modes of thinking in a society that is still largely dominated by men. In doing so, I view feminism as a cultural worldview: that is, as a new way of conceiving of the self and its relationships to others. This implies that I bracket and suspend, temporarily, my own obvious allegiance to feminism in order to understand its impact in destabilizing traditional gender roles and norms through critique and its egalitarian vision of women's and men's rights and duties. Because feminism, along with clinical psychology and consumer culture, has been the most powerful cultural agent shaping and changing the relationships between men and women, it can and should be analyzed like these other two cultural formations.

In her *The Dialectic of Sex*, Shulamith Firestone argues that romantic love not only hides class and sex segregation, but, more importantly, it enables, perpetuates, and strengthens it. In Firestone's words, "[L]ove, perhaps even more than childbearing, is the pivot of women's oppression today."[36] Romantic love has come to be viewed not only as a cultural practice reproducing gender inequality, but also as one of the primary mechanisms through which women are made to accept (and "love") their submission to men. The central concept that has enabled feminism to deconstruct sex and love is the notion of power. In the feminist worldview, power is the invisible, yet highly tangible dimension organizing gender relations, that which must be tracked down and expelled from intimate relationships. "Power" has assumed the status of explaining most of what has been wrong in men's and women's interactions. It is a cultural frame which conceives, and thereby reorganizes and generates social relationships. When viewed as a cultural script which – like the cultural script of "caste" or "blue blood" – organizes and regulates sexual and gender relationships, "power symmetry" can be said to rationalize social bonds in a number of ways. First, it invites men and women to reflect on the rules which organize the routine, taken-for-granted, course of sexual attraction (a routine shaped by centuries-old norms of patriarchal domination) and to monitor reflexively their emotions, language, and conduct. Second, in order to instill symmetry, it invites women to evaluate and measure their own and their partner's contributions to the relationship. Third, it trumps erotic relationships with the values of fairness in the workplace and the polity (the professional status of potential lovers must trump their private desires as individuals). And finally, it calls for a subsuming of erotic relations within neutral procedural rules of speech and conduct, which disembed relations from their particularity and concreteness.

De-Routinizing Power

Perhaps the most visible arena in which the principles of symmetry are exercised is the realm of courtship and sexual initiative. The most conspicuous example of the new principle of organization of intimate relations along the axis of symmetry is to be found in the category of *sexual harassment*, a very good example of the principle of equivalence of power-free and emotionally symmetrical relationships. For example, consider the case of Dave Cass and Claudia Satchel: the former a Professor of Economics at the University of Pennsylvania, and the latter a graduate student. They had been together for five years when in 1994 Cass's appointment to Chair of Graduate Studies was denied on the grounds that his relationship with a student made him unsuitable for this position. In reporting with disapproval on the university prosecution, Barry Dank explains:

> They were in multiple violation of the feminist norms on asymmetrical intimate relationships. These norms hold that it is inappropriate for persons to become intimately involved when there is a significant power differential between the two parties to the relationship. In this framework, asymmetrical relationships represent abuse and make consent suspect and even impossible while symmetrical relationships are viewed as representing equality, and freedom of choice. Dave and Claudia were in a multiple asymmetric relationship since they were in age-differentiated categories – Dave being about 25 years older than Claudia, as well as being in power-differentiated positions in the university, Dave being a professor and Claudia a student.[37]

The cultural/political categories of equality and symmetry – which here conflict with other principles such as freedom of sentiment and privacy – constitute new ways of regulating gender relationships, by making them accountable to new norms of power symmetry and balance.

This entails fresh ways of conceiving the very categories that constitute a sexual bond between two people, for it demands that a concrete interaction be subsumed under an evaluation of a person's abstract position in a social structure. J.M. Coetzee's famous novel *Disgrace* (1999), quoted in the epigraph to this chapter, tells the story of a teacher, Professor Lurie, who has an intense affair with one of his students. As a result of this affair, he undergoes a disciplinary procedure at his college and is forced to resign. Lurie embodies a male character who does not understand the new rules regulating relationships between men and women. This is the exchange he has with one of his colleagues:

> "Don't you think," says Swarts, "that by its nature academic life must call for certain sacrifices? That for the good of the whole we have to deny ourselves certain gratifications?"
>
> "You have in mind a ban on intimacy across the generations?"
>
> "No, not necessarily. But as teachers we occupy positions of power. Perhaps a ban on mixing power relations with sexual relations. Which, I sense, is what was going on in this case. Or extreme caution."
>
> Frodia Rassool intervenes. "[...] Yes, he says, he is guilty; but when we try to get specificity, all of a sudden it is not abuse of a young woman he is confessing to, just an impulse he could not resist, with

no mention of the pain he has caused, no mention of the long history of exploitation of which this is part."[38]

This vignette illustrates the semantic shifts from "irresistible impulse" to the political (and psychological) notion of "abuse," from love for younger people to "intimacy across the generations," from the definition of masculinity as social authority to a prohibition of "mixing power relations with sexual relations," and from the experience of "private pleasure" to the suspicion that it hides a "long history of exploitation." The individual and his/her desires become the bearers of an abstract structure of power which in turn justifies institutional intervention. Along with the language of psychology, feminism has helped enforce norms and procedures to ensure fairness, equality, emotional equity, and symmetry, institutionally and emotionally.

When the Workplace Trumps Feelings

Sexual harassment policies were aimed at protecting women from the abuse of institutional power by men. Sociologically, this had the effect of making the rules of fairness in the workplace trump the private desires of individuals. For example, the policy guidelines of Harvard Graduate School of Education (HGSE) state that:

> HGSE affirms the value of close, caring relationships between members of the HGSE community. At the same time, special questions are raised where one person has direct professional responsibility for another – as a faculty member or teaching fellow does for a student he or she teaches or advises, a supervisor has for a supervisee, or administrators or faculty members may have for one another. In this situation, any romantic relationship is inherently asymmetrical because it involves one person who, by virtue of his or her role within the HGSE community, holds formal power over the other. Because of this power imbalance, such relationships hold potential for exploitation. Such a relationship can also affect other members of the community, who may believe that someone in authority is open to unfair influence, that someone is receiving unfair advantages, or that the romantic relationship puts third parties at a disadvantage academically or professionally. Such assumptions can have detrimental effects even if they are untrue.[39]

Fairness toward the general community of workers must take precedence over individual sentiments, which suggests that the workplace ought to trump the autonomy of erotic relationships. Here, clearly, the workplace takes precedence over private sentiments.

Proceduralism and Neutral Language

The implementation of rules of fairness demanded the use of a neutral language, for neutrality was supposed to purge language of its gender biases and most crucially it was supposed to expose and thus counter the unspoken and invisible assumptions with which men and women have traditionally produced and reproduced their identities and aspirations. For example, consider the University of Pennsylvania student guidelines on sexual harassment, geared to men and women with different power as well as to students with similar power status:

GENERAL QUESTIONS AND ANSWERS ABOUT SEXUAL HARASSMENT

Can I compliment one of my students or coworkers?

Yes, as long as your compliments are free from sexual undertones. Compliments such as "Nice legs" or "You look really sexy in that outfit" can make your co-worker or student feel uncomfortable or threatened. Even if the person you're complimenting isn't bothered by the comments, others might be.

How about asking for a date? Do I have to take "no" for an answer?

You may want to get together socially with someone, from work or from your class, whom you find attractive. This is perfectly acceptable as long as you make sure the desire and attraction are mutual. If you are turned down for a date, you might want to ask the person if a request would be welcome at another time. Be aware, though, that some people don't feel comfortable saying no to that type of question, for fear of offending you, or provoking some type of retaliation. Use your judgment. If the person says no more than once, or is uncomfortable or evasive when you ask, don't use pressure. Accept the answer and move on.[40]

These instructions aim at instilling emotional self-regulation so as to remove the possibility of discomfort in another person. These emotional self-regulations thus end up creating comfort zones around neutral modes of interaction, characterized by emotionally neutral, sex-free and gender-free, language. The ill-described "politically correct" language is thus primarily a *dis-embedding* technique: that is, a linguistic and procedural tool that disrupts the non-conscious rules governing gender relationships and emotions, in order to substitute for them non-contextual, general, and procedural rules of interaction. A famous example of the ways in which rules of consent, symmetry, and reciprocity must now regulate relationships can be found in the Antioch rules, named after the American college in which they originated. In 1990 a feminist group at the college requested that the administration institute a sexual consent policy binding upon all its students. *Newsweek* magazine derisively summarized the purpose of the Sexual Offense Policy as

> to empower these students to become equal partners when it comes time to mate with males. The goal is 100 percent consensual sex, and it works like this: it isn't enough to ask someone if she'd like to have sex, as an Antioch women's center advocate told a group of incoming freshmen this fall. You must obtain consent every step of the way. "If you want to take her blouse off, you have to ask. If you want to touch her breast, you have to ask. If you want to move your hand down to her genitals, you have to ask. If you want to put your finger inside her, you have to ask."[41]

What the article derides is the fact that these rules aim at ensuring procedural equality between partners, and thus end up explicitly engineering erotic encounters by an act of *political will*. Judged from an erotic standpoint, these rules seem to eliminate the tacit ambivalence and spontaneity that normally attend sexual transactions. But the rules also inaugurate new ways of conceiving and marking political will, much like those that emerged during the French Revolution which citizens used to conspicuously fashion, signal, and constitute a new social contract.[42] Such acts of explicit political will stand in contrast to traditional codes and symbols of love, which, because they are not explicitly formulated, seem to be more spontaneous and natural. Spontaneity, however, is indeed nothing but an effect of both the force and the invisibility of social scripts.

New Principles of Equivalence

Intimacy thus conceived entails new modes of evaluating relationships. In particular, it provides new principles by which sentiments are reconceptualized as contributions that can be evaluated, measured, and compared. It introduces what sociologists Luc Boltanski and Laurent Thévenot called new "principles of equivalence": that is, new ways of evaluating an action according to a principle which implicitly organizes objects by grouping them together with others, differentiates them from others, and assigns to them a value, or ranks them.[43] Fairness constituted a new principle of equivalence within romantic and domestic bonds: that is, a new way of introducing a form of metrics by which contributions and sentiments could be evaluated and compared. This principle of equivalence revolved around two objects of evaluation. The most obvious domain that seems easily amenable to this principle of equivalence is that of practical chores and responsibilities. The principle of fairness addressed the question of whether there is an equal distribution of domestic chores: child rearing, house cleaning, and shopping. For example, an Internet site called Sharing Housework states that

> it's important to look at the overall life balance when determining who should handle each household task, including how many hours each person spends working outside the home, tending to children, paying the bills or shopping for the family. [...] When it comes to tallying up and keeping track of who does what, some couples might benefit from using a checklist or spreadsheet.[44]

Clearly, the norm of fairness introduces new ways of evaluating, measuring, and comparing the actions of members of a couple in daily life.

But the most striking illustration of the process of introducing new principles of equivalence is in the far more intangible realm of emotions. While contributions to the household sometimes can be translated into material and measurable components, emotions seem far less amenable to quantification. Yet, despite their intangible character, they have also become the object of principles of equivalence. Domestic and romantic transactions are organized around principles of equivalence and cognitive axes such as "emotional availability," "emotional expressiveness," "emotional investment" – of who invests more energy to keep the relationship alive, whether both parties' emotional needs are adequately expressed and met. Principles of equivalence demand that we compare quantities, that we order and prioritize them, thus enabling a process of evaluating and ranking of emotions. For example, in a book entitled *Lose that Loser and Find the Right Guy*, the author declares: "Remember: Mr Right should care just as much about you as he does about himself."[45] Clearly, to be able to compare the care for oneself and for another requires the mobilization of cognitive tools to evaluate and measure "care." Another example is Lara, a 40-year-old woman with two children, who explains her decision to initiate her recent divorce:

> My husband is in many ways the ideal husband, responsible, handsome, great father, but he never was as warm to me as I wanted him to. During all these years, I kept telling myself I should not try to compare my and his warmth, my and his love, but in the end, I just couldn't. I had everything, and yet he gave me so much less than I wanted, in the end I left.

The implicit norm of emotional symmetry compelled her to seek a divorce.

The demystification of love by political ideals of equality and fairness, by science and by technology, has made sexual relationships into a self-reflexive object of scrutiny and control through formal and predictable procedures. The belief that language should be neutral and purged of its gender biases, that sexual relationships should be free from the long shadow of power, that mutual consent and reciprocity should be at the heart of intimate relationships, and, finally, that impersonal procedures should secure such consent have all had the effect of increasingly subsuming the erotic and romantic experience of love under systematic rules of conduct and abstract categories. Giddens, as we saw in chapter 1, captured these transformations under the glib term of "pure relationship" – a contractual relationship entered and exited at will.[46] Yet, he omitted to grasp the ways in which a pure relationship reflects a rationalization of intimate bonds, and transforms the very nature of desire.

Technologies of Choice

The third cultural force that has contributed to the processes of love's rationalization is to be found in the intensification of technologies of choice, embodied in the Internet. These technologies overlap with and rely heavily on psychological knowledge – a non-artifact-centered technology of choice – and modes of partner selection that derive from the market.[47] That the choice of a mate has become far more rational has often been overlooked, because of the common view that mate selection based on love has entailed a concomitant decrease in the rational criteria involved. In contrast, I would argue counterintuitively that both love and rationality jointly structure modern relationships and that both love and rationality have become rationalized.

To clarify what is rational about the modern choice of a mate, I would ask: what was the pre-modern rationality in the choice of a mate? A pre-modern actor looking for a mate was notoriously rational: s/he typically considered the criteria of dowry size, personal or family wealth and reputation, education and family politics (although from the eighteenth century onward, emotional considerations clearly played an increasingly explicit role in many European countries).[48] But what is often omitted from these discussions is the observation that the calculation stopped here. Given the limited options, beyond the general and rudimentary requirements of character and appearance, actors made very few demands of prospective partners, and, more often than not, settled for the *first available* satisfactory *good-enough* marriage prospect, a rationality which I call *pragmatic rationality*.[49] Thus, to pre-modern authorities on arranged marriage, choice involved little reflexive calculation. Giovanni di Pagolo Morelli, a member of the elite in Renaissance Italy, advised young men not to get carried away by desire, but simply to "take a girl who pleases you."[50] Pragmatic consideration of the prospect's status, reputation, character, and appearance was essential, albeit tempered by the limited pool of potential partners and the mores of the milieu. The decision was based on a rough assessment of the person, not on an extensive attempt to gather information about his or her tastes, personality, and lifestyle. No strong or intense emotion was expected in marriage partner selection. The hope was that partners would gradually develop a general affection for each other. In another Italian advice manual of the period, Lodovico Dolce suggests that fathers put themselves in their "daughters' shoes" when searching for a potential son-in-law.[51] He recognized that there was no way for a father to rationally calculate what type of person his daughter would find attractive and emotionally compatible; instead, this decision ultimately required him to trust his "gut feelings" and make a pragmatic decision about what his daughter would appreciate.

Furthermore, the basic information that was gathered relied a great deal on hearsay and on the general impression formed by others. In the early fifteenth century, an Italian widow writes home to her son regarding the match she is trying to arrange for him: "Everybody says the same thing: whoever marries her will be glad, because she will make a good wife. As far as her looks go, they tell me what I have in fact seen. She has a good, well-proportioned figure. [...] When I asked whether she was a bit rough, I was told that she is not."[52]

From a modern standpoint, what is striking here is how *little* information these pre-modern subjects gathered and had at their disposal before deciding on a prospective partner.[53] A fifteenth-century instructional poem, "'How the Good Wife Taught Her Daughter,' recommends that if only one man courts a girl she should 'scorn him not, whatever he be.'"[54] Physical requirements were often very minimal. "[A]s long as if he does not look like Baronci del Certaldese [a very ugly man] he should be considered handsome by his wife," advises Lodovico Dolce in the Italian advice manual cited above, addressing the task of the bride's father.[55] Attractiveness played a role in mate selection, but given that sex appeal was not a clearly differentiated cultural category, its specifications remained very vague and, by modern standards, quite minimal. Similarly, even if an important consideration for a prospective mate was character, this notion was left very broad and undefined, a far cry from the elaborate psychological requirements people display in modern times.

While many Renaissance parents were heavily swayed by social, financial, and political factors in the selection of mates for their sons and daughters, when it came to issues of personality, pre-modern actors were just looking for "quality" in-laws, a vague term which referred to the basic requirements of character and status. After considering prospective partners' financial standing and social status, English aristocrats in the fifteenth and sixteenth centuries looked for a generally "good" person to marry their son or daughter, not a "perfect" match. Historian Barbara J. Harris presents two examples in her study of women in Renaissance aristocracy:

> [Sir William] Holles stated specifically that he wanted his granddaughter to wed "an honest man, of good name and fame," as well one "of substance." [Sir Anthony] Denny expressed the hope that his daughters would marry his wards, "who being the heirs of my friends, for the good qualities and virtues of their parents [...] I [...] obtained to be coupled in matrimony with mine."

Denny added that his "greatest care was that my posterity and those that should be coupled in matrimony with them might rightly be taught the love and fear of God, their obedience to their sovereign lord, and duty to their country."[56]

According to Frances and Joseph Gies, the peasant class in England similarly counseled its children to find a decent person, although in some cases the objective was simply to find *someone*.[57] The goal for singles was to be satisfied with their selection rather than to find the perfect partner. The emotional expectations for marriage were to avoid excessive suffering, and, in the best of cases, to form an enduring but relatively low-key form of affection.

In sum, pre-modern rationality involved little or no formal "expert" knowledge (except perhaps that of potion-making); it consisted in a rough evaluation of another's economic assets; beyond general traits of pleasantness, people reflected very little about the desired traits of another; the search was not systematic, even when it was conducted outside one's immediate environment; it was a group or family search, not an individualized one; and, finally, the self-interest defended in marital strategies was mostly pecuniary and less clearly emotional. Emotions and self-interest were clearly differentiated categories.

The pre-modern actor looking for a mate seems a simpleton in comparison with contemporary actors, who from adolescence to adulthood develop an elaborate set of criteria for the selection of a mate and very sophisticated means to reach their goals. Such criteria are not only social and educational, but also physical, sexual, and, perhaps most of all, emotional.[58] Psychology, Internet technology, and the logic of the capitalist market applied to mate selection have contributed to create a cultural personality which has considerably refined and multiplied its tastes and capacity for discernment and choice. Psychology in particular has greatly contributed to defining persons as sets of psychological and emotional attributes and intimacy as the sharing of two personalities whose attributes and tastes must be finely matched and attuned. A hyper-cognized, rational method of selecting a mate goes hand in hand with the cultural expectation that love provides authentic, unmediated emotional and sexual experiences. Such a hyper-cognized method of mate selection has become particularly salient in the realm of online dating.[59]

Internet dating sites have become highly popular and profitable enterprises.[60] Online dating represents the most significant trend in modern courtship.[61] Internet dating sites have one goal: to facilitate the search for romance or even true love based on a twin ideal of physical attractiveness and emotional compatibility. Searching for a life partner is no longer about finding someone "who pleases you"; rather it is about finding someone who will satisfy highly elaborate and intense emotional aspirations, supposed to be the outcome of a fine dynamic of sharing of tastes. For example, one popular dating site, Match.com, guarantees to "Make Love Happen."[62] The site advertises success stories with titles such as "He flipped my world upside down and inside out," "We finally are together and plan to be forever," and "We are so ridiculously happy it's not possible to describe." Yahoo! Personals promises, "Dating, butterflies, romance...it all happens here."[63] And eHarmony calls on singles to "experience the joy of true compatibility. Let eHarmony help you begin the journey to your soul mate today."[64] Yet, as I documented in Cold Intimacies, these daunting emotional expectations have actually increased the extent of the rational methods involved in partner selection[65] through a variety of cultural mechanisms:

1   Intellectualization. The profile renders the search process into a list of attributes that can be known, introspected, spelled out, and which, when matched to the right attributes of another, will produce compatibility (the psychological profile).

"Intellectualization" is a central feature of rationalization, and refers to the ways in which implicit features of our experience are brought to our consciousness, named, and subjected to reflexive reasoning.[66]

2 *Rational management of the flow of encounters.* Internet dating involves usually a much larger volume of interactions than real-life dating; this large volume compels actors to develop standard techniques to manage the ongoing flow of interested people more easily and efficiently. As Neil Smelser puts it, the computer serves as a "rationalizing device par excellence."[67]

3 *Visualization.* One of the most important elements contributing to the rationalization of the romantic bond has to do with the fact that users can now see the field of prospective partners in one single snapshot. Whereas in the real world, the market of partners remains virtual – only presupposed, latent and always invisible – on the Net, the market is real and literal, not virtual, precisely because Internet users can actually *visualize* the pool of potential partners and thus compare among them prior to an encounter. The Internet arrays possible choices as if on "a buffet table" and solicits a mode of choice that is derived from the economic sphere, thus interfering with more intuitive or epiphanic modes of knowledge. This rationalization involves conscious, rule-bound comparison and choice among alternative means to a given end. This formal process of reasoning considers the different courses of action we want to take and applies a methodical approach to achieving our goals.[68]

4 *Commensuration.* Combined with the ideology of psychology and that of the market, the Internet institutionalizes a process of *commensuration*. Wendy Espeland and Mitchell Stevens define this as follows: "[C]ommensuration involves using numbers to create relations between things. Commensuration transforms qualitative distinctions into quantitative distinctions, where difference is precisely expressed as magnitude according to some shared metric."[69] The combined effects of psychology, the Internet, and the capitalist market have the cultural effect of making potential partners commensurable, measurable, and comparable with each other according to new techniques and cognitive tools of evaluation.

5 *Competitiveness.* The most obvious effect of visualization of the market is the introduction of ways of ranking which were left implicit in the non-Internet mode of partner selection. In the pre-Internet era, the search for a partner was based largely on what cognitive psychologist Gary Klein refers to as "intuition": "How you turn experience into action [or] the set of hunches, impulses,

insights, gut feelings, anticipations, and judgments stemming from previous events in your life."[70] Intuition is a non-conscious form of judgment and evaluation based on the emotional meaning objects hold for us. In contrast, online dating institutionalizes a formal, conscious, and systematic form of rationality in which people assess others by defining them as a set of attributes, by evaluating them along multiple scales, and by comparing them to others. The Internet enables the development of a comparative mindset, made possible by the fact that the technology lays out choices and offers tools (such as "score cards") to measure the relative merits of each potential partner. If potential partners can be evaluated according to a certain metric, they become interchangeable and in principle can be improved on. That is, the process of settling on a "good-enough" choice becomes increasingly difficult.

6 *Maximization of utilities.* Finally, consistent with the logic of consumer culture, the technology enables and even encourages an increasing specification and refinement of tastes. As one guidebook to Internet dating puts it, "[T]he more experience you have, the more refined your tastes and the fewer people you may be willing to consider."[71] The pragmatic rationalism of pre-modern mate selection has given way to a pervasive calculating, market-based, and highly sophisticated rationality that is motivated by the desire to maximize and refine its utilities. Bourdieu's remark about the general spirit of economy might be an apt one to capture the process at hand: "The spirit of calculation [...] gradually wins out in all fields of practice over the logic of the domestic economy, which was based on the repression, or more precisely, the denial of calculation."[72] Indeed, Internet dating sites display the consumerist logic of increasingly narrowing, defining, and refining tastes, and comparing among alternative possibilities.

By enabling users to investigate a vast number of options, the Internet encourages them to maximize their partner selection in unprecedented ways, in stark contrast to pre-modern methods of mate selection, which settled on the first good-enough choice and chose earlier, from a narrower pool of partners. Maximization of outcomes has become a goal in and of itself.[73] Many respondents declare that the choice available is so large that they get in touch only with people who correspond very precisely to their diverse aspirations, including physical appearance, sexual performance, and psychological and emotional makeup. The majority of respondents report that they aspired to finding "more accomplished" people than at the beginning of their search, suggesting that their tastes and ambitions changed.

Clearly, online dating using the cultural recipes of psychological profiles and consumerist logic illustrates how actors use elaborate rational strategies to achieve their romantic desires. As sociologist Jeffrey Alexander suggests, "The gradual permeation of the computer into the pores of modern life deepened what Max Weber called the rationalization of the world."[74] Like no other technology, the Internet has radicalized the notion of the self as a "chooser" and the idea that the romantic encounter should be the result of the best possible choice. That is, the virtual encounter has become hyper-cognized, the result of a rational method of gathering information to select a mate.

The Internet has become organized like a market, in which one can compare "values" attached to people, and opt for "the best bargain." The values attached to people include their socio-economic and educational achievements as well as their looks, psychological makeup, and lifestyle orientation. The Internet places each person searching for another in an open market in open competition with others, thus radicalizing the notion that one can and should improve one's romantic condition and that (potential or actual) partners are eminently interchangeable. The language of the market is evident in the literature – for example: "In pure marketing terms, the women of Internet dating are faced with an overwhelming number of buying decisions. It's the law of supply and demand."[75] Or: "Internet dating is a numbers game. [...] So, marketing yourself successfully to these women means finding ways to differentiate yourself from other males."[76]

The penetration of marketing language and techniques into the realm of interpersonal relationships marks the move to *technologies of interchangeability*: that is, technologies that expand the pool of choices, enable the rapid move from one partner to another, and set up criteria for comparing partners and for comparing oneself to others. Such practices of evaluation conflict with a conception of love in which the other cannot be apprehended or known through rational methods, which can even be said to constitute the paradigm for a certain model of relationships as defined by Derrida:

> The structure of my relation to the other is of a "relation without relation." It is a relation in which the other remains absolutely transcendent. I cannot reach the other. I cannot know the other from inside and so on. That is not an obstacle but the condition of love, of friendship, and of war, too, a condition of the relation to the other.[77]

Such a conception of the loved other – transcendent and incommensurable – has, however, increasingly been eroded under the assault of the ideology and technologies of choice.

This in turn suggests that it is simultaneously love *and* rationality that have become rationalized, in the sense that pre-modern rational actors had a fairly rudimentary form of rationality to make love and marriage choices in comparison to ours. Technologies of choice mark the demise of non-rational modes of partner selection, chiefly based on the body, in which emotions are put into play with very little knowledge or information about the other, and in which romantic partners are viewed as unique entities, not as units measured along highly cognized criteria and compared with each other.

But a caveat is called for: describing the effects of rationalization on romantic relationships, we should keep in mind the need to differentiate between its different sources. For example, feminism and scientific language have in common the aim of controlling relationships, of making them the object of procedures and rules, of subsuming them under abstract principles and procedures that derive from the legal and economic spheres. Yet, feminism and the rationalization of love by capitalist science and technology have important and different implications for the politics of sentiment. Feminism creates techniques of control that enable the self to monitor power differentials with the ultimate aim of creating dialogical equal relationships. By contrast, capitalist rationalization reproduces and justifies inequalities by creating techniques for ranking others and for reifying one's needs and preferences (i.e., fixating them into a rigid grid). Feminist practice opposes any instrumentalization of bodies and persons; in contrast, a practice of choice based in the lexicon and emotional grammar of the market does not oppose and even encourages instrumentalization. Yet, what *must* be differentiated from a normative standpoint cannot always be differentiated as cultural practices, because scientific language, feminism, and Internet technology all contribute to dis-embed the erotic bond through the formal rules provided by scientific knowledge systems, technology, and contractual proceduralism. I argue that this threefold process of rationalization has deeply transformed the nature of romantic desire and the nature of romantic belief.

Eros, Irony

At face value, this analysis may seem to lead us straight to the argument made by, among others, Cristina Nehring, who laments the loss of passion entailed by new demands for equality. Nehring rightly and elegantly diagnoses a shift in the emotional temperature of modern lovers, and attributes it to the new norms of equality and sameness. She writes: "Perhaps the most difficult situation in romance is the one we are striving so officially and noisily to achieve today: equality."[78] Yet, although the previous analysis may seem congruent with Nehring's diagnostic, it differs from hers in at least two ways. The first is that history has not only examples of Emily Dickinson's famous address to a mysterious lover she names her "Master" (presumably playfully twisting any claim to equality) but also the galvanizing examples of Elizabeth Barrett and Robert Browning, Diderot and Sophie Volland, Harriet Taylor and John Stuart Mill, Sartre and de Beauvoir, for whom partnership and equality were powerful adjuvants to the chemical composition of their love. In fact, there are probably more ways in which inequality is a greater corrosive acid to love than is equality. To suggest that equality is anti-erotic is simply to ignore the many ways in which inequality entails humiliation, shame, and coarseness, hardly conditions conducive to eroticism. But my main source of disagreement with Nehring is that she confuses equality with the more diffuse process of rationalization of love: that is, the fact that romantic life has become regulated by a variety of dis-embedding devices, such as scientific knowledge, technologies of choice, and procedural rules to ensure symmetry, reciprocity, and consent. It is not equality as such that has lowered the temperature of romantic relationships, but the fact that proceduralism, scientific reflexivity, contractualism, and consumer rationality have interfered with the ways heterosexual relationships traditionally have been eroticized. Rationalization conflicts with the regimes of meaning through which, historically, men and women have experienced and expressed sexual desire. It is these regimes I want to unpack now. Because, historically, sexual desire has been coded through male and female inequality, the situation we face in the early twenty-first century is precisely one in which the traditional rituals of sexual interaction and dynamic of sexual desire are disrupted. Below I analyze this traditional dynamic of erotic desire.

Erotics as Thick Difference

Why do romantic practices strongly coded by gender – such as "opening the door for a lady," kneeling to declare one's love, sending large bouquets of flowers – "feel" more erotic than asking permission to touch a woman's breasts? This is because strongly coded gender practices achieve several things at once: they aestheticize the power men have over women; they subsume domination under sentiment and deference – that is, they make power veiled and implicit; they enable the ritualization of relationships between the sexes – that is, they are organized in clear patterns of meaning; and they enable play with meanings, since deference (opening the door) can be erotically alluring only if it is a mock deference – that is, played by the power-ful party (the deference of a slave is not erotically enticing, while that of a powerful man is). Feminist practices de-eroticize gender relations thus understood, because they aim primarily at making power explicit and thus unravel the web of implicit meanings in which power hides and aestheticizes itself. Louis Dumont, one of the finest analysts of modernity, clarifies this dynamic by suggesting there is an intrinsic affinity between power and thick or aestheticized meanings. As he puts it: "[I]t is easy to find the key to our values. Our two cardinal ideals are called equality and liberty."[79] And these values, Dumont suggests, flatten out the perception of social relations:

> The first feature to emphasize is that the concept of the equality of men entails that of their similarity. […] [I]f equality is conceived as rooted in man's very nature and denied only by an evil society, then, as there are no longer any rightful differences in condition or estate, or different sorts of men, they are all alike and even identical, as well as equal.

Recalling de Tocqueville, Dumont adds: "[W]here inequality reigns, there are as many distinct humanities as there are social categories."[80] Dumont is an advocate of the kind of thick differences that are played out between different social and cultural groups in India, for example. In his view, the right and the left hand are not simply polar and sym-metrical opposites; rather, they are different in themselves because they have a different relation to the body. What Dumont suggests, then, is that equality entails a loss of qualitative differences. He uses the analogy of the right and left hand because both are necessary to the body, but each is radically different from each other. In the non-modern, non-egalitarian view, the value of each hand – left and right – is rooted in its relation to the body, which has a higher status.

> This shunning of subordination, or, to call it by its true name, of tran-scendence, substitutes a flat view for a view in depth, and at the same time it is the root of the "atomization" so often complained about by romantic or nostalgic critics of modernity. […] [I]n modern ideology, the previous hierarchical universe has fanned out into a collection of flat views of this kind.[81]

The regime of meaning to which Dumont points is one in which transcendence is produced by the capacity to live in an ordered, holistic and hierarchized moral and social universe. Eroticism – as it was developed in Western patriarchal culture – is predicated on a similar "right-hand/left-hand" dichotomy between men and women, each being radically different and each enacting their thick identities. It is this thick difference which has traditionally eroticized men's and women's relationships, at least since these identities became strongly essentialized. One may further speculate that power produces rich meanings because it almost always needs to be veiled. For that reason, it needs to create complex meanings that simultaneously enforce and evade the violence which it creates. Such evasion is produced by the aestheticization of power-ridden relations, as in the form of the masculine code of "gallantry" and traditional romantic courtship.

Erotics as the Intermittent

Roland Barthes provides an interesting additional definition of the erotic:

> Is not the most erotic portion of the body *where the garment gapes?* In perversion (which is the realm of textual pleasure) there are no "erogenous zones" [...] [I]t is intermittence, as psychoanalysis has so rightly stated, which is erotic; the intermittence of skin flashing between two articles of clothing (trousers and sweater), between two edges (the open-necked shirt, the glove and the sleeve); it is this flash which seduces, or rather: the staging of an appearance-as-disappearance.[82]

The dynamics of erotics is one of revelation and concealment, because, one may speculate, such alternation plays out and rehearses the shift between (erotic) deprivation and satisfaction. In contrast, both sexual liberation and "politically correct" sartorial and bodily practices tend to undermine this dynamic, since they flatten body surfaces, making them equal to each other, either in their exposure (politics of sexual liberation, e.g. being in a nudist camp) or in their concealment (exposing the body becomes a politically illegitimate display of objectified sexuality). Moreover, the gaping garment points to an uncertainty about the question of boundaries, of what is erotic, and of when and where such eroticism is or is not permissible. The intermittent creates a form of semiotic blurring and ambiguity. Here again, the procedures of politically correct speech and dress code eliminate ambivalence, and aim to make speech and the body uni-vocal by clearly defining zones of permissible and non-permissible contact. In short, our new rules tend to eliminate ambiguity.

Absorption and Self-Abandonment

In a very interesting analysis, philosopher Richard Shusterman suggests that erotic experience is actually a form of aesthetic experience. Against the Kantian aesthetics of detachment, he proposes that erotic experiences are aesthetic precisely in the intense absorption they demand and generate.

> Sex can be enjoyed both in terms of its Aristotelian sense of fulfilling, absorbing, undistracted activity and in terms of the attendant pleasurable sensations it gives; it powerfully displays the phenomenological dimension of being subjectively savored but also intentionally directed at an object (typically another human subject) that structures the experience, shapes its quality, and gives it important dimensions of meaning [...]. A cognitive experience providing knowledge of one's own body and mind and also those of one's sexual partners, the sexual act typically displays a distinctive unity both of coherence and completion, a sense of thing developing consistent and powerfully toward a fulfilling consummation. It also stands out distinctively from the flow of ordinary humdrum experience. Sexual experience involves a wide range of affect, some of which is unrivalled in its intensity, and it displays both moments of active self-assertive grasping and self-surrendering absorption.[83]

Sexual/erotic experience is opposed to analytical, rational thought which fragments experience, compartmentalizes it, and disrupts the flow and immediacy of experience. It entirely absorbs the self. Echoing Weber's view, Shusterman contrasts the "self-possessed, rationally controlled pleasure of form and the more passionate delight of an experience that overwhelms the subject."[84] Weber would have strongly concurred, claiming that

> [t]he lover realizes himself to be rooted in the kernel of the truly living, which is eternally inaccessible to any rational endeavor. He knows himself to be freed from the cold skeleton hands of rational orders, just as completely as from the banality of everyday routine. The consciousness of the lover rests upon the ineffaceability and inexhaustibleness of his own experience. The experience is by no means communicable and in this respect it is equivalent to the "having" of the mystic. This is not only due to the intensity of the lover's experience, but to the immediacy of the possessed reality.[85]

Erotics embraces the totality of experience and hence cannot be reduced to categories of knowledge. This means also that modes of explanation that emanate from the erotic sphere are necessarily non-rational. "Non-consummated erotic communion will know itself to be founded in any way other than through a mysterious *destination* for one another: *fate*, in this highest sense of the word."[86] Fate can be the only way to explain love, because it accounts for feelings without explaining them. It makes these feelings inevitable. Erotic experience thus cannot admit a factor extrinsic to its experience. Eroticism is a certain regime of signification in which concreteness, particularity, holistic judgment, and the irreducibility of experience dominate. Rationalized meaning counters the erotic experience because it intellectualizes it and introduces a distance between experience and the knowledge that precedes that experience. It thus undermines intense self-absorption.

Erotics as Waste

When trying to characterize the modern view of love, one is struck by the fact that traditionally, because romantic love was institutionally outside marriage, it stood for values opposite to those of the matrimonial institution, such as self-interest and preservation of a lineage. While marriage may have been motivated by family alliances and economic interest, love as such was viewed as a consummatory experience, which threatened the economic and social order. Georges Bataille's views on utility present a very interesting point of departure for thinking about this. Bataille offers the following hypothesis to analyze a wide number of seemingly disparate phenomena, economic, sexual, aesthetic: namely that productiveness, self-conservation, and self-interest are not primary to the social order. On the contrary, he speculates that unproductive waste and self-destructive and non-utilitarian behavior are more primary. Wars, rituals, luxury, games, sumptuary monuments, are all examples of what he calls "*dépense*," a word with the double meaning of spending and wasting. It is waste, in fact, that gives meaning to these activities, and it is sacrifice which produces sacredness.[87]

Eroticism belongs to that sphere of non-utilitarian behavior in which the self not only abandons itself, but takes the risk of wasting itself, of being hurt. In contrast, the discourses of therapy and feminism share the attempt to render the psyche, especially that of women, useful, and to avoid waste, defined as forms of attachment that do not serve the project of a healthy, autonomous, and self-realized self. What Philip Rieff calls the "psychological man" who carefully counts "his satisfactions and dissatisfactions," and views "unprofitable commitments as the sins most to be avoided,"[88] is thus the man (or woman) who avoids self-sacrificial modes of love contained in erotic and romantic experiences, in which self-abandonment is crucial to their attainment. As Jean-Luc Marion puts it:

> The obstacle that obstructs the opening of the amorous field – an erotic obstacle, not an epistemological or ontic one – consists in reciprocity itself; and reciprocity only acquires this power to set up an obstacle because one assumes, without proof or argument, that it alone offers the condition of possibility for what the ego understands as a "happy love."[89]

But Marion adds that reciprocity is an impossible task because, for him, it takes one out of the realm of love and brings one to the realm of commerce, which is incompatible with love. Such a view of love has become increasingly illegitimate since it appears that self-abandonment and self-sacrifice – wastefulness – are one-sided, and serve as beautifying ideological devices to extract surplus emotional value from women.

Semiotic Certainty

Thick identities and ritualized behavior create semiotic certainty, which, paradoxically, is the condition for the creation of pleasurable ambiguous meanings. That is, power relationships tend to be organized in stable and clear frames of meaning, because power structures tend to reproduce, solidify, and congeal meanings. Ambiguity is made possible when stabilized meanings are played with and twisted. For example, an androgynous man (or woman) is androgynous (and attractive as such) only because the signifiers for masculinity and femininity are otherwise clear and stable. Androgyny cannot be culturally coded if it does not play on well-known signifiers of masculinity and femininity. If masculinity and femininity were semiotically uncertain, androgyny could not be semiotically produced. It is thus semiotic certainty which can create ambiguity, the feeling of play and pleasure. In contrast, the emptying of romantic relationships from power relationships has the semiotic effect of making gender signs less marked, and thus of decreasing the capacity to generate ambiguity, often thought to be an ingredient of seduction. For example, Catherine Townsend laments the lack of passion of the new "sensitive man":

> With the sensitive man, I can't tell if he wants me to sit on him, or in Starbucks discussing the state of the universe. If I want to hear about feelings, I can call a girlfriend. In a brand new love affair, I want hot sex, not hot tea!

> Respect is great, but when it comes to the bedroom, egalitarian doesn't always equal erotic. When Marlon Brando grabbed the butter in Last Tango in Paris, I doubt that he was thinking about political correctness.
>
> Earlier generations of men saw sex as a conquest – bawdy, filthy, funny, and dirty.[90]

Townsend (unwittingly) provides here a rejoinder to Nehring and suggests that equality erases from eroticism both the strongly coded gender identities and their playfulness. She laments the lack of playfulness and ambiguity inherent in the cultural practice of "seduction," as a semi-conscious practice of playing with one's body and language in order to arouse desire in another. In characterizing the perfect seducer, Robert Greene indicates the importance of maintaining the incomplete nature of the romantic interaction, including increasing ambiguity, sending mixed signals, mastering the art of insinuation, confusing desire and reality, mixing pleasure and pain, stirring desire and confusion, toning down the sexual element without getting rid of it, refusing to conform to any standard, delaying satisfaction and withholding total satisfaction.[91]

Ambiguity is essentially a way of maintaining uncertainty with regard to the intention of a speaker. Ambiguity in this sense enables freedom, enabling something to be said without its being meant, and allowing one to have one identity while assuming another. As Shadi Bartsch and Thomas Bartscherer put it (using ambivalence instead of ambiguity): "[A]mbivalence is built into the erotic phenomenon."[92] Seduction often uses ambiguous codes, which make the prototypical seducers of Western culture exemplary of a certain form of freedom from morality because ambivalence and ambiguity are essentially ways of maintaining uncertainty with regard to the intention of the speaker. They enable both power and freedom: that is, the capacity to say something without meaning it, the capacity to imply several meanings at once. Seducers use ambiguous speech because they do not feel accountable to norms of sincerity and symmetry. So-called "politically correct" practices, by contrast, request a form of transparency and lack of ambiguity – so as to ensure maximum contractual freedom and equality, and thus neutralize the traditional rhetorical and emotional halo of seduction.

The rationalization of love has undermined the regimes of meaning on which eroticism and love are based: these include ambiguity, intermittence, veiled language, playfulness, and transcendence. Traditional seduction and eroticism are based on a very partial knowledge of the other, on a certain un-selfconsciousness of the self, on the capacity to produce ambiguity. Summarizing Kant's view on aesthetics, Jeffrey Alexander suggests that "[i]t is the quality of avoiding determination by rational thought or moral understanding, not absolute dissociation from them, that makes an experience aesthetic, the very freedom from a priori determination that, subsequent to the aesthetic experience, allows greater conceptual and moral development in turn."[93]

The fourfold concern for neutral language, symmetrical power relationships, procedural fairness, and explicit consent interferes with and disrupts the rules of implicitness and ambiguity at the cultural heart of libido, understood here *not* as a universal invariant, but as a historically specific way to organize sexual desire: because femininity is defined, by and large, by displays of dependence, power differentials are at the heart of women's and men's desires and erotics (in this, Nehring is entirely correct). That is, the institutional procedures to implement symmetrical displays of power are questioning a very long cultural tradition in which what was eroticized was precisely men's power and women's lack of it, with these power differentials producing richly textured meanings. Let me thus offer the following hypothesis: if "politically correct" language has elicited derision, discomfort, and cultural malaise, it is because it undermines and exposes the ideological glue that held together men's and women's gender identities and power differentials and made them erotic and *pleasurable* – because spontaneous and unreflexive – while leaving intact gender structure and hierarchy. That is, what makes politically correct language unacceptable is that it excludes the emotional fantasies and pleasure on which traditional gender relations are built, but does not fundamentally shake or transform the structure of gender inequalities which gnaw at the emotional core of relationships (letting women care for their children, juggle with part-time jobs, and do all the emotional work of relationships). In other words, equality demands a redefinition of eroticism and romantic desire that has yet to be accomplished.

Uncertainty, Irony, or the Equality's Malaise

The loss of passion and eroticism is associated with two cultural sensibilities which derive from equality, namely uncertainty and irony. If as William James argues, emotions serve to "banish uncertainty from the future,"[94] then, clearly, the process of rationalization has undermined this capacity to gain certainty, with the result that uncertainty and irony dominate the cultural climate of romantic relationships.

Emotional contractualism – a relationship based on free will, equality, and symmetry – paradoxically entails *semiotic uncertainty*: that is, an ongoing preoccupation with the adequacy of one's own conduct and the difficulty to grasp the right rules of conduct in a given interaction. As Maureen Dowd writes:

> My gay friends seem just as flummoxed over modern dating etiquette. As one says: "My team could be a barometer for where your team will head: what happens when desired gender equality really happens. And you know what? It's hell. You are there thinking: If I move too quickly to pick up the check, am I pegging myself as the dominant, aggressive daddy type? If I sit here meekly, do I send out the message: Take care of me, oh, and also, take me?"[95]

Uncertainty here is opposed to ambiguity, which is a regime of meaning generated precisely by shared meanings. Ambiguity is pleasurable and consists of mixing two repertoires of known meanings; uncertainty, by contrast, is painful and derives from the difficulty of knowing the rules that organize interactions. Ambiguity is a property of erotic play because its intent is to say without saying or to say several things at once, based on shared and implicit meanings. Ambiguity is playful and pleasurable because it is a virtuoso way to play with social rules. Uncertainty, by contrast, inhibits sexual desire and entails anxiety, because it makes people focus on and interrogate themselves on the rules of interaction, thus making them less able to let themselves feel emotions elicited by the interaction itself. As a 40-year-old man, based in London, put it:

> All of my male friends are very confused with women these days. They don't know if they should be aggressive or gentle; be masculine-macho or be the sensitive type; we simply have no clue what is expected of us. I think I can say all the men I know are very intimidated by women, by the fact they don't know what the rules are.

Moreover, the norms of equality conflict with the sense of pleasure which derives from enacting semiotically clear gender identity. For example, Claire, a 37-year-old woman painter, born and raised in Europe, said in interview:

> Meeting Israeli men was not easy for me, because it is strange you know, although they are macho, they don't do all the things that macho men do in Europe that make you feel good.

Interviewer: Like what?

Claire: You know like kneeling in front of you, or opening the
               door, or buying you flowers. Even though I think I would
               feel stupid to enjoy these things, I mean, still, I have to
               say, they are enjoyable, and yet, I know I am not sup-
               posed to enjoy them.

Interviewer: Not supposed to enjoy them? Why not?

Claire: Well, you know, because these are not politically correct.

Interviewer: That is so interesting. So you are saying you would stop
               yourself from feeling a certain type of pleasure?

Claire: Oh yes, you know, a lot of my work [painting/sculpture]
               has to do with women and the situation of women, so,
               yes, a part of me would enjoy these things – in fact, more
               than that, I would expect these things to be done, and
               yet a part of me would reprimand the other part, and
               would give almost orders [*laughs*], not to enjoy itself. As
               if I had two selves, a traditional woman self, and a
               modern woman self, you know what I mean?

Interviewer: And these two selves are in conflict with each other?

Claire: [*Long silence*] You could say it this way, it is more that
               I feel very confused. I don't really know what I can and
               should ask from a man: if I tell him why don't you buy
               me flowers or why don't you write me love poems, then
               it feels like I am betraying my identity as a feminist, I
               cannot make these demands because in our age a liberated
               woman like me does not need this stuff, or at least cannot
               ask for it anymore. So it really is about what you feel
               entitled to ask for. So a part of me wants certain things,
               but another part says I shouldn't feel this way. So I often
               don't really know what I want or what I should want or
               even what I feel.

The superposition of two cultural structures creates tensions and
uncertainty about the very content of one's desires, between what is
actually pleasurable and the norms against which this pleasure is
evaluated. This superposition makes it difficult for the woman to
know which rules should govern her interactions. As philosopher
Robert Pippin suggests: "[T]here is something about eros that cannot
be accommodated easily within Christian or liberal-egalitarian
humanism."[96] In more sociological terms: equality produces social
anxiety because it generates uncertainty about rules of interaction,

which thus undercuts the spontaneity that was historically produced by thick identities and ritualized rules.

Uncertainty in turn generates irony as a dominant trope with which to discuss love. In Western culture, the first manifestation of an ironic, disenchanted condition of love can be found in *Don Quixote* (1605–15). This novel introduced a breach within the very capacity of the reader to believe in the love experience of the knight errant. This difficulty in believing in love was accentuated with the advent of modernity; the modern romantic condition resembles more often the "sobering up" described by Marx than the fervor and frenzy of pre-modern lovers, with love increasingly becoming the object of ironic gloss. Modern love has become the privileged site for the trope of irony. The process of rationalization of love is at the heart of the new ironic structure of romantic feeling which marks the move from an "enchanted" to a disenchanted cultural definition of love. Structures of feeling, the highly felicitous expression coined by Raymond Williams, designate social and structural aspects of feelings and the feelings of social structures. They are "social experiences in *solution*."[97] An ironic structure of romantic feeling makes it difficult to subscribe not just to the idea of passion, but also to a passionate and self-sacrificing commitment to a loved person which has characterized the Western idea of love for the last few centuries.

Irony is a literary technique that feigns ignorance, but counts, for its effect, on the knowledge of the hearer (otherwise irony would be taken literally as meaning what it says, when it in fact means the opposite). It is thus the trope of the person who refuses to subscribe to the beliefs inscribed in a situation. Modern romantic consciousness has the rhetorical structure of irony because it is saturated with disenchanted knowledge which prevents full belief and commitment. Irony cannot take seriously a belief central to love, namely its self-proclaimed claim to eternity and totality. The following example of irony from Catherine Townsend describes both the desire to believe in the eternity of love (desiring that her ex-boyfriend would do something dramatic to keep her from leaving) and the impossibility of believing in it:

> How could I have fallen for the fantasy? I've always said that if *Pretty Woman* had a sequel, I'm willing to bet that it would feature Julia Roberts living on the street after Richard Gere got bored and promptly dumped her.
>
> But they know just how to get you back, because we've all seen it in movies: by pulling a grand gesture.[98]

This type of cultural reflexivity – vis-à-vis cinematic formulas and vis-à-vis the grip that cultural myths have on us – deflates the pathos of Townsend's desire to stay through self-irony. Indeed, the German Romantic philosopher Schlegel views the awareness of the finitude of love as central to irony: "True irony is the irony of love. It arises from the feeling of finitude and one's own limitation and the apparent contradiction of these feelings with the concept of infinity inherent in all true love."[99] This definition makes sense in light of the fact that Schlegel, like Kierkegaard, viewed the essence of love as residing in the sentiment of its own infinitude, "for what distinguishes all love from lust is the fact that it bears an impress of eternity."[100] In contrast, we could say that the rationalization of love has had the effect of creating a culture of the finitude of love – stressing its psychological, biological, evolutionary, political, and economic limits. The relativization of love through various processes of rationalization was bound to make irony central to the new romantic sensibility. What is likely to have increased the consciousness of the finitude is the expansion of technologies of choice, the awareness of partners' commensurability and interchangeability, and the use of scientific expert systems that deflate claims to eternity. Irony thus impinges on the very possibility of belief. As David Halperin writes:

> Some experiences [...] are incompatible with irony. In order to have them at all, it is necessary to banish any hint of irony. Conversely, the arrival of irony signals the end of the experience, or its diminution. Irony's opposite is intensity. In moments of intense, overwhelming sensation, we have little awareness of context and no attention to spare for more than one set of meanings. In such states, we become literalists: we can experience only one kind of thing. The three cardinal experiences that demand the elimination of irony, or that cannot survive the irony, are raw grief or suffering, religious transport, and sexual passion.[101]

If Halperin is correct, irony is incompatible with the emotional and bodily experience of passion and intensity. Irony has become the dominant cultural experience of our time, because of the threefold process of rationalization described in this chapter, which impinges on the emotional structure of enchanted love.

Conclusion

In his *Symposium*, Plato famously argues that love is the path to knowledge and wisdom, and thus is entirely compatible with reason.

Plato's metaphor of the ladder of love[102] postulates that to love a single beautiful body is to love the idea of beauty and perfection itself and that, in that sense, reason and love could be intertwined. The threefold process of rationalization described above demands a reformulation of the Platonic view that love and reason are compatible, because reason, and, more exactly, rationalized reason, has undermined the ways in which romantic and erotic desire has been historically constructed and experienced as constructed of thick and ambiguous meanings, as enabling the performance of real masculine and feminine roles, as oscillating between exposing and hiding, and as ostentatiously displaying waste.

Love has lost its cultural pathos, and passion, as a disorderly movement of the mind and the body, has been disciplined by a vast cultural process of proceduralism and rationalization. In that sense, romantic suffering has also lost its pathos and poignancy. As the critic Vivian Gornick writes in *The End of the Novel of Love*:

> When Emma Bovary was loosening her stays with a man other than her husband, or Anna Karenina running away from hers, or Newbold Archer [*sic*] agonizing over whether to leave New York with Ellen Olenska, people were indeed risking all for love. Bourgeois respectability had the power to make of these characters social pariahs. Strength would be needed to sustain exile. Out of such risk-taking might come the force of suffering that brings clarity and insight. Today, there are no penalties to pay, no world of respectability to be excommunicated from. Bourgeois society as such is over.[103]

This commentator suggests that love's suffering has lost its cultural force and pathos and can no longer provide existential clarity because it does not articulate a conflict between society and the individual, is not opposite to the calculus of economic action, and does not command the self to sacrifice or surrender its usual mechanisms of self-control; rather it points only to the self and its utilities. If in chapters 2 and 3 I described a de-structuration of the romantic will, in chapters 4, 5, and 6 I point to a de-structuration of romantic desire, caught between self-doubt, irony, and a hyper-sexualized culture, and in which the traditional terms of emotional and sexual passion have become undone.

6

From Romantic Fantasy to Disappointment

No love is original.
Roland Barthes, *A Lover's Discourse*[1]

Heard melodies are sweet, but those unheard are sweeter.
John Keats, "Ode on a Grecian Urn"[2]

The exercise of imagination, no less than reason, has been central to the rise of a modern consciousness, and, I will argue, to modern emotional life.[3] In an interesting twist to Weber's disenchantment thesis, Adorno suggests that imagination was central to bourgeois society because it became a force of production and consumption, a component of the aesthetic culture of capitalism. In *The Positivist Dispute in German Sociology*, Adorno argues that through its deployment of cultural technologies, bourgeois modernity tamed the unregulated associative form of thought, and that in the eighteenth century, imagination, having become central to discussions of aesthetics, also became confined to that realm. From the late eighteenth century, imagination became an institutionalized practice in the realm of aesthetics and later in mass culture. In this view, the regulated, institutionalized, commodified exercise of imagination is a central dimension of a modern bourgeois consumer society. The so-called postmodern subject is characterized by a multiplication of desires which result from the institutionalization of imagination. More: this institutionalization has transformed the very nature of desire in general, and romantic desire in particular. It has much more clearly codified the cultural fantasies through which love as a story, as an event, and as an emotion is imagined, and it has made imaginary longing its perpetual condition. As an emotion and a cultural cognition, love increasingly contains imaginary objects of longing: that is, objects deployed by and in imagination. But Adorno also speculates that in becoming incorporated into the consumer circuit, imagination became defamed outside the realm of aesthetics. "[T]he defamation of fantasy or its relegation to a special domain, marked off by the division of labour, is the original phenomenon of the regression of the bourgeois spirit."[4] Romantic love and fantasy have become the object of cultural suspicion because "fantasy is only tolerated when it is reified and set in abstract opposition to reality."[5] It is precisely because it has become difficult or even impossible to disentangle the imaginary from the real in the experience of love that imagination, in love, has been and continues to be defamed. It is this assumption – that collective fantasies burden the romantic experience – that I want to examine in this chapter. More precisely, I want to try to understand the relationship between the emotion of love and its scripting in mass-manufactured fantasies, and the impact of such scripting on the nature of romantic desire.

Imagination, Love

What is imagination? A common view is that it is a normal activity of the mind. Jeffrey Alexander described imagination as "intrinsic to the very process of representation. It seizes upon an inchoate experience from life, and forms it, through association, condensation, and aesthetic creation, into some specific shape."[6] Imagination is viewed here not as the freewheeling activity of the mind, but rather as consisting of the very stuff through which we organize thought and experience or anticipate the world. Alexander's definition emphasizes that the activity of imagination does not invent cultural scenarios and constructs as much as uses pre-established ones. Moreover, far from being disconnected from the real, imagination entertains a close relationship with sensory or "real" experience and is often a substitute for it. Hobbes described imagination as like "decayed senses," a faint copy of some original perception. In the *Psychology of Imagination*,[7] Jean-Paul Sartre pursues this theme, noting that imagination, while often viewed as a more powerful faculty than ordinary perception, is actually a pale echo of the senses. Close your eyes and imagine the face of someone you love, says Sartre; whatever image will be conjured up will seem "thin," "dry," "two dimensional," and inert.[8] The imagined object simply lacks what Elaine Scarry calls the vivacity and vitality of the object that is perceived: that is, the object perceived with the senses.[9] In this view, imagination is the capacity to substitute for the "real" experience of the real object, by feeling sensations that are close to what they would be in real life. Imagination thus does not annul reality, but, on the contrary, tries to imitate it by relying on the sensations, feelings, and emotions which make present that which is absent.

Yet the most widespread view of imagination presents it as a fanciful creation which takes hold of the mind far more intensely than ordinary sense perceptions and separates us from reality. Shakespeare famously illustrates this view in *A Midsummer Night's Dream* (1600):

> And as imagination bodies forth
>
> The forms of things unknown, the poet's pen
>
> Turns them to shapes, and gives to airy nothing
>
> A local habitation and a name.[10]

Here imagination is the capacity to invent something that was not there before, to magnify and intensify our lived experience by acts of invention and creation that give "shape" to the formless. This view of imagination is especially salient in the realm of love, in which the object of love and imagination has much vigor and vitality. Both ordinary experience and a vast corpus of philosophical and literary writing attest to the fact that when loving another, the imaginary invocation of the beloved is as powerful as its presence, and to the fact that when in love, to a large extent we invent the object of our desires. Perhaps nowhere more clearly than in love can we observe the constitutive role of imagination: that is, its capacity to substitute for a real object and to create it. It is precisely because love can create its object through imagination that the question of the authenticity of the emotions activated by imagination has reverberated throughout Western culture. This is why the authenticity of the love experience and sentiments was such an interesting site of inquiry in the twentieth century, resonating with an older tradition that questions the sources of the love sentiment. From Heidegger to Baudrillard via Adorno and Horkheimer, modernity has been viewed as the increasing splitting of experience and its representation, and as the subsumption of the former by the latter.

The *locus classicus* of the concern for the epistemic status of imagination in love can be found, again, in *A Midsummer Night's Dream.*

Despite its festive character, its profusion of fairies and mythological creatures, *The Dream*, as actors refer to it, is a dark comedy about the human heart and its vagaries. This darkness derives from the specific way in which the concept of imagination articulates the opposition between reason and love. Bottom says to Titania, "reason and love keep little company together nowadays," and it is this time-honored opposition that structures the play. A superficial reading of this opposition would suggest that *The Dream* re-enacts the *topos* that what makes love a dangerous or ridiculous emotion is that its choices are not rational because the prime site of reason is in the mind, and love presumably is based on and triggered by the senses. But Shakespeare offers the opposite (and highly modern) view. Helena, in a monologue, claims to be as "fair" as Hermia, yet, to have been systematically denigrated and shunned as a love object.

Through Athens I am thought as fair as she.

But what of that? Demetrius thinks not so;

He will not know what all but he do know:

And as he errs, doting on Hermia's eyes,

So I, admiring of his qualities:

Things base and vile, folding no quantity,

Love can transpose to form and dignity:

Love looks not with the eyes, but with the mind;

And therefore is wing'd Cupid painted blind:

Nor hath Love's mind of any judgement taste;

Wings and no eyes figure unheedy haste:

And therefore is Love said to be a child,

Because in choice he is so oft beguiled.

As waggish boys in game themselves forswear,

So the boy Love is perjured every where:

For ere Demetrius look'd on Hermia's eyne,

He hail'd down oaths that he was only mine;

And when this hail some heat from Hermia felt,

So he dissolved, and showers of oaths did melt. (emphasis added)[11]

Shakespeare's *Dream* offers a very interesting twist on the familiar *topos* of the irrationality of love in suggesting that what makes it irrational is precisely that it is located *in the mind, not in the senses.* "Love looks not with the eyes, but with the mind": because love is located in the mind, it is less amenable to the rational criteria of discussion than if it had been located in the eyes. What is meant by the mind is the set of intricate associations subjectively generated, impermeable to the outside world. The eyes, by contrast, mediate between the self and the surrounding reality: the object of sight is, as it were, objectively established, and in that sense the eyes rely on the world external to the subject. Helena requests that love be based in the senses (the eyes), and not in the mind, because the mind is precisely that which detaches the process of evaluating/loving another from its value in an objective world of objects. The mind here is not only the site for the exercise of imagination, but also its source. What makes love a form of madness is that it bears no connection to the real.

Following sixteenth-century medical discourse, *The Dream* suggests that romantic imagination is a form of madness precisely because it lacks an anchor, either physical or psychic. For Freud, romantic imagination, however irrational, has such an anchor – the early image of a parent, the need and desire to master an early trauma – but in Shakespeare's play the irrationality of love is radical because imagination makes it into an arbitrary emotion, not amenable to explanation, and not a constitutive event, even of the psychoanalytical variety. In *The Dream*, love is an experience on which we cannot get a grip, neither rational nor irrational. Nor, pre-Freud, does it respond even to the logic of the unconscious. The key to the play is that there is no real distinction between sane and mad love, for "sane" love does not fundamentally differ from the frenzied feelings of Puck's victims. Romantic imagination here is a code for madness and turns love into an irrational and self-generated emotion, oblivious to the identity of the person loved. This view of love highlights what, in subsequent views of love and imagination, both resembles and differs from the suspicion of imagination. Shakespeare's play anticipates the interrogation of the nature of emotions activated by imagination, but does not make any mention of the themes which were to preoccupy philosophers and writers from the eighteenth century onward, namely the roles of cultural technologies and fiction in shaping imagination, the anticipatory character of imaginary emotions, and, even more crucially, the problem of shifting from an imagined object to ordinary reality.

Modern institutions of imagination actively solicit and encourage a low-key form of daydreaming, mostly through the unprecedented production of print and visual media, which provide visual displays of powerful narratives of the good life. Modernity, to a great extent, has consisted in the capacity to imagine social-political bonds in new ways.[12] These new imagined bonds include not just political relationships, but, perhaps more importantly, utopias of private happiness. The utopian imagination is activated in the realm of private life and presupposes a definition of the subject as endowed with private thoughts, feelings, and longings; especially the realm of domesticity and sentiments is made into the object and the site of imagination. Love and emotional fulfillment became the objects of utopian fantasy. Imagination goes hand in hand with the democratization and generalization of the ideal of happiness – understood as a material and emotional state. Consumer culture – which forcefully articulates an emotional project of personal self-fulfillment – organizes the private modern emotional subject around his or her emotions and daydreams and locates the exercise of one's freedom in an individuality to be achieved *and* fantasized. It legitimizes the category of desire and fantasy, making them the basis of action and volition, and makes consumption and commodities the institutional support to achieve or simply experience such desire. A "life project" is the institutionalized projection of one's individual life into the future through imagination. Modernity institutionalizes the subject's expectations and capacity to imagine his/her life chances in the cultural practice of imagination. Emotions are turned into objects of imagination in the sense that a life project is not just an imagined cultural practice but can include sometimes elaborate emotional projects. Imagination thus transforms longing and anticipatory projection of a perpetual condition of love and disappointment into a threat to the very capacity to desire.

It is precisely this role of culture and technology in feeding a self-generated romantic imagination that has preoccupied moralists and philosophers in Western Europe since the seventeenth century. The intricate relationship between love and imagination acquired a particular poignancy with the spread of the printed book, the codification of the genre and formula of romance, and the progressive formation of a private sphere. The emotion of love became increasingly intertwined with technologies which freed the activity of imagination and simultaneously codified it by organizing it within clear narrative formulas.[13]

The capacity of the novel to elicit identification and imagination – and its preoccupation with the themes of love, marriage, and social mobility – made romantic imagination a topic of public concern. Increasingly, imagination was viewed as having a destabilizing effect, socially and emotionally. The spread of readership among women was greeted throughout the eighteenth century with a slew of denunciations about the moral perniciousness of the novel, which contained the barely disguised fear that it changed the very nature of women's emotional and social expectations.[14] The feminization of this genre, owing to its predominantly female audience and the emergence of women novelists, exacerbated the view that novels encouraged unreal and dangerous sentiments.[15]

Increasingly reflecting on the impact of their own literary genre, many nineteenth-century novels incorporated critiques about the socially disruptive character of the novel, its capacity to create dangerous sentimental and social aspirations, in short to create anticipatory emotions. In Pushkin's *Eugene Onegin* (1833), which became notorious for its discussion of the relationship between life and art, Tatiana, a simple provincial girl, falls desperately in love with Eugene, a sophisticated and dissolute city dweller; the narrator, mimicking Eugene's coolness, ironically observes:

> She early had been fond of novels;
>
> For her they replaced all;
>
> She grew enamored with the fictions
>
> Of Richardson and of Rousseau.
>
> Her father was a kindly fellow
>
> Who lagged in the precedent age
>
> But saw no harm in books.[16]

> The time had come – she [Tatiana] fell in love.
>
> Thus, dropped into the earth, a seed is quickened by the fire of spring.
>
> *Long since had her imagination, consumed with mollitude and yearning,* craved for the fatal food;
>
> Long since had the heart's languishment
>
> Constrained her youthful bosom;
>
> Her soul waited – for somebody. (emphasis added)[17]

Clearly, Tatiana's love was a pre-made form, waiting to be filled by a passing object, which was the seemingly romantic Eugene. George Eliot describes Hetty Sorel in *Adam Bede* (1859) thus: "Hetty had never read a novel; how then could she find a shape for her expectations?"[18] Similarly, in *Northanger Abbey* (1818), Jane Austen mocks the genre of gothic romances in the character of Catherine Morland, who entertains fanciful ideas all inspired by the novels she has read. These and other authors describe and ironize about the power of novels to shape love by anticipation: that is, to shape the ways in which the exploration of imaginary worlds creates feeling.

The book that captured most fully contemporary concerns over imagination and the intricate relationship between imagination, the novel, love, and social aspiration is *Madame Bovary* (1856), which provides the ultimate description of the misery of a properly modern consciousness saturated with imaginary scenarios of love and their fate when they confront the real. As an adolescent, Emma Bovary read novels secretly, and this shaped her conceptions of love and her dreams of luxury.

> They [the novels] were filled with love affairs, lovers, mistresses, per-
> secuted ladies fainting in lonely country houses, post-riders killed at
> every relay, horses ridden to death on every page, dark forests, palpi-
> tating hearts, vows, sobs, tears and kisses, skiffs in the moonlight,
> nightingales in thickets, and gentlemen brave as lions, gentle as lambs,
> virtuous as no one really is, and always ready to shed floods of tears.
> For six months, at the age of fifteen, Emma soiled her hands with this
> dust from all lending libraries. Later, with Sir Walter Scott, she devel-
> oped a passion for things historical and dreamed of wooden chests,
> palace guards and wandering minstrels. She wished she could have
> lived in some old manor house, like those chatelaines in low-waisted
> gowns who spent their days with their elbows on the stone still of a
> Gothic window surmounted by a trefoil, chin in hand, watching a
> white-plumed rider on a black horse galloping toward them from far
> across the countryside.[19]

Flaubert's description of imagination is very modern: it is highly structured, an activity of daydreaming that has clear, vivid, and repeti-tive images; and it produces the same diffuse longing experienced by Tatiana, Hetty Sorel, and Catherine Morland. This longing is struc-tured by language – in the form of narrative plots and sequences – and by mental images – the moonlight, the pastoral landscape, the pas-sionate embraces. In fact, what makes love uniquely modern is the extent to which it is an anticipatory emotion: that is, it contains well-rehearsed emotional and cultural scenarios, which shape the longing both for an emotion and for the good life attendant on it. (A pre-modern equivalent might have been perhaps the kind of anticipatory emotions of dread or hope one may have felt in contemplation of death and the other-worlds of hell and paradise.) Thus, when Emma Bovary commits her first act of adultery, she experiences it only in the mode of the literary genres that permeated her imagination:

She repeated to herself, "I have a lover! I have a lover!" [...] She was entering a marvelous realm in which everything would be passion, ecstasy and rapture; she was surrounded by vast expanses of bluish space, summits of intense feeling sparkled before her eyes, and everyday life appeared far below in the shadows between these peaks.

She remembered the heroines of novels she had read, and the lyrical legion of those adulterous women began to sing in her memory with sisterly voices that enchanted her. It was as though she herself were becoming part of that *imaginary world, as though she were making the long dream of her youth* come true by placing herself in the category of those amorous women she had envied so much. [...] [N]ow she was triumphing, and love, so long repressed, was gushing forth abundantly with joyous effervescence. She savored it without remorse, anxiety or distress. (emphasis added). [20]

This imagination shapes through anticipation the emotions which, as a married woman, will both make Emma disappointed in her life and encourage her to fall in love with Leon and Rodolphe. *Madame Bovary* was one of the first novels to question the relationship between imagination and the tasks and duties of daily domestic life. Don Quixote fantasizes and daydreams far more than Emma, but his romantic fantasies do not challenge his duties as a father or husband or endanger a domestic space or unit. Also in contrast to Don Quixote, Emma is first of all the wife of a kind and mediocre provincial doctor, and her daydreams – which occupy prime place in her inner life – intertwine an emotional and socially upwardly mobile project: "The drabness of her daily life made her dream of luxury, her husband's conjugal affection drove her to adulterous desires."[21] Imagination here is both private/emotional and social/economic. It is the very engine of the colonization of the future; it grounds present choices based on one's image of the future, and in turn shapes that future. One of the most interesting transformations to the institutionalization of imagination in mass culture can be characterized by its being increasingly shaped by technologies and cultural genres that generate desire, longing, and anticipatory emotions, emotions about emotions to come, and cognitive scripts about how they should feel and be enacted.

Imagination affects and shapes the present precisely in making the potentialities of the present – what it could or should be – cognitively ever more salient. As the narrator in *Madame Bovary* makes clear, this romantic imagination has two effects: it makes love an anticipatory emotion – that is, an emotion felt and dreamed about before it actually happens; and this anticipatory emotion, in turn, shapes the evaluation of the present because it allows real and fictional emotions to overlap and substitute for each other.

> [A]s [Emma] wrote, she saw in her mind's eye another man, a phantom composed of her most passionate memories, her most enjoyable books, and her strongest desires; at last, he became so real and so tangible that she was real and amazed, yet he was so hidden under the abundance of his virtues that she was unable to imagine him clearly.[22]

Emma's imagination makes Leon a character poised between reality and fiction, turning the reality of her own sentiments into the rehearsal of imaginary cultural stereotypes and scripts.

Emma cannot distinguish between her love and her images of love. Prefiguring postmodern laments, her love seems to be nothing but the repetition of empty signs, themselves repeated by the then-emerging cultural industries. In contrast to Hobbes' and Sartre's claims, her imagination is far more vivid and far more real to her than her daily life. In fact, it is her daily life that seems to be a pale, barely perceptible copy of the imaginary original, a prolegomenon to Baudrillard's fear that the real has been reduced to its simulations. In modernity, the activity of imagination affects the relation to the real, deflating it, making it a thin and pale reflection of the scenarios lived out in the mind.

The problem of imagination thus points to the organization of desire: *how* people desire, how culturally salient cognitions shape desire, and how such culturally induced desires in turn create ordinary forms of suffering, such as chronic dissatisfaction, disappointment, and perpetual longing. Imaginary anticipation of experience poses two problems: an epistemological one (Do I experience the thing in itself or its representation?) and an ethical one (How does it affect my capacity to live a good life?). The question of the emotional impact of technologies of imagination is all the more acute since the twentieth century was marked by a spectacular acceleration in the technologies of imagination. The cinema perfected what the novel had started – that is, techniques of identification with characters, exploration of unknown visual settings and behaviors, and images of daily life organized within aesthetic vignettes – which expanded the range of techniques to imagine and shape one's aspirations. More than any other culture in human history, consumer culture has actively and even aggressively elicited the exercise of imagination and daydreaming. Indeed, less customarily remarked in Emma Bovary's story are the ways in which her imagination is the engine driving the debts she incurs with Lheureux, a wily merchant who sells her fabrics and trinkets. Emma's imagination feeds directly into the early consumer culture in nineteenth-century France precisely through the mediation of romantic desire.

As suggested by Adorno, quoted at the beginning of this chapter, imagination has been both disciplined and relentlessly excited through bourgeois commodified culture. Colin Campbell and other sociologists claim that consumption is driven by dreams and fantasies that connect the individual to the question of who s/he is. In his *The Romantic Ethic and the Spirit of Modern Consumerism*, Campbell argues that consumer culture has placed center stage the "romantic self," a self full of feeling and longing for authenticity which stimulates emotions, imagination, and daydreams.[23] In his discussion of anticipated consumer experiences, Campbell declares that "the essential activity of consumption is [...] not the actual selection, purchase or use of the products, but the imaginative pleasure-seeking to which the product image lends itself."[24] The consumer and the romantic self are thus historically conjointly set.

Campbell does not specify exactly how this kind of low-key daydreaming is set in motion, but we can suggest four sources whose intertwining creates powerful cognitive mechanisms for it. The first source is the commodities which are the endpoint in a complex and rich process of meaning-making through advertising, branding, and other media outlets. This process associates commodities with identity-making and the good life. That is, in consumer culture it becomes difficult to separate the fantasy about a commodity (say, a racy car) from the fantasies with which the object is relentlessly associated (say, sex with a beautiful woman). Material and emotional fantasies are bundled, with each activating and reinforcing the other. A second source of daydream is a double one: it contains the stories and the images distributed through the print and visual media which offer images of beautiful people struggling, often successfully, to achieve emotional happiness. These characters enact clear narrative scripts and vivid visual imagery around which their emotion of love is organized: that is, it becomes anticipated as a narrative script and a series of visual vignettes. Finally, since the 1990s, the Internet has been a site for the mobilization of imagination, enabling the imaginary projection of the self through a variety of sites, and the imaginary simulation of actual experiences. All four media – commodities, narrative plots, images, Internet sites – variously contribute to position the modern individual as a desiring subject, longing for experiences, daydreaming about objects or forms of life, and living experiences in an imaginary and virtual mode. The modern subject increasingly apprehends his or her desires and emotions in this mode, through commodities, media images, stories, and technologies, and these multiple mediations in turn have an impact on the structure of desire, how and what is desired, and the role of desire in the psyche. Fantasy becomes a means of experiencing both pleasure and the emotions institutionalized through the consumer market and mass culture.

I offer a sociological definition of imagination as an organized and institutionalized cultural practice. First, it has a social organization: for example, men's and women's imaginations may be activated in different ways and may contain different objects (say, love for women, social success for men). Second, it is institutionalized – it is stimulated and circulated by specific cultural genres and technologies, in print and visual forms – and pertains to institutionalized social domains such as love, domesticity, and sex. Third, it is systematic in its cultural content and has a clear cognitive form – it revolves around well-trodden narrative formulas and visual clichés. Fourth, it has social effects: for example, estrangement from one's husband or experiencing everyday life as dull. And finally it is embodied in emotional practices – anticipatory and fictional emotions that bind the emotions to real life in specific ways. Imagination is thus a social and cultural practice which constitutes a significant part of what we call subjectivity – desire and volition. It shapes emotional life, and impacts on one's perceptions of daily life.

Fictional Emotions

In order to think about the emotional and cognitive process that is activated through imagination, our starting point must be the immense role of fiction in socialization. Imagination is of particular interest to a cultural sociology of love because it is deeply intertwined with fiction and fictionality and because institutionalized fiction (in television, comic books, movies, and children's literature) has become so central to socialization. This fictionality shapes the self, the ways in which it emplots itself, lives through stories, and conceives of the emotions that make up one's life project. One of the chief, yet understudied, topics of the sociology of culture is to understand the ways in which ideas are infused with emotionality, and, vice versa, the ways in which emotions have absorbed an ideational, narrative, and fictional content. This process is contained in what I call fictional emotional imagination.

Strictly speaking, "fictional imagination" is the imagination deployed when reading or interacting with fictional material, and which in turn generates emotions. In the context of fictional reading, Bijoy Boruah defines imagination as a "species of unasserted thought – a truth that is indifferent to truth on referential considerations and is merely entertained."[25] Unasserted beliefs are beliefs about actions and characters which we know do not exist. Yet, Boruah continues, these "unasserted beliefs" – imagination – provoke real emotions. Boruah suggests that fictional imagination can trigger action through a specific subset of emotions he calls "fictional emotions." Certainly, fictional emotions are contiguous to "real-life" emotions – they mimic them – but they are not equivalent to them in that they can be triggered by things we know to be unreal, and even impossible ("I cry at the end of *Anna Karenina*, even though I know she never existed"; "I left the movie happy because the main protagonists managed to reunite at the end"). Fictional emotions may have the same cognitive content as real emotion, but they are generated by involvement with aesthetic forms and are self-referential: that is, they refer back to the self, and are not part of an ongoing and dynamic interaction with another. In that sense, they are less negotiable than real-life emotions, which may be the reason why they have a self-contained life of their own. These fictional emotions in turn constitute the building blocks for the cultural activity of imagination. One imagines and anticipates emotions that have been elicited through exposure to media content.

Representations of love can be condensed around a few key stories and images. Love is presented as a strong emotion, which not only bestows meaning on actors' actions but also motivates them from within. It is, in many ways, the ultimate narrative motivation of a plot. Love is presented as surmounting inner or outer obstacles, as a state of bliss. Characters fall in love at first sight, and their beauty is often what binds the viewer and the lovers. Love is expressed in clear and recognizable rituals; men love, and very quickly yield to the realm of women. People are in touch with their feelings and act on them. Love entails usually perfect love-making, and beautiful settings.

Fictional emotions – those that arise when we identify with stories and characters – come to form the cognitive templates of anticipatory emotions. For emotions to be shaped through imaginary scripts, two main conditions must be met: vividness and narrative identification.

Vividness

Perhaps the most obvious characteristic of modern imagination is to be found in the fact it has a high degree of resolution or vividness. Kendall Walton argues that vividness is the main reason why fictional content elicits emotions.[26] Vividness is defined as the ability of some representations to provoke the mind by relating, contrasting, and invoking clear objects. Images create vivid mental content because they enable visualization of an anticipatory experience and endow it with emotional meaning. Some claim that images are more successful than linguistic content in generating emotions, which leads us to speculate that it is largely the visual character of many stories in the mass media that gives them their emotional stimulus.[27] Moreover, vividness is accentuated by realism (which itself is often associated with visuality). Indeed, realism has been the dominant cultural style in contemporary visual culture. Finally, fictional emotions are likely to be particularly vivid when they rehearse widely resonant images. The mental images with which one forms ideas about love are clear and repetitive. This is because the images of love available in culture have an extraordinary cultural saliency: they exist in a vast array of cultural arenas (advertising, movies, low-brow popular fiction; high-brow literature; television; songs; the Internet; self-help books; women's magazines; religious stories; children's literature; opera); love stories and images present love as an emotion conducive to happiness, the most desired state; love is associated with youth and beauty, the most admired social characteristics of our culture; love is viewed as the core of the most normatively prescribed institution (marriage); and in secular cultures, love defines both the meaning and the goal of existence. Finally, inasmuch as love is associated with situations, gestures, or words which potentially could be erotic, they elicit a particular state of emotional and physiological arousal, which in turn contributes to the vividness of these images when consumed. In short, these different conditions – cultural spread, cultural resonance, cultural legitimacy, cultural meaningfulness, realism, bodily arousal – explain why the mental imagery of love is likely to inscribe itself in one's cognitive world in a particularly intense way. In the words of Anna Breslaw, writing for the *New York Times'* "Modern Love" column: "Due to the noticeable absence of men in my family, for years the men in my aunt's VHS collection were the only men I knew, the tumultuous romances and cathartic, hard-earned endings the only relationships I saw. [...] [I am] conditioned to reject nice men and kiss someone passionately only if my city is burning in the background."[28]

Narrative Identification

Modern emotions are fictional because of the prevalence of narrative, images, and simulation technologies to engineer longing. We have all become Emma Bovarys in the sense that our emotions are deeply embedded in fictional narratives: they develop in stories and as stories.

If "we all live out narratives in our lives and [...] we understand our own lives in terms of the narratives that we live out,"[29] then we can say that the narrative shape of our emotions, especially the romantic variety, is provided and circulated by stories in the media and consumer culture. Emotions are inextricably intertwined with fiction (embodied in various technologies): that is, they are lived as narrative life projects. What enables these emotions to develop as narratives is the fact that they develop in stories that mobilize strong mechanisms of identification.

Keith Oatley proposes two definitions of identification:

> Meaning 1 is recognition, and Meaning 2 is imitation. In Freud's idea of identification a person learns of an action and identifies (Meaning 1) a reason or desire for it in him- or herself. Then, by a kind of unconscious inference from this desire, he or she also becomes drawn towards the same kind of behavior or attitude, imitating it (Meaning 2) and becoming like the person who was the model for the identification.[30]

According to Oatley, identification is at the heart of what he calls simulation, by which he means that we simulate the feelings of the protagonists in the novel, similar to simulations run on a computer. Empathy, identification, and simulation entail four basic processes: adopting the goals of the protagonist ("A plot is the working out of such plans in the story world," i.e., engaging with a plot means trying to figure out a specific way of connecting intentions with goals); imagining a world, presenting vividly a world that one can imagine; speech acts to the reader through which the narrator makes the narrative more credible; and the synthesizing of different elements of the story into some "whole." It is through this fourfold process of identification and simulation, according to Oatley, that we feel emotions. In other words, imagination generates emotions through culturally scripted narratives which mobilize the mechanism of identification with characters, plots, characters' intentions, and the subsequent emotional simulation. It is this mechanism which, when combined with visual vividness, inscribes some narrative vignettes in our mental schemas, and thus makes them more likely to become a part of our way of imagining and anticipating. To the extent that we encounter many of our own emotions in and through media culture, we can say that a part of our emotional socialization is fictional: we come to develop and anticipate feelings through the repeated cultural scenarios and stories we encounter. That is, we come to anticipate the rules through which emotions are expressed, how important some emotions are for one's life narrative, and the vocabulary and rhetoric that express these emotions.

Fictional emotions emerge through the mechanism of identification – with both characters and storylines – activated by templates or schemas to evaluate new situations, to reminisce about life events, and to anticipate them. In that sense, imaginary anticipation provides templates for the fictional emotions that form the basis of life projects. This scripted anticipation shapes the projected narrative used to organize incoming life events, the emotions subsequently attached to this narrative, and the expected goal of the narrative. Life projects, therefore, are embedded with fictional emotions.

A 37-year-old woman interviewee, a translator, talked, with a tinge of humor:

Bettina: When I meet a man, after the second or third encounter, sometimes even before, can you believe it, I imagine the wedding, the dress, the invitation cards, all that kitsch, sometimes even a few minutes after having met him.

Interviewer: Is this a pleasurable feeling?

Bettina: Well, yes and no; yes, because it is great to fantasize about anything, I love to fantasize; but sometimes I feel I get carried away without even wanting it, I'd like to be more careful, to have a better hold on the whole thing, but my fantasies, that mushy kitsch in my head always takes me to places I don't want to be in.

Interviewer: What kind of "mushy kitsch?"

Bettina: Like there is this great love waiting for me, I see the whole script in front me, sitting together in the evening and holding hands, drinking a glass of champagne, traveling together to amazing places, crazy love-making, just have a great life, great sex, you know, like in the movies.

This woman is saying that she is unable *not* to experience her attraction to a man as a story that gets deployed in her imagination with a force of its own, as if such emotional intensity imposes itself on her. What ignites this imagination and the attendant emotions is the mental rehearsal of well-codified images and narrative scripts.

Similarly, relating an encounter with a former boyfriend and her hope of rekindling the relationship, Catherine Townsend describes her state of mind before the meeting in terms that suggest both the vividness of the mental images she has and their capacity to transform reality into a disappointing experience.

I blame Hugh Grant's character in Four Weddings and a Funeral for my obsession with British men. I learnt that no matter how bumbling and repressed they seemed, they would come through in the end and declare their love, probably in the rain.

After all, this is the land of Shakespeare even if most of the men I've met here think that "courtly love" has something to do with Kurt Cobain.

Another common fantasy is the Sliding Doors moment, the idea that, while on a mundane Tube journey, my eyes will meet those of a Colin Firth lookalike.

Never mind that most of the men who start conversations with me in the Tube tend to be asking for spare change. I keep hoping that somewhere, crammed among the sweat-stained masses, I will meet a man who won't balk at the idea of having to give up his seat to the elderly man with a cane. (If he does, that's an instant deal breaker.)

My ex-boyfriend had always had trouble expressing his feelings, so when he invited me to meet him in Las Vegas, for some reason I thought that being forced to spend time together in a zany, crazy environment would bring us closer together.

If our weekend had been a cheesy romantic comedy, such as What Happens In Vegas, we would have hit the jackpot on a slot machine and married in a drunken ceremony, and the wacky adventures we spent together would have made him realise how much he loved me. Maybe this could even be a crazy story we told our grandchildren one day. After all, Ross and Rachel got married drunk on Friends, and it worked out for the best in the end.

When I got to the airport, Virgin very kindly gave me an upgrade, which I took as a good omen. I spent the entire flight sipping champagne and fantasising about my dress, which looked like the one Sharon Stone wore in Casino when she was shooting craps.

Perhaps the biggest myth that romantic movies perpetuate is the "moment of truth", that magical instant when a totally unsuitable couple realizes that they are meant to be together, despite the fact that their relationship was totally dysfunctional up to that point. Usually this involves one or the other disrupting someone's wedding, or stopping them from boarding a flight at the airport.

The reality of Vegas was much more mundane. My ex and I had a nice time that weekend, but we didn't hit the jackpot. We had the same discussions we'd had back in London, and even after drinking the contents of the minibar our relationship problems did not disappear.[31]

Here, the narrative structure of anticipation clearly is shaped by the genre of the screwball comedy in which dislike and conflict are the psychological and narrative precursors to true love. Townsend describes how a specific narrative formula – the romantic comedy –

raises expectations that "problems" will be overcome in an epiphanic moment. It is the projection of the self in these narrative scripts that explains their capacity to generate expectations and anticipation and activate daydream and imagination. This in turn resonates with the common claim that movies and cinematic culture do not portray everyday relationships realistically, that they instill high expectations, that they tend to omit the portrayal of problems, offer narrative formulas in which love triumphs against all odds, and finally generate disappointment. Indeed, as Reinhart Koselleck argues, modernity is characterized by the increasing distance between reality and aspiration,[32] which in turn generates disappointment and makes it a chronic feature of modern lives. Viewed thus, modern imagination becomes a code for "raised expectations" and disappointment. Imagination has changed and raised the thresholds of women's and men's expectations about the desirable attributes of a partner and/or about the prospects of shared life. It has therefore become aligned to the experience of disappointment, a notorious handmaid of imagination and, especially in the realm of love, a major source of suffering.

Disappointment as a Cultural Practice

Socio-biologists, the Panglosses of our time, would explain the association of fantasy and disappointment as a result of inevitable biological mechanisms that serve grander evolutionary purposes. As we noted in chapter 5, when in love, the brain releases various chemical substances which produce the euphoria and the propensity to fantasize about another.[33] Because these substances do not remain in the body beyond a limited amount of time (up to two years), romantic fantasy and euphoria soon transform into either a calm attachment or what some experience as disappointment. The perhaps more common view suggests that love, more than other sentiments, must cope as insistently with the presence of another in institutionalized, routine frameworks and operate the shift from intensity to continuity, from novelty to familiarity, thus making "disappointment" existentially inherent in the experience of love.

I argue that disappointment in one's partner, one's life, one's lack of passion, is not only a psychological private experience, or an expression of the determinism of hormones, but is also a dominant emotional trope. Marshall Berman views the difference between premodern and modern selfhood as follow: "[T]he man whose whole future life is laid out for him at birth, who came into the world only to fill a pre-existing niche is much less likely to be disappointed than a man living under our own system [...] where the limits for ambition are not socially defined." This is because, although "membership in a rigidly organized society may deprive the individual of opportunities to exercise his particular gifts, it gives him *an emotional security* which is almost unknown among ourselves" (emphasis added).[34] Another way to say that modern relationships lack emotional security is to say that they are always on the verge of disappointment.

More than that, it is not only disappointment, but the anticipation of disappointment that is a modern feature of love. As a protagonist in *Sex and the City* puts it: "[E]very time a man tells me he's a romantic, I want to scream. All it means is that the man has a romanticized view of you, and as soon as you become real and stop playing into his fantasy, he gets turned off. That's what makes Romantics dangerous. Stay away."[35] This character displays her modernity in her anticipation of another's (or her own) disappointment, differing from Emma Bovary in precisely this aspect.

I suggest that for daydreaming and imagination to be disappointing, they have to be connected to the real in specific ways, by which I mean that there must be a particular means – and difficulty – to shift from the imaginary to the real.

In his celebrated *Imagined Communities*,[36] Benedict Anderson suggests that ways of imagining communities differ not according to whether they are true or false, but rather according to *their style*. Imagination, or the culturally and institutionally organized deployment of fantasy, is not an abstract or universal activity of the mind. Rather, it has a cultural form which connects it to the real in specific ways. To put it differently, disappointment is not inherently associated with the activity of imagining. This can be illustrated, *a contrario*, by using the example of medieval imagination. Medieval imagination was preoccupied with hell and paradise. Paradise was a place of flow and abundance, which was defined and discussed as a geographical space, not as a story with a clear-cut narrative line. Much of the discussion around paradise had to do with where it was located and who dwelt there. The imagination deployed revolved around mythical locales. As Jean Delumeau put it, paradise was not only present but even amplified well into the seventeenth century. The dream was about "the golden age, the Happy Isles, the fountain of youth, idyllic pastoral scenes, and a land of plenty. [...] [N]ever before in the West had gardens had so prominent a place and been so highly regarded."[37] Thus, paradise was cognitively imagined as a geographical entity, defined by its waters and lush vegetation. In the fifteenth century, it became a place of eternal youth and eternal love, outside space and time. This imaginary construction of paradise has two characteristics: it is not centered on clear characters and plot lines; and it is not subject to disappointment *per se*. Medieval imagination believed that paradise was real, that it existed somewhere far away from Europe's coasts, and did not have to be confronted by real time, in the sense that it did not have to cope with the question of how to operate the shift from imagined content to reality.[38] When paradise was lost, sometime during the sixteenth century (i.e., when people stopped believing it was located somewhere in the world), it became the object of nostalgic longing. Paradise was deployed as a means of consolation, or as a way of beautifying daily life, but it did not connect culturally to anticipatory emotions felt in real life, nor did it connect to the cultural problem of disappointment. Rather, the exercise of imagination became a source of disappointment when it was mobilized by novels. More exactly, when imagination became more realistic – that is, oriented to real, everyday objects – and when it became democratic – geared to objects or experiences in principle attainable by anyone – it became plagued by the problem of navigating between imagined expectations and the limitations of daily life. Disappointment became concomitant with the experience of love, precisely as the exercise of imagination within that sphere grew and its relationship to everyday life became stronger.

To start to understand the nature of disappointment, I want to distinguish between disappointment as a one-time event – meeting a person who falls short of our expectations – and disappointment as a fuzzy emotion extending over a long time span. The first is sharply and clearly articulated, and can happen on an initial encounter (increasingly the case with the extensive use of Internet dating sites); the second is built through the accumulated experience of everyday life. These two forms of disappointment differ because they involve different cognitive styles. The former is related to the formation of a usually clear mental image about a person prior to a meeting; the latter arises from a tacit comparison of one's everyday life to the core of one's general and fuzzy narrative expectations about how one's life should be.

Disappointed Lives

What are the factors that contribute to create a sense of disappointment as the dominant experience accumulated in and through daily life? I start this discussion with the distinction made by Daniel Kahneman and colleagues, who argue that there is a disparity between two forms of consciousness: one that lives life in an endless stream of moments; and one that memorizes and organizes experience into forms.[39] For example, patient A, who submits to a painful procedure that ends abruptly, will remember the procedure as more difficult than patient B, whose painful procedure lasted longer, but whose pain was reduced progressively.[40] This suggests that in order to decide if an experience is pleasurable or not, people attend to its cognitive structure more than to the experience itself. Although Kahneman et al. do not develop the implications of their research, these findings point clearly to the ways in which consciousness that organizes content into pre-established cultural and cognitive forms differs from consciousness that attends a shapeless flow of experience. The capacity to organize experience in form – in a narrative with specific sequences or in visual snapshots – gives a different texture and meaning to that experience, thus suggesting that for an experience to be experienced and remembered as more pleasurable, we need to organize it in a cultural and cognitive form.

Clearly, the problem of imagining is similar in nature, with the difference that imagination organizes experience prospectively rather than retrospectively. If memory obliterates some aspects of experience and privileges others, making us remember only those elements "that fit the script," imagination creates anticipation only of certain forms and shapes of experience, thus making us oblivious to other aspects of that experience when it is actually lived or making us evaluate the experience negatively. Disappointment therefore is either the inability to find the anticipated (aesthetic) form in the actual experience, or the difficulty to sustain it in real life. This difficulty is due to the ways in which the two forms of consciousness are made to connect – or not – with each other. But this problem, I would argue, has much to tell us about *both* the nature of the imagination and the nature of the everyday experience with which our mental anticipation must cope. While a long tradition makes us suspicious of imagination and has made us assume implicitly that daily life must be accommodated, I argue that we should pay no less attention to the structure of everyday existence for creating a large gap between these two forms of consciousness.

The Failure of Daily Life

In the claim that media culture unduly raises expectations through imagination, imagination is always implicitly at fault; "reality" has the last word and is viewed as the ultimate yardstick by which the exercise of imagination is judged. Psychoanalysis, for instance, makes the "reality principle" the code that ultimately must govern the psyche. According to James Jones: "Since it involves an 'over-evaluation,' romantic love, with its idealization, involves a break with reality-testing and so is always immature and dangerous."[41] But this affirmation of the real against the imagined does not question the structure of the "real" with which imagination must cope. Disappointment is always viewed as the result of "unrealistic expectations," yet the structure of the real that makes those expectations unrealizable is never questioned. I would precisely question the assumption that the real intrinsically and inevitably lacks the resources to satisfy imagination. Or if it does, I would ask why.

In a book entitled *Can Love Last?*,[42] the psychoanalyst Stephen Mitchell argues that from the experience of his practice, most marriages become difficult because they end up passionless, which he attributes to most people striving simultaneously to achieve security and adventure. The passionlessness of marriage derives from the ways in which we orchestrate our need for security. Security is often seen as incompatible with passion, or even as leading to its demise. But I would argue that this need for "security" and/or for "adventure" is not an invariant constituent of the psyche; or if it is, then security and adventure take on changing shapes in different cultural structures. They are also outcomes of the social organization of the psyche. Security derives from the capacity to control and to predict one's environment; adventure, by contrast, derives from feeling challenged, either in one's social identity or in the ways in which one knows how to do things. What Mitchell calls security is an effect of the profound rationalization of daily and domestic life, the routinization of tasks and services that help maintain the ongoing operation of a household. The rationalization of domestic households is manifest in the discipline of time (waking up at a fixed hour; coming home at a fixed hour; taking children to regular activities; having meals at set times; watching regular news or sitcoms; having a particular day for grocery shopping; planning social activities; having predictable leisure times, etc.) and the rationalization of space (shopping in malls which are highly controlled environments; living in homes in which space is homogeneously planned, rationally divided and organized according to the functional use of objects; living in neighborhoods that are surveilled and free from potential sources of chaos, etc.). Modern domestic lives are highly predictable, and their predictability is engineered by an array of institutions organizing daily life: home deliveries (food, newspapers, catalog shopping); television with its regular programs; sociability, mostly pre-planned; and standardized leisure and vacation times. Thus, what Mitchell calls security is actually a rationalized way of organizing everyday existence: that is, "security" is achieved both psychically and sociologically as a byproduct of the rationalization of daily life.

This rationalization of daily life is often conducive to disappointment because it is ongoingly, incessantly compared to widely available different models and ideals of emotional excitement and emotional expressiveness, which make people evaluate themselves and their lives negatively. Indeed, research shows that people are more likely to perceive their own rationalized daily experience negatively as a result of exposure to media images. The mechanism for this is complex. Research on the impact of media images on how individuals perceive their bodies suggests that images of perfect bodies have negative effects on self-esteem and self-concept because watching these images suggests to people both that others can achieve them more easily (competitiveness) and that others view them as important (normative legitimacy). Media images thus become a source of disappointment through the implicit mediation of what we think they say about others' expectations of us and about their achievements compared to ours. Widespread images of love may instill ideas that others achieve love when we do not, and that achieving love is normatively important for successful life. The dissatisfaction induced may fuel chronic disappointment. Thus, the rationalization of daily life produces boredom, which in turn is ongoingly, implicitly compared to media models of emotional excitement, intensity, and plenitude.

Irritations

Along with security and rationalization, shared daily domestic life produces irritations. In *Gripes*, the French sociologist Jean-Claude Kaufmann analyzed the irritations or the little annoyances of everyday life that couples experience.[43] He describes these irritations as concerning either the character of a person ("Why do you read your newspaper when I am cleaning?" or "Why do you always accuse me of being insufficiently attentive to you?") or ways of doing things ("Why don't you close the jar properly?" or "Why do you always sniff your food before eating it?"). These irritations – that is, their object (relatively small or insignificant gestures or words) – seem to be a peculiarly modern experience, which reflects a new way of conceiving of and organizing relationships.

Kaufmann's analysis does not offer insights into the reasons why modern everyday life is such fertile ground for "gripes." I would suggest that these come from the ways in which domesticity is organized through what we may call institutionalized closeness and intimacy.

Intimacy is produced by a number of linguistic strategies, all of which aim at reducing the distance between two persons: revealing the deeper layers of the self; telling each other one's innermost secrets; revealing and baring one's psyche; sharing the same bedroom and bed; and, mostly, using the sphere of leisure as common ground to spend time together and share the same space. The extraordinary expansion of leisure in the twentieth century cannot be divorced from the ways in which leisure increasingly is used as a meeting ground for men and women to build shared experiences and familiarity. Indeed, familiarity and closeness are the main goals of couplehood and intimacy. Combined with the rationalization of everyday life, familiarity institutionalizes selves in such a way that it abolishes the distant, the unfamiliar, or the unpredictable in another person. But familiarity and closeness, I argue, counter-intuitively, are actually conducive to greater gripes.

One can substantiate this *a contrario*. Research shows that long-distance relationships are more stable than close dating relationships. The reason offered by researchers for this is that it is easier to idealize one's partner when s/he is at a distance.[44] Idealization is negatively correlated with frequency of interaction. Positive ruminations about another are easier in another's absence. In contrast, partners who live together institutionalize their relationship through proximity in a number of ways: they share the same space, room, and bed; they participate in the same leisure activities; and they perform their authentic self through ritual expressions of authenticity. This contrasts to patterns of domesticity among the gentry up to the mid- or late nineteenth century: men and women did not necessarily share the same bedroom; they were segregated in their leisure; and they did not ongoingly communicate their emotions and interiority. As an illustration of a different cultural pattern in the nineteenth century, consider this letter from Harriet Beecher Stowe to her husband, summarizing the "problems" of their marriage:

> In reflecting upon our future union – our marriage – the past obstacles to our happiness – it seems to me that they are of two or three kinds. 1st those from physical causes both in you and in me – such on your part as hypochondriac morbid instability for which the only remedy is physical care and attention to the laws of health – and on my part an excess of sensitiveness and of confusion and want of control of mind and memory. This always increases on my part in proportion as I blamed and found fault with and I hope will decrease with returning health. I hope that we shall both be impressed with a most solemn sense of the importance of a wise and constant attention to the laws

of health. Then in the second place the want of any definite plan of mutual watchfulness, with regard to each other's improvement, of a definite time and place for doing it with a firm determination to improve and be improved by each other – to confess our faults one to another and pray one for another that we may be healed.[45]

By contemporary standards, this description of problems in a relationship seems both unemotional and distant: that is, it does not presume that either of the two selves should understand the unique makeup of the other, and strive for maximum fusion. Rather, it takes the view that these two selves must strive to "improve" themselves and each other. This contrasts with contemporary norms and cultural models of closeness and intimacy.

Describing the structure of the everyday lives of many couples, researchers claim that "[t]hrough everyday talk, partners 'check out one another's lusts, desires, and attitudes; announce their values; reveal the structure of their concerns; uncover their attachment styles; and otherwise discourse freely on a multitude of topics that both openly and subtly reveal their own, and give clues to other people's meaning.' Empirical evidence appears to validate the importance of everyday talk."[46] This form of talk – that is, baring the soul and exposing one's preferences – has the effect of creating intense forms of familiarity that are at odds with the capacity to sustain distance. Cognitively, familiarity is to emotions what visual closeness is to cognitions. That is, being distant from an object allows us to organize it in a cultural form which can better grab our focus and attention. Closeness to an object, by contrast, makes one focus on the discrete components of experience. Transposed to daily life and romantic relationships, I would argue that closeness makes one attend more closely to the single and discrete moments in everyday existence and makes one less able to attend to and focus on their cognitive form, on the cultural shape that renders them able to generate emotional vividness. In other words, the institutionalization of intimacy and closeness produces irritations and disappointments, making partners ongoingly focus on each other and less able to focus on the cultural shape of their emotions.

One of the reasons why distance enables idealization is that it activates the "other" form of consciousness: that is, the memory which reminisces about good experiences, and anticipation which organizes it in aesthetic vignettes. Distance enables the anticipation of a meeting according to memory scripts and cognitive forms which aestheticize everyday life, and which dissolve in the cognitive open-endedness of daily reality. Because emotions are better formed by interacting with sharply defined ("aesthetic") forms, distance enables sentiments to be more intense, precisely because they are organized in clear and sharp cognitive patterns.

Psychological Ontology

There is a deeply entrenched cliché that suggests that excessive imagination and expectations make us unable to cope with the real, and that expectations are intrinsically unrealistic. In a story in the *New York Times'* "Modern Love" column, a woman suggests that she separated from a man who was a very good match for her precisely because of her increasingly raised expectations:

> As I took in my cramped surroundings and snoozing boyfriend, a version of our future together flashed before me – a life that struck me as being, well, average. And I wanted more. [...] In New York, and especially in the movie business, it's hard to dispel the fantasy that there's always someone better just around the corner. Yet by embracing this notion, I had allowed my life to become an ongoing cycle of shallow disappointments that left me longing for someone like my Tim Donohue, who could be satisfied with exactly what he had and who he was. Even more, I longed to be that kind of person again, too.[47]

The gap between anticipation and reality is often viewed and addressed in terms of inflated expectations about the qualities of a mate, an inflation which, as this story illustrates, is activated by the institutionalized hope to improve one's position. Writing about the difficulty of finding a mate, *The Atlantic Magazine* writer Lori Gottlieb made a plea for women to lower their expectations. As summarized by another commentator, her plea was that "women have to learn to look for the good qualities of men who may not fit with their exigent *dream lists*, but with whom they know they get along" (emphasis added).[48] The problem here is that men and women looking for a partner have very elaborate and cognitively clear pre-existing sets of criteria, but missing from this recommendation is an understanding of the mechanism that makes these expectations not only very clearly formulated and cognitively salient but also a hindrance to actual relationships. No less than in Hollywood imagery, one of the central mechanisms generating disappointment in the real is what we may call a *psychological ontology* of the self: that is, the fact that others are approached as having stable, nameable, knowable psychological properties. In this ontology, the self has fixed attributes; the self must know its own fixed attributes and transact with what are perceived as the fixed attributes of another. Consequently, one searches for people with definite, knowable, stable qualities. Thus two categories in particular are ontologized: selves and relationships.

A 42-year-old divorcee evaluated her prospects of finding a "good" man as follows:

> *Barbara:*   It is so difficult to find good men, you know, or at least, men that would suit me. I sometimes think it would take a miracle for this to happen.
>
> *Interviewer:* Why? What would these men need to be like?
>
> *Barbara:*   For one, they would need to fit my complex psyche. I have anxieties of all kinds, and needs of all kinds, like, on the one hand, I am very independent, I need my space, I need to feel I can organize my life as I want, on the other hand, I also need to be cuddled, to feel supported. It is not easy to find someone who would know to give both. I need a guy very strong, very sure of himself, but also very soft with me.

Her search here is clearly motivated by a psychological ontology of the self. Despite her self-proclaimed contradictory needs, her knowledge of herself is highly stabilized; it is fixed through a psychic ontology, which solidifies her sense of self and creates clear cognitive tools with which to evaluate potential partners. I asked her:

> So when you are looking for someone on a site, how do you know if that person can fit your needs, as you just said.
>
> *Barbara:*   That's difficult; but, for example I would pay attention to how they react if I don't write quickly; if a guy makes a remark about it, he is out. I'm very annoyed by that. Or how they sign their mails, if they use some sweet funny words, but it's easier to know these things once you meet them.
>
> *Interviewer:* So when you meet them, what do you pay attention to?
>
> *Barbara:*   Difficult to say, but it has to do with whether he is comfortable with himself, if he pays attention to me, if he talks nervously or not, if he bitches about others, if something about him is possessive, if he projects self-esteem or lack of self-esteem, things of that sort.

This very fine tuning to the behavior and identity of others is made possible by the fact that she uses fixed cognitive categories and boundaries which become difficult to negotiate, because they fix interactions into fixed psychological properties and personality attributes. For example, consider this exchange with Susan, a 42-year-old psychologist:

> I met this guy at a dinner party, and I liked him quite a bit, he is very good looking, and he kept cracking up these jokes that made all of us laugh hysterically. When he asked for my number, I was thrilled, just thrilled. Then we met for lunch, in a café with a garden. He preferred to sit in the garden, and I preferred to sit inside. So we sat in the garden. But I really couldn't sit in the sun, because I did not have sunglasses, and I am very sensitive to sunlight, but he said he was sun-deprived, and kept insisting we sit in the sun, and you know what, I felt actually I was not attracted to him anymore.

Interviewer: Can you say why?

Susan: I felt this would be a person with whom it would be difficult to compromise. That he would always push his interests first.

Interviewer: So from that episode, you felt you were able to see who he was.

Susan: Absolutely. If you have good instincts and psychological acumen, you can see who people are quickly and in small details, maybe especially in small details.

In the *New York Times*' "Modern Love" column, a woman recounted how she "fell in love" with a man during a Vipassana workshop, and then finally spoke to him: "I glanced sidelong at him and saw the pens wedged in his pants pocket – not one pen, but many, crowded together. It was this odd detail that drove home just how crazy he might be."[49] Clearly, here, the "small detail" is translated into a psychological and emotional ontology.

Such a minute, fine-grained, psychologized mode of evaluating others is rampant. For example, Catherine Townsend's boyfriend was evaluated by her female friends in this way: "Look, I don't think he's an evil guy. I'm sure that he would protect you, after considering it for about 20 minutes and going over the pros and cons. But don't you want someone to whom that comes instinctively?"[50] Obviously, this dismissal requires an elaborate psychological script of what the psychological essence of a man should consist of. Or finally, consider this answer from Hellen, a 35-year-old writer:

[I]n many ways, I have the ideal boyfriend. I don't mean that he's smart, attractive, and lots of fun; he is all that, by the way. But I say this because he is very much in love with me, you have no idea the SMS he sends me every day, twice or sometimes five times a day, they are real poetry, I could publish them, I'm sure. But what drives me crazy about him is his relationship with his mother, any time something happens to him, good or bad, he tells me and his mother, almost at the same time. Sometimes he sends the same SMS to both of us, and I find it really annoying. More than annoying. I almost broke up with him over this issue.

Interviewer: Can you say why?

Hellen: It's as if he's not yet separated from his mother and is still deep into his Oedipus. A 50 years old man should be able to be emotionally mature enough to not involve his mother every single step he makes. I just don't find it attractive because of what it says about him and his emotional maturity.

"Calling his mother" is "ontologized" here under the category of "Oedipus" and the notion of "emotional maturity," both of which indicate that behaviors and emotions are evaluated in reference to a well-elaborated model of a healthy self, endowed with fixed attributes. All of the answers above ontologize the self based on therapeutic modes of evaluation in which forms of behavior are viewed as more or less healthy.

This leads in turn to the emergence of a new cultural category which we can call the category of the "relationship." A relationship has come to acquire a cultural status of its own, distinct from that of the person (although they are of course closely connected). As one divorced interviewee, Irina, 48, put it, "My ex-husband is a great person, truly, I can still see today what I saw the first time, he is a great guy, but our relationship just never worked. We were never able to connect deeply." Psychological selves have fixed properties and in turn they produce relationships, a cognitive construct supposed to be the tangible expression of a psychological entity. Relationships, as a cultural category, become a new self-conscious object of observation and evaluation. A "relationship" is evaluated according to how smoothly it runs – scripts of relationships – and according to hedonic principles – the pleasure and well-being it provides. What some sociologists have called "emotional work" – a mostly female prerogative – is based on "emotional ontology," an evaluation of what relations are according to scripts and models of healthy and satisfying emotionality and relationships. Emotional work is the reflexive monitoring of a relationship, reflected in the practice of conversations, complaints, requests, expressions of needs, understanding of another's needs. Emotional ontology implicitly contains a comparison with media ideals and stories through a socio-psychological process of tacit comparison with others. More crucially, such emotional ontologies constitute tools to monitor relationships, and to compare them with what they should or could be, to criticize them and hold them accountable for failing to be what they ought. Modern romantic relationships are incessantly captured in such ontological evaluations.

To sum up: everyday life is structured in such a way that it does not enable the activation of a stylized form of consciousness that sustains the intensity of emotions and preserves the idealized image of another. Moreover, cultural ontologies – of selves, emotions, and relationships – militate against ordinary interactions following the fluidity of actual experience as they are ongoingly implicitly compared to existing models of what they should be.

Imagination and the Internet

If there is a history of the imagination of the bourgeois subject, the advent of the Internet must mark a decisive phase in it. The Internet constitutes, undoubtedly, one of the most significant transformations in the style of romantic imagination. In the context of contemporary culture, I would distinguish between at least two forms of anticipatory imagination that are produced by modern culture. The first is an anticipation based on a synthesis of a multitude of images, stories, and commodities, such as when we anticipate, say, the purchase of a luxury item or a vacation, or a love story. This anticipation can be diffuse or cognitively highly structured, through either commodities, the invocation of mental images, or narratives: for example, the desire for a love story that follows a specific sequence, or visual vignettes with high levels of resolution, such as the romantic kiss or the romantic dinner. The second form of anticipatory imagination is produced by the attempt to engineer and mimic the actual experience virtually, using technology. This imagination is anticipatory in that it attempts to imitate the actual encounter. It covers online games and Internet dating sites which engineer and mimic actual sexual/romantic encounters.

According to a 2010 BBC World Service global poll which surveyed close to 11,000 Internet users in nineteen countries,[51] 30% of all Web users at any point in time are looking for a boyfriend or

girlfriend; in some countries, such as Pakistan and India, the proportion is 60%. In one of their college love stories contests, the *New
York Times* noticed a sweeping change in modes of interaction, from
casual sexual hook-ups, to relationships mediated by Internet
technology.

> In February [2011], Sunday Styles [of the *New York Times*] asked
> college students nationwide to tell us – through their own stories, in
> their own voices – what love is like for them. When we first held this
> contest three years ago, the most popular essay topic was hooking up:
> the "no strings attached" sex that for many wasn't turning out to be
> so carefree. The question that seemed to hover over hundreds of such
> accounts was: How do we get the physical without the emotional?
>
> What a difference three years make. This time the most-asked ques-
> tion was the opposite: How do we get the emotional without the
> physical? The college hookup may be alive and well, but in these
> entries the focus shifted to technology-enabled intimacy – relationships
> that grow and deepen almost exclusively via laptops, webcams, online
> chats and text messages. Unlike the sexual risk-taking of the hookup
> culture, this is love so safe that what's most feared is not a sexually
> transmitted disease but a computer virus, or perhaps meeting the object
> of your affection in person.[52]

The Internet and the different technologies available to follow
someone and see them through a screen seem to play an outstandingly
important role in new forms of courtship.

But as another *New York Times* article by the same writer also
stated:

> Large numbers of people report approaching online dating with great
> trepidation, then quickly embracing it for the great fun and smorgas-
> bordlike temptation it presents, then allowing themselves to imagine
> that the person with whom they are corresponding is their one true
> love, and finally facing *profound disappointment* when the process
> ends in a face-to-face meeting with an actual, flawed human being who
> doesn't look like a JPEG or talk like an e-mail message. (emphasis
> added)[53]

As I argue in *Cold Intimacies*,[54] the style of imagination that is
deployed in and by Internet dating sites must be understood in the
context of a technology that dis-embodies and textualizes encounters,
linguistic exchange being the means to produce psychological intimate knowledge. The intimacy that is produced is not experiential
or centered on the body but rather derives from the production of
psychological knowledge and modes of relating to each other.

The Internet imagination relies on a mass of text-based cognitive knowledge according to the premium it puts on defining subjects as entities endowed with discernible, discrete, and even quantifiable attributes – psychological and lifestyle. Where traditional romantic imagination once was characterized by a mix of reality and imagination, based on the body and accumulated experience, the Internet splits imagination – as a set of self-generated subjective meanings – and the encounter with the other, by having them happen at different points in time. Knowledge of another is also many times split because the other is apprehended first as a self-constructed psychological entity, then as a voice, and only later as a moving and acting body.

Internet imagination is not opposed to reality; it is opposed to a kind of imagination based on the body and on intuitive emotions: that is, emotions based on quick and non-reflexive evaluations of others. It is opposed to a retrospective imagining: that is, an imagination which tries to capture *in absentia* the sensory and bodily affects provoked by the real bodily presence of another. This form of imaginary projection is triggered by an incomplete and intuitive knowledge of another person. The Internet, by contrast, offers a prospective form of imagination, in which one imagines a specific object whose physical presence has yet to be encountered. Retrospective imagination of the kind described here is information-thin whereas the Internet-based prospective imagination is information-thick.

Traditional romantic imagination was based on the body, synthesized past experience, mixed and combined the present object with images and experiences located in the past, and focused on a few "revealing" details about the other, both visual and linguistic. As a result, such imagination consisted of mixing one's past images and interactions with a real person. As mental and emotional processes, this specific form of imagination, in common with desire, needs little information to be activated. Also like desire, it is better activated through a little rather than a lot of information. As psychoanalyst Ethel Spector Person puts it: "[I]t may be the way someone lights a cigarette in the wind, tosses her hair back, or talks on the phone."[55] In other words, bodily gestures and motions, inflections of the voice, do the work of eliciting romantic fantasies and sentiments. For Freud, the capacity to be moved by small and seemingly irrational details results from the fact that, "in love, we love a lost object."[56] It is likely that this is the result of deep parental schemas and cultural familiarity with certain forms of bodily postures and behavior that get engraved in our consciousness. "The enormous power the beloved seems to exert on the lover can in part be explained by the love object having been invested with the mystique of all the lost objects from the past."[57] In the cultural configuration in which Freud was working, love and fantasy were closely intertwined through their capacity to mix past and present experiences in solid, embodied interactions. Judgments based on attractiveness often consist of reactivating intuitive judgments based on accumulated experience. "Intuition denotes the ability to make judgments about stimulus features or discriminate between stimulus categories better than chance without being able to describe the basis of the judgments verbally. [...] [F]rom an introspective perspective intuitive judgments seem to occur spontaneously and without being mediated by conscious reasoning."[58]

Intuition is a form of judgment that activates unconscious knowledge: that is, knowledge whose structure and attributes are not immediately available to one's consciousness. Perhaps because some forms of imagination are information-thin, they can easily over-evaluate: that is, attribute to the other an added value, or what we commonly refer to as "idealizing" someone. This act of idealization can be based on a few, rather than many, elements of another person.[59]

By contrast, prospective imagination mediated by the Internet is loaded with information. The Internet can be said to stand in contrast to an information-thin imagination, because it enables and in fact demands knowledge of another that is not holistic but based on attributes, and enables systematic comparisons of people and their attributes, which tends to dampen the process of idealization. Internet imagination is prospective: that is, it addresses someone not yet met. It is based not on the body but on linguistic exchange and textual information. Evaluation of another is based on an accretion of attributes, rather than being holistic. In this particular configuration, people have too much information and seem less able to idealize. For example, this is how Stephanie, a 26-year-old graduate student, recounts her first date with someone she met on the Net.

> *Stephanie*: I met him fairly quickly after a very intense exchange of mails and one telephone call, where I liked his voice. We met in a café, near the sea, the setting was perfect, and although I was ready to find him less good-looking than in the pictures, because that's always how it happens, actually I found him as good-looking as in his pictures. So it started very well, but it is so strange, in the course of the evening, we spent two and half hours together, I felt I just didn't click, there was nothing different really from the guy I had known on the Net, he seemed to have the same sense of humor, he had the same credentials, was smart, good-looking, but I didn't click.

Interviewer: Can you say why?

Stephanie: Well I hate to say this, but maybe he was too sweet? There was something about his sweetness that was too sweet [*laughs*], like a bit too eager to please, or maybe, I don't know. I love sweetness, but it has to be mixed with a little bit of roughness, otherwise, maybe he does not feel masculine enough, you know what I mean?

This is an interesting response: although this man satisfies her dream list of attributes, she still rejects him, in the absence of a "click" (an important concept in modern romance), itself explained by the fact the man was lacking a specific and ineffable quality ("masculinity"), which, one could speculate, consists of recognizing established visual and bodily codes. The criteria of "masculinity" (or "femininity") – and more generally of "sexiness" – demand the type of holistic judgment that has become the hallmark of Gestalt psychology. Masculinity, femininity, sexiness, can be identified only in the ways in which the various movements and postures of the body are connected to each other. They are identified visually and cannot be processed linguistically. This approach to the real is preceded by abstract, verbal knowledge of the other, and has difficulties in making the transition to a visual holistic approach. Too much psychological-verbal knowledge of another may not be conducive to feeling attracted to him or her. Thus in traditional love, based on the body and an information-thin imagination, emotions are generated through four basic processes. First, there is an attraction based on the body. Second, this attraction mobilizes the subject's previous relationships and experiences. (Where Freud understood these past experiences to be strictly psychological and biographical, I, like Bourdieu, view them as social and collective.) Third, this process in turn takes place at the semi-conscious or unconscious level, thus bypassing the rational *cogito*. Finally, and almost by definition, there is an idealization of the other person, perceived as unique. (Such idealization often takes place based on a mix of what we do and do not know about the other.) In other words, it is the very core of how desire is organized – by information-thin imagination – which gets changed: the roles of visual and bodily cues are demoted, partial information is substituted with an abundance of information, and the ensuing capacity to idealize is diminished.

By contrast with traditional romantic imagination, Internet imagination is dominated by a verbal overshadowing, a prevalence of language in the processes of evaluation, some, or most, of which is based on visual perception and cues. Language is heavily used, with people presenting themselves through a depiction but also through a linguistic profile, through the activity of knowing and labeling others and through email exchanges. Language interferes with the processes of visual and bodily evaluation and recognition. Verbal overshadowing is the interference of verbal modes of evaluation from the processes of visual recognition. In experiments, researchers show that individuals who have used words to describe faces of others whose pictures they have seen perform less well in recognizing these faces than do individuals who are asked to pick these people out without any prior verbal processing. This suggests that text-based, linguistic, and attribute-based knowledge of another can interfere with the capacity to put into motion the mechanisms of visual recognition of attractiveness.

We may say that this marks a shift in the core of romantic desire. I argue that romantic desire is increasingly less determined by the unconscious. The ego with its seemingly endless capacity to enunciate and refine criteria in mate selection is a highly conscious entity, made incessantly aware of and responsible for choice, for spelling out rationally desirable criteria in another. Desire is structured by choice, as a dual rational and emotional form of action. Moreover, one might suggest that idealization – as a process central to the experience of love – is becoming increasingly difficult to achieve, precisely because of the ontologization of selves, which encourages the scrutiny of others' makeup, and a parsing into discrete attributes, which prevents holistic evaluation of another. Finally, the overwhelming sentiment of uniqueness which was once characteristic of the love sentiment has changed, as suggested by the opening epigraph from Barthes, drowned in the sheer numbers of potential partners.

Autotelic Desire

I would claim, therefore, that it is increasingly difficult for desire, imagination, and the real to connect with each other, and for two main reasons. The first is that imagination has become progressively more stylized and based on genres and technologies that activate fictional emotions, encourage identification, and anticipate narrative formulas and visual settings. The second is related to the fact that everyday life uses cultural and cognitive categories that make it difficult to organize romantic experiences and relationships into a holistic cognitive form. The upshot of this is that fantasy and imagination have become increasingly autonomous of their objects. But I would also claim that fantasy and imagination have become not only self-generated, but also autotelic, becoming their own (pleasurable) goals. Here are examples. Robert, a 50-year-old divorced man in interview:

Interviewer: You said earlier that the older you get, the more addicted to fantasy you become. What do you mean? What do you mean by fantasy? Do you mean a love that cannot be fulfilled?

Robert: Yes, and I think the older I get, the more I like these unfulfilled loves.

Interviewer: That's very interesting. Can you say why?

Robert: I get an enormous pleasure from it.

Interviewer: Can you explain why?

Robert: It solves the existential problem of the symbiosis between the emotional and the intellectual. If it is not fulfilled sexually, but it is fulfilled psychically, it provides satisfaction. What is deeply satisfying is precisely the fact it is not satisfied, that the love remains unrealized. The fact that the promise has not been fulfilled, makes any small gesture, any smile, any waving of the hand full of meaning, an SMS in the morning which says " Good Morning!" this becomes endowed with a lot of meaning.

[…]

Interviewer: Have you been in love with women who were not available?

Robert: Yes, absolutely.

Interviewer: Do you find it more attractive?

Robert: Difficult to say because when I fall in love, it seems to be always the biggest love. But yes, on the whole, I would say yes. Because I can fantasize about them more.

Desiring and fantasizing here are one and the same as they coalesce around the fact that love remains unfulfilled. Imagination becomes a mode and a vector to experience desire, and, vice versa, desire is more acutely experienced in the mode of imagination. Desiring and fantasizing are not only intertwined; they have become autotelic activities. Or in the words of another respondent, Daniel, the same man quoted in chapters 3 and 4:

I hate one-night stands. It feels empty. I need the whole package that enables me to fantasize. I need to fantasize. […] Without love, I have no inspiration in my work; it is my drug. I cannot be alone. I mean I cannot be alone in my head. Not alone physically. I have no interest whatsoever in intimacy between four walls. I am done with the whole business of domesticity. But not with fantasy.

Here, clearly, fantasy is opposed at once to pure sexual relations (one-night stands) and to domesticity, because, I would argue, both have in common that they do not enable the deployment of imagination, in turn facilitated by narrative/aesthetic shape. Or as Marianne, a 44-year-old French woman, describes her long-distance relationship with a man living in the United States: "[I]it is much more convenient for me to have him be away; I have the feeling that our relationship will forever remain beautiful, because most of it is lived in our minds." These men and this woman suggest that at the heart of the hyper-modern imagination is the desire of desire, the fact that one is kept in a state of perpetual desire, and chooses to defer the gratification of one's desire precisely in order to maintain one's desire and to maintain the desired object with an aesthetic shape. Note that fantasy is intertwined with emotional intensity: that is, the capacity to imagine produces strongly felt emotions. Domesticity is rejected precisely because it threatens this capacity to live emotions through imagined scenarios. Moreover, in these accounts, the fantasy seems to aim not at the possession of an object, but only at itself: that is, the fantasmatic pleasures it provides. As John Updike puts it, "An imagined kiss is more easily controlled, more thoroughly enjoyed, and less cluttery than an actual kiss."[60] Echoing this view, a 47-year-old woman talked about an extra-marital affair in the following way:

> *Veronica*:   You know, the most pleasurable part of it, maybe, were the emails we sent to each other from home, each of our spouses not knowing, and it was all the sweet agony of waiting to see him, to fantasize about him endlessly at night, and when waking up, and at work. Being in this situation where you can't talk to each other, and see each other when you want, really makes you long for him. Sometimes I even wondered if I did not like him more in my imagination than in real life, because the fantasy felt so much more intense.
>
> *Interviewer*: Can you say why?
>
> *Veronica*:   Wow, what a question, that's so hard to say. [*Pausing for a long time.*] I guess that's because you can control everything in a much neater way; it all looks the way you want it to look; when you write you write as you want to appear, you make no mistakes, of course you can agonize if he does not answer you, but it feels like you write down

> yourself your own script, whereas when you see him, it
> becomes immediately so much more complicated, you get
> more anxious, more irritable, you want to be with him,
> you want to run away, you like him, you don't like him,
> somehow in writing, all the feelings are what they are
> supposed to be like.

Fantasy and imagination are associated not with disorder, as has
often been thought in the long cultural history of condemnation of
imagination, but with control, with the capacity to master and shape
one's thoughts, to give the experience a stable and aesthetic shape.
Moreover, these men's and women's fantasies are autotelic, lived for
their own sake, and viewed as a source not of suffering, but rather
of pleasure.

There is also the example of Orit, a 38-year-old woman working
as a secretarial assistant in an NGO. She tells the story of how she
fell in love with a man she met on the Internet three years prior to
the interview.

> We corresponded for a long time and I came to feel that
> I knew him very well.

Interviewer: Did you actually meet each other?

Orit: No. Once, I think it was two years ago, we decided to
meet but at the last minute he canceled.

Interviewer: And you did not see him since then?

Orit: No. I don't really know why he canceled. I think he got
cold feet or something.

Interviewer: Did this change your feelings toward him?

Orit: Not at all. I kept loving him all the same. All these years,
I feel he is the only one I love. I feel very close to him,
even if we do not correspond anymore. I feel I know him
very well, and understand him.

Interviewer: You feel close to him.

Orit: Yes. I do.

Interviewer: But how, if you have never met him?

Orit: Well first of all, he told me a lot about him. We emailed
back and forth a lot. You see, with all these new technologies, you can get to know a lot about a person. On
Facebook, I can see his friends, what he did, which

> vacations he spent; his pictures; often I feel almost that
> he is with me in the room, I can see when he is on gmail,
> I can see when he logs in; when he is busy on Skype; I
> can see which music he downloaded and what he is listen-
> ing to. It's like he is near me, in my room, all the time. I
> can see what he is doing, what he listens to, which con-
> certs he went to, so, I feel really close to him.

It is not clear to what extent Orit is interacting with a real or an imaginary character. Her emotions, I would argue, have an epistemologically intermediary status: to the extent that she has never met this man and that her emotions are largely self-generated – not generated by an actual interaction, even a virtual one – they are fictional. Yet, to the extent that she interacts with real technological devices (gmail, the pictures on Facebook, etc.), we can say that it is a kind of interactional fictional emotion, anchored in technological objects that objectify and make present the virtual person. We may say that technology here plays the role of creating fictional emotions by "presencing absence." The Internet seems to sustain relationships precisely through the ways it creates a phantasmatic presence. A phantom limb is a limb that has been amputated but whose neurological presence is still felt by the subject. Similarly, the technology of the Internet creates phantom sentiments – sentiments that are lived as sentiments based in real-life stimuli, but whose actual object is absent or non-existent. This is made possible through technological devices that mimic presence. While the novel and movies created sentiments through strong mechanisms of identification, the new technologies create sentiments by abolishing distance and by mimicking presence, and by providing objective anchors to emotions. More than any other cultural technology, the Internet enables the imagination, based on little sensory contact, to generate emotions that become autotelic, and feed and sustain themselves. If imagination is the capacity to make present that which is absent, the Internet offers a radically new way of managing the relationship between presence and absence. Indeed, one of the main dimensions along which imagination may be said to vary and can be said to have a history is precisely along the lines of the differences and innovations in the ways in which presence and absence are managed and in the ways in which imagination can sustain itself. An autotelic imagination becomes impervious to real-life interactions and is organized by fictional material and technological artifacts.

Conclusion

This chapter documents several processes: the increased codification and mobilization of daydream as an ordinary cognitive and emotional activity in love; the connection between disappointment and the structure of daily life and of intimacy in hampering the shift and transition from imagination to everyday existence, thus generating disappointment; the rationalization of imagination and desire by information-thick technologies; and the progressive autonomization of desire and imagination – that is, the fact that they become their own ends themselves, with no specific aim or object. Imagination as a cultural practice has thus become both highly institutionalized and highly individualized, a property of increasingly monadic individuals whose imaginations lack specific real objects, or at least have difficulties fixating on a single object. Thus, while concrete relationships are increasingly made sense of and organized under procedural rules, the exercise of imagination has been, in parallel, increasingly solicited toward a form of autotelic desire, a desire that feeds itself and has little capacity to operate the shift from fantasy to daily life. These changes decompose the classical structure of desire, based on volition and oriented toward an object, the core of which managed the tensions between imagined objects and reality, and the shifts and passages from one to the other.

7

Epilogue

If I can stop one heart from breaking
I shall not live in vain
If I can ease one Life the Aching
Or cool one Pain

Or help one fainting Robin
Unto his Nest again
I shall not live in vain.

Emily Dickinson, "No. 982"[1]

If there is a non-academic ambition to this book, it is to "ease the aching" of love through an understanding of its social underpinnings. In our times, such a task can begin only if we stop issuing instructions and prescriptions to individuals already overburdened with the tyrannical imperative of living healthy and painless lives and loves. I hope to have shown that the "fear of love" or the "excess of love," the anxieties and disappointments inherent in so many experiences of love, find their causes in the social reorganization of sexuality, of romantic choice, of the modes of recognition inside the romantic bond and of desire itself.

But before I recapitulate the nature of these changes, let me settle a few possible misunderstandings which this book may have unwittingly elicited.

Under no circumstance does this book make the claim that modern love is always unhappy or that Victorian love is a better or preferable option to our own. The stylized letters and novels of the past have served me mostly as analytical tools to highlight the sociological characteristics of the modern condition, not as normative yardsticks. More than that: we should always remember that women in the past, however worshiped, were in a state of dependence and sometimes despondency which cannot be mourned. Not only are there many modern forms of happy love, but these loves are no less modern in their happiness than they are in their predicaments. I did not write about them because unhappiness more urgently demands a scholar's attention. Equality, freedom, the search for sexual satisfaction, the gender-blind display of care and autonomy – all are all expressions of the fulfilled promises of modern love and intimacy. When men and women – in heterosexual or homosexual relationships – fulfill such promises, I believe their relationships are happy not only because they are adapted to the normative conditions of modernity, but also because they enact ideals that are normatively superior to those of previous times.

Moreover, although this book takes the perspective of women, and, to a great extent, explicates their predicaments, under no circumstance does it argue that men do not struggle in love. I have focused on women because they are more familiar terrain to me; because women have been the endless target of an industry of psychological self-fashioning and urgently need to stop incessantly scrutinizing the so-called "faultiness" of their psyches; and because, like many others, I believe emotional suffering is connected – albeit in complex ways – to the organization of economic and political power. If there is one fundamental puzzle or source of unease this book has tried to account for, it is the fact that the feminist revolution – which was necessary, salutary, and is unfinished – has not fulfilled men and women's deep longing for love and passion. Both freedom and equality must remain at the heart of our normative ideals of love, but whether and how these political ideals can organize passion and commitment remains a cultural conundrum which this book has sought to clarify. Middle-class heterosexual women are thus in the odd historical position of having never been so sovereign in terms of their body and emotions, and, yet, of being emotionally dominated by men in new and unprecedented ways.

The third potential misunderstanding this epilogue would like to dispel is the claim that unhappy love is a new phenomenon associated with modernity or even that people suffer more in love today than they did in the past. The pangs of love suffering are tropes of world literature as old as the representation of love itself, and the past has its many examples and models of the agony of love. Yet, in the same way that modern self-inflicted pain differs from medieval rituals of self-flagellation, modern romantic pain contains new social and cultural experiences. This is not to say, obviously, that some of these experiences do not retain elements that resist change, but if all research implies deliberate decisions to focus on certain aspects of a phenomenon and to ignore others, this book, likewise, has deliberately focused on what in romantic suffering is novel. It has thus argued that romantic love is the site of a paradoxical process. Modern selves are infinitely better equipped to deal with the repeated experiences of abandonment, break-ups, or betrayals than ever in the past through detachment, autonomy, hedonism, cynicism, and irony. In fact, from a young age, most people expect the road to romantic love to be a highly bumpy one. Yet, my point in this book has been that *because* we have developed many strategies to cope with the fragility and interchangeability of relationships, many aspects of contemporary culture deprive the self of the capacity both to enter and to live the full experience of passion and to withstand the doubts and uncertainties attendant to the process of loving and getting attached to someone. Love has changed its form in the sense that it has changed the ways in which it hurts.

Finally, although this book has tried to provide an ample account of men's evasion and their difficulty to enter strong emotional bonds, it is neither a rejoinder to the cultural lament of "where have the good men gone?" nor an indictment of sexual freedom as such. It is rather an attempt to understand the social forces that shape men's emotional evasiveness and the consequences of sexual freedom in a way that does not presume that men are inherently insufficient creatures or that freedom should be the ultimate value of our practices. If – as many agree – the cult of freedom in the economic realm can and does sometimes have devastating consequences – producing uncertainty and large income inequalities, for example – then we should at the very least similarly inquire about its consequences in the personal, emotional, and sexual realms. The critical examination of freedom in one realm ought to be symmetrically undertaken in others. A radical mind should not shy away from examining and questioning the unintended consequences of one's deepest and most cherished norms and beliefs, here freedom. In the same way that freedom in the economic realm creates inequalities and makes them invisible, freedom in the sexual realm has had the same effect of obscuring the social conditions which make possible the emotional domination of men over women. One of the main points of this book is fairly simple: in conditions of modernity, men have far more sexual and emotional choice than women, and it is this imbalance that creates emotional domination. Thus, the point of this book has been to bring sociology where psychology traditionally reigns, and to try to do what sociologists of culture are best at: that is, to show that the deepest recesses of our subjectivity are shaped by such "big" entities as the transformation of the ecology and architecture of sexual choice. Ordinary experiences of emotional suffering – feeling unloved or abandoned, struggling with the detachment of others – are shaped by the core institutions and values of modernity. The grand ambition of this book is thus to have done to emotions – at least to romantic love – what Marx did to commodities: to show that they are shaped by social relations; that they do not circulate in a free and unconstrained way; that their magic is social; and that that they contain and condense the institutions of modernity.

We should not, obviously, overdraw the distinction between the modern and pre-modern; after all, pre-modern men and women married each other with a certain amount of freedom, loved each other, left each other, and operated with a relative sense of choice. Yet, as I hope to have shown, sociology tries to make sense of the direction and broad tendencies of culture, and is thus in a position to suggest that beyond the subjectivity of particular people, something fundamental about that freedom – that is, about the ways in which it has been institutionalized in the modern cultural category of choice – has changed, and such institutionalization in turn has changed the terms of emotional bargaining and exchange between men and women. Men's and women's romantic unhappiness contains, stages, and enacts the conundrums of the modern freedom and capacity to exercise choice. These conundrums are complexly structured around the following key processes:

The transformation of the ecology and architecture of choice. For reasons that are normative (the sexual revolution), social (the weakening of class, racial, ethnic endogamy), and technological (the emergence of Internet technologies and dating sites), the search for and choice of a partner have profoundly changed. The idea of a "great transformation of love" is an analytical tool to grasp the ways in which the social organization of pre-modern and contemporary choice differs. Contrary to conventional wisdom, I have argued here that in modernity, choice – as a cognized and reflexive category – has become far more salient to the process of looking and finding an object of love. This salience is the result of the transformation of the ecology of choice, characterized by a number of elements: the

considerable enlargement of the samples from which one can choose
and the resulting open-endedness of one's sense of possibilities; the
fact that the process of settling on a choice is longer and more
complex; the fact that tastes in a variety of domains – sexual, physical, cultural – have become increasingly mobilized and refined; the
fact that the process of evaluation of others is more cognized and
individualized; and the fact that the perception of one's chances for
improving one's choice has become structurally embedded in relationships. All of these have transformed the search process, in making it
cognized, both more rational and more emotional, and more tightly
dependent on tastes. At the heart of modern love thus lies a new
process of evaluation: the self relies on ontologized emotions – that
is, on knowable and fixed emotions in turn supposed to be the guide-
posts for action. It makes complex and elaborate evaluations of
persons along multiple scales. These changes set up the conditions
for the transformation of the nature of desire and the will, of the
ways in which people make promises, anticipate the future, use their
own past to make decisions, consider and assess risk, and, more
fundamentally, think about what they feel, want, and will when they
love another.

The emergence of sexual fields. Sexual fields are social arenas in
which sexuality becomes an autonomous dimension of pairing, an
area of social life that is intensely commodified, and an autonomous
criterion of evaluation. Sexual fields imply that actors participating
in them do an incessant work of evaluation of others, know they are
in competition with many others, and evaluate them in such a state
of competition. In a sexual field, actors compete with each other (a)
for the sexually most desirable partners, (b) in accumulating partners,
and (c) in displaying their own sexual attractiveness and sexual
prowess. Marriage markets include these dimensions of the competition for pairing but include other dimensions as well, such as socio-
economic status, personality, and cultural competence. In a marriage
market, choice is made following criteria of economic status, physical
attractiveness, education, income, and less tangible attributes such as
personality, "sexiness," or "charm." That marriage is a market is a
historical not a natural fact, caused by the transformation of the
ecology of romantic choice. Never before in history have men and
women of different social classes, religions, races met as if on a free,
unregulated market where attributes – of beauty, sexiness, social class
– are rationally and instrumentally evaluated and exchanged.
Marriage markets always coexist with sexual fields; however, sexual
fields often predate and therefore interfere with them, such that men

and women linger in these fields or prefer them to marriage markets. A sexual field as such is dominated by men because they can stay in them longer and can have a broader sample of women to choose from. This greater availability of choice makes men – especially upper-middle-class men – dominate the sexual field. Such a domination is manifest in their greater reluctance to enter long-lasting bonds. This dynamic of sexual fields and the new ecology and architecture of choice create the conditions for emotional domination of women by men and have given men an advantage, for three main reasons. First, men's social status now depends much more on their economic achievement than on having families and children. Second, men are not biologically and culturally defined by reproduction, thus their search can span a much longer time frame than can women's. Finally, because men use sexuality as status, because norms of sexiness put a premium on youth, and because age discrimination gives an advantage to men, the samples of potential partners from which men can choose are much larger than they are for women. Middle-class heterosexual men and women thus approach the sexual field in different ways. Because men are more directly dependent on the market for their economic survival than on marriage, and because they are not – or are less – bound by the imperative of romantic recognition, use sexuality as a status, and display autonomy, they tend to have a cumulative and emotionally detached sexuality. Women, by contrast, are caught in more conflicted strategies of attachment and detachment. Men's emotional detachment and commitment phobia are thus an expression of their position in sexual fields, created by a new ecology of choice.

New modes of recognition. The inequalities arising from this new ecology revolve precisely around new modes of recognition. As in all social fields, success leads to the accrual of status and self-worth. Attractiveness and sexual capital are now used to signal and build social worth and thus have become central to processes of recognition. Conversely, failure to succeed in such fields can threaten one's sense of worth and identity. Thus love becomes an aspect of the dynamic of moral inequalities: that is, inequalities in one's sense of self-worth. These inequalities divide men and women – with men dominating the field – and they divide also the more from the less successful men and women. In other words, this inequality is both between the sexes and within one's own sexual group. Moreover, because modernity has been marked by the constitution of a private sphere that both shaped women's identity and disconnected it from the public world, love is central to their social sense of self-worth.

In free-market conditions, therefore, women both need more love for self-validation and want to commit more intensely and earlier. The transformation of the ecology and architecture of choice, and the connection of love and social worth, suggest that gender inequality is now enacted around emotional, rather than social, inequalities. The widespread literature on Mars and Venus is nothing more than an attempt to understand in psychological terms what is in fact a sociological process, namely the reorganization of gender differences around love as a source of worth for women or sexual capital for men.

The cooling of desire and the weakness of will. Irony, commitment phobia, ambivalence, disappointment – all central themes of this book and central features of the experience of love – constitute the four main components of what I have called the de-structuration of the will and desire, whose orientation has shifted from the formation of intense bonds to the formation of cool individuality. All four components have in common the fact they express the difficulty of mobilizing the totality of the self in desiring another, the affirmation of autonomous selfhood in the deepest recesses of subjectivity, and the more general cooling of passion. Indeed, the very capacity to activate desire, to settle on a love object, to subscribe to the culture of love, has changed. It is desire itself that has changed its intensity and the ways in which it radiates from the self. First, faced with greater choice, desire relies on highly cognized forms of introspection and self-scrutiny. Second, comparisons between different possible choices dampen strong emotions. Third, desire now takes place in a cultural environment dominated by proceduralism: that is, abstract and formal rules by which to conduct relations to others and one's own emotional life. Fourth, while pre-modern desire was governed by an economy of scarcity, it is now governed by an economy of abundance caused both by sexual normative freedom and by the commodification of sex. Finally, because desire has migrated to the realm of imagination, the possibility to sustain desire in real interactions is threatened. In that sense, desire becomes both weaker and stronger: weaker because it is not backed up by the will – choice tends to enervate rather than embolden the will – and stronger when it migrates to the vicarious realm of virtual and vicarious relationships.

This book can thus appear to be an indictment of love in modernity. But it would be more useful to read it as an attempt to counter the reigning views that men are psychologically and biologically naturally inept at connecting and that women are better off changing their psychic makeup to find and keep love. In fact, biology and psychology – as modes of explanation and legitimation of the difficulties of romantic relations – are parts of the problem, not an answer to them. If men's and women's emotional inequality is inscribed in biology, evolution, or inadequate psychic development, these differences have been largely amplified and to a certain extent justified by the culture and institutions of modernity, most conspicuously owing to the transformation of patterns of economic survival, the commodification of sex, and the normative freedom and equality between men and women. Thus the Mars and Venus terminology with which we have tried to explain and soothe our differences will obviously not do; in fact, it only serves to further naturalize the culturally engineered differences between men and women. Such terminology posits that men and women are fundamentally different, that men like to solve problems while women like to be acknowledged, and that the solution is that men should listen to and validate women, while women should respect men's need for autonomy. This may seem to provide disoriented men and women with a useful way to navigate the high sea of gender differences, but in many respects it only reinforces the view of men as emotionally inept, and of women as in need of fixing their emotional makeup.

This is not to say, obviously, that men and women should not be held personally responsible for their actions. In no way does this book disparage or discount the notion of personal responsibility and accountability in interpersonal relations. On the contrary, it argues that understanding the larger set of forces operating on men and women may help avoid the burdens of over-responsibilization, and better locate the locus for personal and ethical responsibility. Indeed, the critical reader, as many readers of this book will undoubtedly be, will want to know what my political recommendations are. One main normative assumption standing behind this work is that the loss of passion and emotional intensity is an important cultural loss and that the cooling of emotions may make us less vulnerable to others, but makes it more difficult to connect to others through passionate engagement. I rejoin here Crista Nehring or Jonathan Franzen's view that passionate love implies pain and that such pain should not anguish us. As Franzen puts it beautifully: "[P]ain hurts but it doesn't kill. When you consider the alternative – an anesthetized dream of self-sufficiency, abetted by technology – pain emerges as the natural product and natural indicator of being alive in a resistant world. To go through a life painlessly is to have not lived."[2]

The goal of gender equality is not equal detachment but an equal capacity to experience strong and passionate emotions. Why would that be the case? After all, there is no lack of philosophical or ethical models preaching moderation in all things, and especially in the passions. Although this work rejects entirely the idea that the institutionalization of relations is the only viable framework to organize them, it views the capacity to love in a way that mobilizes the entirety of the self as a crucial capacity to connect to others and to flourish, thus as an important human and cultural resource. The capacity to derive meaning from relationships and emotions, I believe, is better found in those bonds that totally engage the self, enabling it to focus on another person in a way that is self-forgetful (as in the models of ideal parenthood or friendship, for example). Moreover, passionate love dispels the uncertainty and insecurity inherent in most interactions, and in that sense provides a very important source for understanding and enacting what we care about.[3] This kind of love radiates from the core of the self, mobilizes the will, and synthesizes a variety of one's desires. As Harry Frankfurt put it, loving frees us from the constraints and difficulties inherent in the fact of not knowing what to think, and, I would add, what to feel. Passionate love ends that state of indecisiveness, releases us from "the blockage of irresolution."[4] This kind of love is character-building, and ultimately is the only one to provide a compass by which to lead one's life. The state of indecisiveness about what we love – caused by the abundance of choice, by the difficulty to know one's emotions by self-scrutiny, and by the ideal of autonomy – prevents passionate commitment and ends up obscuring who we are to ourselves and to the world. For these reasons, I cannot take at face value the cult of sexual experience that has swept over the cultural landscape of Western countries, mostly because I believe such a kind of intensely commodified sexual freedom interferes with the capacity of men and women to forge intense, all-involving meaningful bonds, which provide one with a knowledge of the kind of persons one cares about.

Radical and liberal feminism must respond to the current situation in a way that is both analytical and normative: given that women are not yet willing to check out on the idea of romantic love, and given that they meet men in an open sexual field, the accumulation of sexual capital must be discussed and questioned so as to devise new strategies to cope with emotional inequalities and meet women's larger social and ethical goals. From the standpoint of both a feminist and a Kantian ethics, we should question the cultural model of the accumulation of sexual capital. If the second wave of feminism opened the gates of sexual constriction and repression, it is now time we re-examine the state of estrangement and alienation created by the interaction and intersection of emotions, sexual freedom, and economics. As long as the institutions of economy and biological reproduction in the framework of heterosexual families institutionalize gender inequality, sexual freedom will be a burden for women. What should be discussed, then, is the question of how sexuality should be made a domain of conduct regulated both by freedom and by ethics. The sexual revolution, anxious to put taboos aside and to reach equality, has by and large left ethics outside the realm of sex. Ultimately, this book suggests that the project of self-expression through sexuality cannot be divorced from the question of our duties to others and to their emotions. We should thus not only stop viewing the male psyche as inherently weak or unloving, but also open for discussion the model of sexual accumulation promoted by modern masculinity and too enthusiastically endorsed and imitated by women; we should also rearticulate alternative models of love, models in which masculinity and passionate commitment are not incompatible and are even synonymous. Instead of hammering at men their emotional incapacity, we should invoke models of emotional masculinity other than those based on sexual capital. Such cultural invocation might in fact take us closer to the goals of feminism, which have been to build ethical and emotional models congruent with the social experience of women. For when detached from ethical conduct, sexuality as we have known it for the last thirty years has become an arena of raw struggle that has left many men and especially women bitter and exhausted.

There is, then, a paradox which this book has tried to account for: there has been a cooling of emotionality, of love and romance. Passion looks faintly ridiculous to most men and women, who would recoil in mockery or vague disgust at the rhetoric of eighteenth- and nineteenth-century love letters. Yet, as I have tried to show, love in many ways is more crucial than ever to the determination of self-worth. Given that so much in our culture points a finger at our psyches, we are deemed to be insufficiently competent when a love story fails, and for this reason, love failures threaten the foundations of the self, which is why modern love demands psychotherapies, endless friends' talks, consultations and consolations. Love is more than a cultural ideal; it is a social foundation for the self. Yet, the cultural resources that make it constitutive of the self have been depleted. Precisely for that reason, ethics is urgently demanded back into sexual and emotional relations, exactly because these relations are now so crucial to the formation of self-worth and self-respect.

This book is thus a sobered endorsement of modernity through love. It recognizes the necessity of values of freedom, reason, equality, and autonomy, yet is also forced to take stock of the immense difficulties generated by the core cultural matrix of modernity. Like all waking up after heavy drinking, a sobered endorsement of modernity does not have the fervor of utopias or of denunciations. But it offers the quiet hope that with lucidity and self-understanding, we can better live these times and perhaps even reinvent new forms of passion.

Notes

Chapter 1   Introduction: The Misery of Love

1   S. Firestone, *The Dialectic of Sex: The Case for Feminist Revolution* (New York: Bantam, 1970), p. 129.
2   E. Brontë, *Wuthering Heights* (Oxford: Oxford University Press, 2008 [1847]).
3   G. Flaubert, *Madame Bovary* (New York: Courier Dover Publications, 1996 [1857]), p. 145.
4   S. de Beauvoir, *The Second Sex* (New York: Vintage Books, 1970 [1949]).
5   See note 1.
6   T.-G. Atkinson, "Radical Feminism and Love" (1974), in Susan Ostrov Weisser (ed.), *Women and Romance: A Reader* (New York: New York University Press, 2001), pp. 138–42.
7   C.A. MacKinnon, *Sexual Harassment of Working Women: A Case of Sex Discrimination* (New Haven: Yale University Press, 1979); A. Rich "Compulsory Heterosexuality and Lesbian Existence," *Signs*, 5(4) (1980), 631–60; S. Schecter, "Towards an Analysis of the Persistence of Violence against Women in the Home," *Aegis: Magazine on Ending Violence against Women* (July/August 1979), p. 47; S. Schecter, *Women and Male Violence: The Visions and Struggles of the Battered Women's Movement* (New York: South End Press, 1983).
8   See A. Swidler, *Talk of Love* (Chicago: University of Chicago Press, 2001) for an excellent answer to that question.
9   H. Frankfurt, *The Reasons of Love* (Princeton: Princeton University Press, 2004), p. 5.
10 E. Chowers, *The Modern Self in the Labyrinth* (Cambridge, MA: Harvard University Press, 2003).

11 Quoted and translated in P. Wagner, *A Sociology of Modernity: Liberty and Discipline* (London: Routledge, 1994), p. xiii.

12 M. Weber, "Religious Rejections of the World and Their Directions," in H.H. Gerth and C.W. Milles (eds and trans), *From Max Weber* (London: Routledge, 1970 [1948]), pp. 323–59.

13 This is also the theoretical and sociological perspective of various sociologists such as Giddens, Beck and Gernsheim-Beck, and Bauman.

14 See R. Bellah, W. Sullivan, A. Swidler, and S. Tipton, *Habits of the Heart: Individualism and Commitment in American Life* (Berkeley: University of California Press, 1985).

15 E. Illouz, *Saving the Modern Soul: Therapy, Emotions and the Culture of Self-Help*, (Berkeley: University of California Press, 2008).

16 U. Frevert, "Was haben Gefühle in der Geschichte zu suchen?" *Geschichte und Gesellschaft*, 35 (2009), pp. 183–208 (p. 202).

17 G. Motzkin, "Secularization, Knowledge and Authority," in G. Motzkin and Y. Fischer (eds), *Religion and Democracy in Contemporary Europe* (Jerusalem: Alliance Publishing Trust, 2008), pp. 35–53.

18 M. Macdonald, *Mystical Bedlam: Madness, Anxiety and Healing in Seventeenth-Century England* (Cambridge: Cambridge University Press, 1983), p. 98.

19 F. Cancian, *Love in America* (Cambridge: Cambridge University Press, 1987); A. Giddens, *The Transformation of Intimacy* (Cambridge: Polity Press, 1992); L. Stone, *The Family, Sex and Marriage in England, 1500–1800* (New York: Harper and Row, 1977).

20 Giddens, *The Transformation of Intimacy*.

21 Motzkin, "Secularization, Knowledge and Authority," p. 43.

22 A. Douglas, *The Feminization of American Culture* (New York: A.A. Knopf, 1978), pp. 6–7.

23 A. Giddens, *Modernity and Self-Identity* (Stanford: Stanford University Press, 1991), pp. 70–108; Giddens, *The Transformation of Intimacy*, pp. 49–64.

24 See R. Girard, *Le Sacrifice* (Paris: Bibliothèque nationale de France, 2003); R. Girard, *A Theatre of Envy: William Shakespeare* (New York: Oxford University Press, 1991).

25 W. James, *The Principles of Psychology, Vol. 1* (New York: Cosimo, 2007 [1890]), p. 224.

26 See Swidler, *Talk of Love*.

27 A. Kleinman, V. Dass, and M. Lock (eds) *Social Suffering* (Berkeley: University of California Press, 1997).

28 A. Schopenhauer, *Essays and Aphorisms* (Harmondsworth: Penguin, 1970), p. 44.

29 For example, one may speculate that egalitarian cultures with an egalitarian cultural imaginary and a mobile social structure generate more psychic suffering than caste societies, in which individuals develop few or fewer expectations.

30 I. Wilkinson, *Suffering* (Cambridge: Polity Press, 2005), p. 43.

31 In religion, this has been the main function of religious theodicy, which explains why people suffer, and, more crucially, why it is right that they suffer. In the realm of romance, clinical psychology has occupied the function of theodicy, explaining why we suffer, thus making it not only intelligible but acceptable as well.

32 My data are varied and include 70 interviews with people living in three large urban centers in Europe, the US, and Israel; a wide variety of web-based support groups; nineteenth-century and contemporary novels; a large sample of contemporary guidebooks to romance, dating, marriage, and divorce; Internet dating sites; and, finally, an analysis of the *New York Times* weekly column "Modern Love" for a period of two years. The interviewees comprised 60% women and 40% men, and because the interviewer needed to be trusted, I used a snowball procedure. All interviewees were college graduates and their ages ranged from 25 to 67. The sample included single people never married, single people who had been divorced, and married people. Pseudonyms are used for interviewees to protect their anonymity. National differences are not discussed for two reasons: the first is that I found the type of predicaments faced by men and women remarkably similar (in itself a finding); and the second is that if all research implies choices to focus on certain aspects of a phenomenon and to ignore others, my choice was to focus on precisely what united rather than divided the experience of these men and women in different national contexts.

Chapter 2   The Great Transformation of Love or the Emergence of Marriage Markets

1 F. Dostoevsky, *Poor Folk* (Teddington, UK: Echo Library, 2003 [1846]), pp. 16–17.

2 P. Roth, *Indignation* (New York: Houghton Mifflin, 2008), p. 58.

3 H.M. Markus and S. Kitayama, "Models of Agency: Sociocultural Diversity in the Construction of Action," in V. Murphy-Berman and J. Berman (eds), *Cross-Cultural Differences in Perspectives on the Self* (Lincoln: University of Nebraska Press, 2003), pp. 1–58.

4 See C.R. Sunstein and R.H. Thaler, *Nudge: Improving Decisions about Health, Wealth, and Happiness* (New Haven: Yale University Press, 2008).

5 This concept was formulated independently of Sunstein and Thaler's concept (see previous note), and signifies something different.

6 For examples of the rise of new ways of attending to the remote consequences of one's actions, see N. Elias, *The Civilizing Process: Socio-genetic and Psychogenetic Investigations* (Oxford: Blackwell, 1969 [1939]); T.L. Haskell, "Capitalism and the Origins of the Humanitarian Sensibility, Part 1," *The American Historical Review*, 90(2) (1985), 339–61; T.L. Haskell, "Capitalism and the Origins of Humanitarian

Sensibility, Part 2," *The American Historical Review*, 90(3) (1985), 547–66.

7   S.C. Chang and C.N. Chan, "Perceptions of Commitment Change during Mate Selection: The Case of Taiwanese Newlyweds," *Journal of Social and Personal Relationships*, 24(1) (2007), 55–68. For a comparable case, see D. Lehmann and B. Siebzehner, "Power, Boundaries and Institutions: Marriage in Ultra-Orthodox Judaism," *European Journal of Sociology*, 50(2) (2009), 273–308.

8   See K. Savani, H. Markus, and A. Conner, "Let Your Preference Be Your Guide? Preferences and Choices are More Tightly Linked for North Americans Than for Indians," *Journal of Personality and Social Psychology*, 95(4) (2008), 861–76.

9   J. Austen, *Emma* (Whitefish, MT: Kessinger Publishing, 2004 [1816]), p. 325.

10   Ibid.

11   J.D. Hunter, *Death of Character: Moral Education in an Age without Good or Evil* (New York: Basic Books, 2000), p. 21.

12   Ibid., p. 19.

13   Quoted in ibid.

14   J. Austen, *Pride and Prejudice* (Cambridge, MA: Harvard University Press, 2010 [1813]), p. 40.

15   J. Austen, *Persuasion* (Oxford: Oxford University Press, 2004 [1818]), p. 54.

16   A.O.J. Cockshut, *Man and Woman: A Study of Love and the Novel, 1740–1940* (Oxford: Oxford University Press, 1978), p. 67.

17   The notion of character should be differentiated from Wahrman's contention that during the eighteenth century there existed an *"ancien régime"* of identity which later transformed into the modern, interiorized, unique self. In his conception, as I understand it, the *"ancien régime"* is a wide-ranging cultural understanding of identities as "hollow" or a lack of a core self, "a play of surfaces without real substance, referent or true value" (D. Wahrman, *The Making of the Modern Self: Identity and Culture in Eighteenth-Century England* [New Haven: Yale University Press, 2004], p. 207). By contrast, the notion of character I discuss has a more stable core, even if it must be performatively displayed and affirmed.

18   J. Wood, "Inside Mr Shepherd," *London Review of Books*, 26(21) (2004), 41–3.

19   M.D. Sanford, *Mollie: The Journal of Mollie Dorsey Sanford in Nebraska and Colorado Territories, 1857–1866* (Lincoln: University of Nebraska Press, 2003), p. 57.

20   A. MacFarlane, *Marriage and Love in England: Modes of Reproduction, 1300–1840* (Oxford: Basil Blackwell, 1986), p. 294.

21   S. Harris, *The Courtship of Olivia Langdon and Mark Twain* (Cambidge: Cambridge University Press, 1996), p. 72.

22   This was true also of the poorer classes, who had no or little land to exchange in marriage. Indeed, in his study of an early seventeenth-

century doctor/astrologer's treatment of various forms of distress, Michael MacDonald suggests that obedience to parents and community standards, even if not always observed in practice, was always in the background or foreground of young people's decision to marry. See M. MacDonald, *Mystical Bedlam: Madness, Anxiety, and Healing in Seventeenth-Century England* (Cambridge: Cambridge University Press, 1983), pp. 96–7.

23   A. Giddens, *The Constitution of Society: Outline of the Theory of Structuration* (Cambridge: Polity Press, 1986).

24   In his novel *On Chesil Beach*, Ian McEwan portrays a couple on their wedding night, before the much-awaited and -dreaded act of sexual intercourse. This wedding night ends as a fiasco (it remains unconsummated) and is the pretext for the narrator to reflect about the shift to the "new" sexual morality from an "old" sexual morality imbued with rituals: "Even when Edward and Florence were alone, a thousand unacknowledged rules still applied. It was precisely because they were adults that they did not do childish things like walk away from a meal that others had taken pains to prepare. It was dinner time, after all." See I. McEwan, *On Chesil Beach* (New York: Vintage, 2008), p. 8.

25   S. Coontz, *Marriage, a History: From Obedience to Intimacy or How Love Conquered Marriage* (New York: Viking, 2005), p. 199.

26   One reason may be that at least until the American Civil War, men outnumbered women in most areas.

27   W.M. Reddy, "Emotional Liberty: Politics and History in the Anthropology of Emotions," *Cultural Anthropology* 14(2) (1999), 256–88; W.M. Reddy, "Against Constructionism: The Historical Ethnography of Emotions," *Current Anthropology*, 38(3) (1997), 327–51.

28   E.K. Rothman, *Hands and Hearts: A History of Courtship in America* (New York: Basic Books, 1984), p. 34.

29   M. Yalom, *A History of the Wife* (New York: HarperCollins, 2001), p. 206.

30   M. Berman, *The Politics of Authenticity: Radical Individualism and the Emergence of Modern Society* (New York: Atheneum, 1970), p. xix.

31   J.H. Young , *Our Deportment* (Charleston, SC: BiblioBazaar, 2008 [1879]), p. 155.

32   Austen, *Persuasion*, p. 195.

33   T. Kenslea, *The Sedgwicks in Love: Courtship, Engagement, and Marriage in the Early Republic* (Boston: Northeastern University Press, 2006), p. 7.

34   R.H. Frank, *Passions within Reason: The Strategic Role of the Emotions* (New York: Norton, 1988), p. 4.

35   MacDonald, *Mystical Bedlam*, p. 94.

36   Louis Dumont, *Homo Hierarchicus: The Caste System and Its Implications* (Chicago: University of Chicago Press, 1970 [1966]).

37   *Wahrman, The Making of the Modern Self.*

38   M. Kaplan, *The Marriage Bargain: Women and Dowries in European History* (New York: Harrington Park Press, 1985), p. 2.

39 Ibid., p. 4.
40 Ibid., p. 9.
41 The following conceptualization and analysis are based on the ground-breaking work of Michèle Lamont, who showed the centrality of repertoires of evaluation to identity formation, social structures, and cultural boundaries. See M. Lamont, "National Identity and National Boundary Patterns in France and the United States," *French Historical Studies*, 19(2) (1995), 349–65.; M. Lamont and L. Thévenot, *Rethinking Comparative Cultural Sociology: Repertoires of Evaluation in France and the United States* (Cambridge: Cambridge University Press, 2000).
42 R. Craig, *Promising Language: Betrothal in Victorian Law and Fiction* (Albany: State University of New York Press, 2000), p. 58.
43 S. Shapin, *A Social History of Truth* (Chicago: University of Chicago Press, 1994).
44 Austen, *Persuasion*, p. 155.
45 Ibid., p. 194.
46 E. Wharton, *Summer* (Whitefish, MT: Kessinger Publishing, 2004 [1917]), p. 105.
47 M. Twain, *Mark Twain's Letters: 1867–1868*, Vol. 2, ed. E.M. Branch, M.B. Frank, and K.M. Sanderson (Berkeley: University of California Press, 1988), p. 357.
48 G.S. Frost, *Promises Broken: Courtship, Class, and Gender in Victorian England* (Charlottesville: University of Virginia Press, 1995).
49 A. Trollope, *Doctor Thorne* (London: J.M. Dent and Sons, 1953 [1858]), p. 19.
50 E. Wharton, *The Age of Innocence* (Ware, UK: Wordsworth, 1994 [1920]), p. 198.
51 Sanford, *Mollie*, p. 145.
52 Yalom, *A History of the Wife*, p. 260.
53 R. Bellah, W. Sullivan, A. Swidler, and S. Tipton, *Habits of the Heart: Individualism and Commitment in American Life* (Berkeley: University of California Press, 1985).
54 A. Sen, "Rational Fools: A Critique of the Behavioral Foundations of Economic Theory," *Philosophy and Public Affairs*, 6(4) (1977), 317–44 (p. 326).
55 These mechanisms are more likely to have been present in Protestant countries than in Catholic ones, in which the ideal of companionate love as the foundation for marriage was less prominent.
56 L. Stone, *The Family, Sex and Marriage in England, 1500–1800* (New York: Harper and Row, 1977).
57 K. Polanyi, *The Great Transformation* (Boston: Beacon Press, 1944).
58 As Kierkegaard writes, "In spite of the fact that love is essentially based on the sensuous, it is noble, nevertheless, by reason of the consciousness of eternity which it embodies." S. Kierkegaard, *Either/Or* (Princeton: Princeton University Press,1944 [1843]), p. 21.

59 See J. Markus, *Dared and Done: The Marriage of Elizabeth Barrett and Robert Browning* (New York: Knopf, 1995).
60 For an early discussion on the role of beauty in love see Plato's *Symposium*. However, the discussion had mostly to do with the beauty of boys, and not with beauty as a criterion for marriage.
61 J. d'Emilio and E. Freedman, *Intimate Matters: A History of Sexuality in America* (New York: Harper and Row, 1988), p. 291.
62 K. Peiss, "On Beauty . . . and the History of Business," in P. Scranton (ed.), *Beauty and Business: Commerce, Gender, and Culture in Modern America* (London: Routledge, 2001), pp. 7–23 (p. 10).
63 K. Peiss, *Hope in a Jar: The Making of America's Beauty Culture* (New York: Henry Holt, 1998), p. 142.
64 For example, in the cosmetics industry, Max Factor advertised by using movie stars. "All advertisements [for Max Factor] prominently featured screen stars, their testimonials seemed in an arrangement with the major studios that required them to endorse Max Factor." Ibid., p. 126.
65 "[M]ovie studios struck agreements with clothing manufacturers to highlight new styles. If a dress received particular notice from fans – like one worn by Bette Davis in *Letty Lynton* – it was quickly manufactured at popular prices and featured in department stores." Peiss, "On Beauty," p. 13.
66 Peiss, *Hope in a Jar*, p. 249.
67 Ibid., p. 114.
68 Ibid., p. 142.
69 Ibid.
70 L. Banner, *American Beauty* (New York: Knopf, 1983), p. 264.
71 T. Pendergast, *Creating the Modern Man: American magazines and consumer culture, 1900–1950* (Columbia: University of Missouri Press, 2000); B. Osgerby, "A Pedigree of the Consuming Male: Masculinity, Consumption, and the American 'Leisure Class,'" in B. Benwell (ed.), *Masculinity and Men's Lifestyle Magazines* (Oxford: Blackwell, 2003), pp. 57–86 (pp. 61–2).
72 Osgerby, "A Pedigree of the Consuming Male," p. 62.
73 Ibid., p. 77.
74 Peiss, *Hope in a Jar*, p. 126.
75 J.F. Gerhard, *Desiring Revolution: Second-Wave Feminism and the Rewriting of American Sexual Thought, 1920 to 1982* (New York: Columbia University Press, 2001).
76 W. Camp, *Prospects of Love* (London: Longmans, Green, 1957).
77 http://www.brainyquote.com/quotes/authors/s/sophia_loren.html, last accessed September 29, 2011.
78 J. Nevid, "Sex Differences in Factors of Romantic Attraction," *Sex Roles*, 11(5/6) (1984), 401–11 (p. 401). See also A. Feingold, "Gender Differences in Effects of Physical Attractiveness on Romantic Attraction: A Comparison across Five Research Paradigms," *Journal of Personality and Social Psychology*, 59(5) (1990), 981–93; A.M. Pines,

"A Prospective Study of Personality and Gender Differences in Romantic Attraction," *Personality and Individual Differences*, 25(1) (1998), 147–57.

79 P. Eastwick and E. Finkel, "Sex Differences in Mate Preferences Revisited: Do People Know What They Initially Desire in a Romantic Partner?" *Journal of Personality and Social Psychology*, 94(2) (2008), 245–64; N.P. Li and D.T. Kenrick, "Sex Similarities and Differences in Preferences for Short-Term Mates: What, Whether, and Why," *Journal of Personality and Social Psychology*, 90(3) (2006), 468–89.

80 D.M. Buss, T.K. Shackelford, L.A. Kirkpatrick, and R.J. Larsen, "A Half Century of Mate Preferences: The Cultural Evolution of Values," *Journal of Marriage and the Family*, 63(2) (2001), 491–503.

81 Hence, if a considerable amount of contemporary psychological research has consistently shown that sexual attraction is an important factor in mate selection, it is because, as is often the case, it confuses history for nature and naturalizes the former under the guise of the latter.

82 The three cultural forces of consumer culture, psychology, and politicization of sexuality coalesced and gave rise to what sociologists have called *recreational sexuality*. "Broadly defined, the concept of recreational sexuality refers to a pleasure-based repertoire of practices and attitudes that reshapes sexual lives in late modernity. [...] Rather than rigid sexual identities, communities or politics, which characterize 'procreational sex', at the heart of this 'plastic sexuality' [...] lie more fluid sexual preferences, or 'flows of desire' – 'the desire to have new relationships with different types of persons and to experiment with alternative ways of relating to oneself and others' [...]. There is, in other words, a non-linear replacement of procreational sexual models with recreational ones." D. Kaplan, "Theories of Sexual and Erotic Power" (unpublished manuscript, forthcoming), pp. 3–4. See also D. Kaplan, "Sexual Liberation and the Creative Class in Israel," in S. Seidman, N. Fischer, and C. Meeks (eds), *Introducing the New Sexuality Studies* (second edition; London: Routledge, 2011), pp. 357–63.

83 Webster and Driskell refer to *beauty* as status, and I suggest expanding the concept to *sexiness* as status, combining it with Zetterberg's observations. See M. Webster and J.E. Driskell, "Beauty as Status," *American Journal of Sociology*, 89 (1983), 140–65; H. Zetterberg, "The Secret Ranking," *Journal of Marriage and the Family*, 28(2) (1966),134–42.

84 For an extensive analysis of morality and class, see M. Lamont, *Money, Morals, and Manners: The Culture of the French and American Upper-Middle Class* (Chicago: University of Chicago Press, 1992). For a different aspect, see N.K. Beisel, *Imperiled Innocents: Anthony Comstock and Family Reproduction in Victorian America* (Princeton: Princeton University Press, 1998).

85 Zetterberg, "The Secret Ranking," p. 136.

86 This is the theme of D.H. Lawrence's *Lady Chatterley's Lover* and of Tennessee Williams' *A Streetcar Named Desire*.

87 See J. Alexander, "Iconic Consciousness: The Material Feeling of Meaning," *Environment and Planning D: Society and Space*, 26 (2008), 782–94.

88 G.S. Becker, "A Theory of Marriage: Part I," The Journal of Political Economy, 81(4) (1973), 813–46 (p. 814).

89 N. Wolf, *The Beauty Myth: How Images of Beauty Are Used Against Women* (New York: Random House, 1990).

90 F. Attwood, *Mainstreaming Sex: The Sexualization of Western Culture* (New York: I.B. Tauris, 2009); A.C. Hall and M.J. Bishop, *Pop-Porn: Pornography in American Culture* (Westwood, CT: Greenwood Publishing Group, 2007); B. McNair, *Striptease Culture: Sex, Media and the Democratization of Desire* (London: Routledge, 2002); P. Paul, *Pornified: How Pornography is Transforming Our Lives, Our Relationships, and Our Families* (New York: Times Books, 2005); C.M. Roach, *Stripping, Sex, and Popular Culture* (Oxford: Berg Publishers, 2007).

91 Zetterberg, "The Secret Ranking," p. 135.

92 Webster and Driskell, "Beauty as Status."

93 See A. Green, "The Social Organization of Desire: The Sexual Fields Approach," *Sociological Theory*, 26(1) (2008), 25–50.

94 Ibid., p. 29; J. Levi-Martin and M. George, "Theories of Sexual Stratification: Toward an Analytics of the Sexual Field and a Theory of Sexual Capital," *Sociological Theory*, 24(2) (2006), 107–32.

95 J. Kilmer-Purcell, "Twenty-Five to One Odds," in M. Taeckens (ed.), *Love Is a Four Letter Word: True Stories of Breakups, Bad Relationships, and Broken Hearts* (New York: Plume, 2009), pp. 106–19 (p. 108).

96 G. Christina, "Are We Having Sex Now or What?" in A. Soble and N. Power (eds), *The Philosophy of Sex: Contemporary Readings* (Totowa, NJ: Rowman & Littlefield, 2008), pp. 23–9 (p. 24).

97 D. Kaplan, *Sex, Shame and Excitation: The Self in Emotional Capitalism* (unpublished manuscript, n.d.), p. 2.

98 C. Hakim, *Work–Lifestyle Choices in the 21st Century: Preference Theory* (Oxford: Oxford University Press, 2000), pp. 160–3; R. Erikson and J.H. Goldthorpe, *The Constant Flux: A Study of Class Mobility in Industrial Societies* (Oxford: Clarendon Press, 1993), pp. 231–77; C. Thélot, *Tel Père, Tel Fils? Position Sociale et Origine Familiale* (Paris: Dunod, 1982).

Chapter 3   Commitment Phobia and the New Architecture of Romantic Choice

1 F.W. Nietzsche, *The Genealogy of Morals* (New York: Courier Dover Publications, 2003 [1887]), p. 34.

2 M. Dowd, "Blue Is the New Black," *New York Times*, September 19, 2009.

3 See A. Honneth, *Das Recht der Freiheit* (Frankfurt: Suhrkamp Verlag, 2011).

4   M.J. Sandel, "The Procedural Republic and the Unencumbered Self," *Political Theory*, 12(1) (1984), 81–96; C. Taylor, *Sources of the Self* (Cambridge: Cambridge University Press, 1992); M. Waltzer, *Spheres of Justice: A Defense of Pluralism and Equality* (New York: Basic Books, 1983).

5   A. Giddens, *Modernity and Self-Identity* (Stanford: Stanford University Press, 1991); B.S. Turner and C. Rojek, *Society and Culture* (London: Sage, 2001); M. Weber, *The Protestant Ethic and the Spirit of Capitalism* (London: Routledge, 2002 [1930]).

6   See, e.g., D. Cornell, *At the Heart of Freedom: Feminism, Sex, and Equality* (Princeton: Princeton University Press, 1998).

7   Pascal Bruckner reminds us that freedom in the sexual and emotional realm contains a range of various and complexly related meanings: freedom from external authority (that of parents, community, or men); being open and available to multiple life and sexual options; or living to the fullest one's fantasies and pleasure. See P. Bruckner, *Le Paradoxe Amoureux* (Paris: Grasset & Fasquelle, 2009). Pepper Schwartz illustrates the practice of such sexual relations in what she calls "peer marriages." See P. Schwartz, *Love between Equals: How Peer Marriage Really Works* (New York: Free Press, 1994).

8   D.T. Elwood and C. Jencks, "The Spread of Single-Parent Families in the United States since 1960," in D.P. Moynihan, T.M. Smeeding, and L. Rainwater (eds), *The Future of the Family* (New York: Russell Sage Foundation, 2006), pp. 25–64.

9   A. Thornton, "Changing Attitudes toward Family Issues in the United States," *Journal of Marriage and the Family*, 51(4) (1989), 873–93.

10 D. Yankelovich, *New Rules: Searching for Self-Fulfillment in a World Turned Upside Down* (New York: Random House, 1981), quoted in R. Bellah, W. Sullivan, A. Swidler, and S. Tipton, *Habits of the Heart: Individualism and Commitment in American Life* (Berkeley: University of California Press, 1985), pp. 90–3.

11 Ibid.

12 The number of cohabiting households increased from 1.1 million in 1977 to 4.9 million in 1997. Cohabiting households made up 1.5% of all households in 1977, increasing to 4.8% by 1997. See L.M. Casper and P.N. Cohen, "How Does POSSLQ Measure Up? Historical Estimates of Cohabitation," *Demography*, 37(2) (2000), 237–45.

13 R. Schoen and R.M. Weinick, "Partner Choice in Marriages and Cohabitations," *Journal of Marriage and the Family*, 55(2) (1993), 408–14.

14 Bellah et al., *Habits of the Heart*, pp. 89–90.

15 Chapter 4 of *Habits of the Heart* draws mainly on Ann Swidler's research on love and marriage. See ibid., pp. 85–112.

16 D. Harding and C. Jencks, "Changing Attitudes toward Premarital Sex: Cohort, Period, and Aging Effects," *Public Opinion Quarterly*, 67(2) (2003), 211–26.

17 Debate on the meaning and consequences of these changes has been ongoing since the 1980s. For example, Bellah et al. (*Habits of the*

Heart) argue that these changes undermine commitment through the use of therapeutic language and the ideal of self-realization. Francesca Cancian, meanwhile, criticizes them for over-emphasizing the model of individual independence and neglecting the model of mutual inter-dependence, and argues that commitment remains a central feature of marriage. See F.M. Cancian, *Love in America* (Cambridge: Cambridge University Press, 1987). However, in this chapter I explore the issue of commitment in contemporary romantic relations and marriage from a different perspective – I ask how the structure of commitment in these relationships has changed, and for what reasons.

18 N.F. Cott, "Passionlessness: An Interpretation of Victorian Sexual Ideology, 1790–1850," *Signs: Journal of Women in Culture and Society*, 4 (1978), 219–36 (p. 222).

19 S. Richardson, *Pamela: or Virtue Rewarded* (Harmondsworth: Penguin Books, 1985 [1740]).

20 Montesquieu's *Persian Letters* prefigured this theme of virtuous resis-tance, telling us that Roxanne became Usbeck's favorite wife by resist-ing his advances and thus displaying her virtue.

21 I. Watt, "The New Woman: Samuel Richardson's *Pamela*," in R.L. Coser (ed.), *The Family: Its Structure and Functions* (New York: St Martin's Press, 1964), pp. 281–2, cited in Cott, "Passionlessness," p. 223.

22 Cott, "Passionlessness," p. 228.

23 Ibid., p. 233.

24 E.K. Rothman, *Hands and Hearts: A History of Courtship in America* (New York: Basic Books, 1984), p. 32.

25 Ibid., p. 34.

26 Ibid.

27 Ibid., p. 35.

28 Ibid., p. 11.

29 Ibid., p. 33.

30 Ibid., p. 70.

31 Ibid., p. 71.

32 T. Kenslea, *The Sedgwicks in Love: Courtship, Engagement, and Mar-riage in the Early Republic* (Boston: Northeastern University Press, 2006), p. 49.

33 L.A. Gaeddert, *A New England Love Story: Nathaniel Hawthorne and Sophia Peabody* (New York: Dial Press, 1980), p. 81.

34 K. Lystra, *Searching the Heart* (New York: Oxford University Press, 1989), p. 21.

35 L. Stone, *Broken Lives: Separation and Divorce in England 1660–1857* (Oxford: Oxford University Press, 1993), p. 88.

36 S. Chojnacki, "Dowries and Kinsmen in Early Renaissance Venice," *Journal of Interdisciplinary History*, 5(4) (1975), 571–600.

37 Stone, *Broken Lives*.

38 In nineteenth-century England, women were more likely to be respon-sible for breach of promise to marry. See ibid.

39 A. Hannay, *Kierkegaard: A Biography* (Cambridge: Cambridge Uni-versity Press, 2001), pp. 158–9.

40 *http://www.lipstickalley.com/f41/how-go-casual-committed-138565/*, last accessed October 10, 2011.

41 *http://www.urbandictionary.com/define.php?term=Commitment*, last accessed October 10, 2011.

42 US Census Bureau Report: *Number, Timing and Duration of Marriages and Divorces: 2001*, February 2005.

43 R. Schoen and V. Canudas-Romo, "Timing Effects on First Marriage: Twentieth-Century Experience in England and Wales and the USA," *Population Studies*, 59(2) (2005), 135–46.

44 The proportion of one-person households increased by 9%, from 17% in 1970 to 26% in 2007. Including other non-family households, this category is estimated to be a third of total households in the US. See US Census Bureau Report: *America's Families and Living Arrangements: 2007*, September 2009.

45 According to the US Census Bureau Report, *Number, Timing and Duration of Marriages and Divorces: 2001*, by age 40, about 15% of men and women born between 1935 and 1939 had been married two or more times. This proportion increased to 22% for those in the first baby-boom cohort born between 1945 and 1949. In the next ten years, the proportion remained mainly unchanged for women but fell to 17% for men born between 1955 and 1959.

46 C. Strohm, J. Seltzer, S. Cochran, and W. Mays, "Living Apart Together: Relationships in the United States," *Demographic Research*, 21(7) (2009), 177–214.

47 Andrew Cherlin conceptualizes this change as a move from a companionate model of marriage to an individualized one. See A.J. Cherlin, "The Deinstitutionalization of American Marriage," *Journal of Marriage and Family*, 66(4) (2004), 848–61.

48 Commitment phobia is most common in upper-middle-class men who control the social, cultural, and economic resources, and middle-class, educated, and economically independent women who are interested in the heterosexual model of family. Thus, the description in this chapter is less relevant to men and women who do not fit into these categories.

49 J. Bernard, *The Future of Marriage* (New Haven: Yale University Press, 1982).

50 S.F. Berk, *The Gender Factory: The Apportionment of Work in American Households* (New York: Plenum Press, 1985).

51 S.L. Nock, *Marriage in Men's Lives* (Oxford: Oxford University Press, 1998).

52 G. Kaufman and F. Goldscheider, "Do Men 'Need' a Spouse More Than Women? Perceptions of the Importance of Marriage for Men and Women," *Sociological Quarterly*, 48(1) (2007), 29–46.

53 G.S. Becker, *A Treatise on the Family* (Cambridge, MA: Harvard University Press, 1981). For a critique of this theory, see V.K. Oppenheimer, "Women's Employment and the Gain to Marriage: The Specialization and Trading Model," *Annual Review of Sociology*, 23 (1997), 431–53.

54 Conversely, the theory predicts that an increase in men's wages should exert a strong influence on marriage and divorce, hastening marriage and increasing its overall prevalence.

55 For similar academic explanations, see D.M. Buss and D.P. Schmitt, "Sexual Strategies Theory: An Evolutionary Perspective on Human Mating," Psychological Review, 100 (1993), 204–32; D. Symons, *The Evolution of Human Sexuality* (Oxford: Oxford University Press, 1979); R. Trivers, *Social Evolution* (Menlo Park, CA: Benjamin/ Cummings, 1985).

56 M.S. Kimmel, *The Gender of Desire: Essays on Male Sexuality* (Albany: SUNY Press, 2005), p. 32.

57 A. Vincent-Buffault, *History of Tears: Sensibility and Sentimentality in France* (New York: St Martin's Press, 1991); Cancian, *Love in America*; E. Illouz, *Consuming the Romantic Utopia: Love and the Cultural Contradictions of Capitalism* (Berkeley: University of California Press, 1997).

58 N. Chodorow, *The Reproduction of Mothering: Psychoanalysis and the Sociology of Gender* (Berkeley: University of California Press, 1979); N. Chodorow, "Oedipal Asymmetries and Heterosexual Knots," *Social Problems*, 23(4) (1976), 454–68.

59 S. Firestone, *The Dialectic of Sex: The Case for Feminist Revolution* (New York: Bantam, 1970), p. 127.

60 A. Rich, "Compulsory Heterosexuality and Lesbian Existence," *Signs*, 5(4) (1980), 631–60.

61 B. Latour, *We Have Never Been Modern* (Cambridge, MA: Harvard University Press, 1993).

62 B. Latour, *Pandora's Hope: Essays on the Reality of Science Studies* (Cambridge, MA: Harvard University Press, 1999), pp. 145–73.

63 J. Tosh, *Manliness and Masculinities in Nineteenth-Century Britain: Essays on Gender, Family and Empire* (London: Pearson Longman, 2005), p. 35.

64 Ibid., p. 35.

65 Here I should clarify that I do not refer to sexuality as male status as a process of social distinction, employed as a substitute for traditional male distinction mechanisms. Rather, I claim that there are two parallel processes that create a matrix: the attenuation of traditional male status symbols, on the one hand, and the centralization of sexuality as status, on the other.

66 F. Fukuyama, *The Great Disruption: Human Nature and the Reconstitution of Social Order* (Glencoe, IL: Free Press, p. 121).

67 This indeed is what makes the historical figure of Casanova so modern, precisely the fact that although having no personal fortune, he was able to gain sexual access to a large number of women from different socio-economic levels.

68 Fukuyama, *The Great Disruption*, p. 121.

69 M. Donaldson, "What is Hegemonic Masculinity?" *Theory and Society*, 22(5) (1993), 643–57 (p. 645).

70 S. Hite, *The Hite Report on Male Sexuality* (New York: Ballantine Books, 1981), p. 479.

71 F. Attwood, *Mainstreaming Sex: The Sexualization of Western Culture* (London: I.B. Tauris, 2009); A.C. Hall and M.J. Bishop, *Pop-Porn: Pornography in American Culture* (Westport, CT: Greenwood Publishing Group, 2007); B. McNair, *Striptease Culture: Sex, Media and the Democratization of Desire* (London: Routledge, 2002).

72 E. Blackwood, "The Specter of the Patriarchal Man," *American Ethnologist*, 32(1) (2005), 42–5 (p. 44).

73 R. Collins, "A Conflict Theory of Sexual Stratification," *Social Problems*, 19(1) (1971), 3–21 (p. 3).

74 S. Brownmiller, *Against Our Will: Men, Women, and Rape* (New York: Bantam Books, 1976); Chodorow, "Oedipal Asymmetries and Heterosexual Knots" and *The Reproduction of Mothering*; Rich, "Compulsory Heterosexuality and Lesbian Existence".

75 A. Rossi, "Children and Work in the Lives of Women" (paper delivered at the University of Arizona, Tucson, February 1976) cited in Rich, "Compulsory Heterosexuality and Lesbian Existence," p. 631.

76 Rosanna Hertz illustrates another strategy addressing this problem in which middle-class, educated, and economically independent women separate motherhood and marriage (or any other form of relationship), and choose to become mothers "on their own." This is another possible reaction to the same ecology of choice constraining women. See R. Hertz, *Single by Chance, Mothers by Choice: How Women Are Choosing Parenthood Without Marriage and Creating the New American Family* (Oxford: Oxford University Press, 2008).

77 Elwood and Jencks, "The Spread of Single-Parent Families in the United States since 1960."

78 Obviously, this claim should be greatly nuanced as women in Spain and Italy are opting out of motherhood, while American women are still oriented to it.

79 *http://sleeping-around.blogspot.com/search?updated-min=2008-01-01T00%3A00%3A00Z&updated-max=2009-01-01T00%3A00%3A00Z&max-results=50*, last accessed October 11, 2011 (no longer online).

80 H. Fielding, *Bridget Jones's Diary* (London: Thorndike Press, 1998), p. 34.

81 J. Easton, J. Confer, C. Goetz, and D. Buss, "Reproduction Expediting: Sexual Motivations, Fantasies, and the Ticking Biological Clock," *Personality and Individual Differences*, 49(5) (2010), 516–20.

82 Undoubtedly, advances in reproductive technologies are now pushing these age constraints and limits further. But by and large, these remain marginal.

83 *http://seductiontutor.blogspot.com/2006/09/4-women-to-avoid.html*, last accessed October 11, 2011.

84 This refers, of course, to commitment to a relationship *with* children, not just to a romantic partner or relationship.

85 C.A. MacKinnon, *Sexual Harassment of Working Women: A Case of Sex Discrimination* (New Haven: Yale University Press, 1979).

86 However, Robert Schoen and Robin Weinick ("Partner Choice in Marriages and Cohabitations") demonstrate that in cohabitations there is a slight tendency toward male hypergamy, reinforcing the belief that in cohabitation the education of the female is as important as that of the male.

87 K. Peter and L. Horn, *Gender Differences in Participation and Completion of Undergraduate Education and How They Have Changed Over Time* (NCES 2005–169) (US Department of Education, National Center for Education Statistics, Washington, DC: US Government Printing Office, 2005); A. Sum, N. Fogg, and P. Harrington, with I. Khatiwada, S. Palma, N. Pond, and P. Tobar, "The Growing Gender Gaps in College Enrollment and Degree Attainment in the US and Their Potential Economic and Social Consequences" (prepared for the Business Roundtable, Washington DC: Center for Labor Market Studies, 2003).

88 S.K. Lewis and V.K. Oppenheimer show that women residents in educationally less favorable marriage markets are more likely to marry men with lesser education compared to them, and their chance of doing so increases with age more than for residents in more favorable markets. See S.K. Lewis and V.K. Oppenheimer, "Educational Assortative Mating across Marriage Markets: Non-Hispanic Whites in the United States," *Demography*, 37(1) (2000), 29–40; V.K. Oppenheimer, "Women's Rising Employment and the Future of the Family in Industrial Societies," *Population and Development Review*, 20(2) (1994), 293–342.

89 Eric D. Gould and M. Daniele Paserman show that higher male wage inequality in a city lowers the marriage rate of women and makes them search longer for their first and second husbands. See E.D. Gould and M.D. Paserman, "Waiting for Mr Right: Rising Inequality and Declining Marriage Rates," *Journal of Urban Economics*, 53 (2003), 257–81.

90 This probably explains also why since 1980 there has been an increase in the number of marriages in which women are better educated than their husbands, a trend away from the traditional reverse practice. See Z. Qian, "Changes in Assortative Mating: The Impact of Age and Education, 1970–1990," *Demography*, 35(3) (1998), 279–92. As Qian notes, there is an age differentiation in women's pairing strategy: women who form unions at younger ages tend to follow the traditional pattern of educational hypergamy, whereas women who form unions at older ages (above 30) tend to be similar to their male counterparts in educational assortative mating (p. 291).

91 Qian notes also that in 1990, for unions involving men who were older than their partners, the odds of cohabitation were less than the odds of marriage, whereas for partnerships where the woman was older, cohabitation was twice as likely as marriage (ibid., p. 283).

92 Lewis and Oppenheimer, "Educational Assortative Mating across Marriage Markets," p. 36.

93 This category includes two aspects: out of a relationship, and while in a relationship. While both indicate fragmentation of commitment, the

latter can be situation-bound, a short-term and implicit commitment to an undefined relationship, or a specific and explicit commitment, on a scale of "seriousness" measured by degree of obligation.

94 *http://www.nytimes.com/2008/05/04/fashion/04love.html*, last accessed October 11, 2011.

95 Firestone, *The Dialectic of Sex*, p. 130.

96 *http://www.ivillage.com/men-confess-what-makes-them-fall-love-0/4-a-283713*, last accessed October 11, 2011.

97 E. Faison, "The Neglected Variety Drive: A Useful Concept for Consumers' Behavior," *Journal of Consumer Research*, 4(3) (1977), 172–5.

98 For example, R.W. Firestone and J. Catlett, *Fear of Intimacy* (Washington, DC: American Psychological Association, 1999); M.D. Sherman and M.H. Thelen, "Fear of Intimacy Scale: Validation and Extension with Adolescents," *Journal of Social and Personal Relationships*, 13 (1996), 507–21.

99 R. Schenk at *http://ingrimayne.com/econ/Introduction/Scarcity NChoice.html*, last accessed October 11, 2011.

100 Fielding, *Bridget Jones's Diary*, p. 102.

101 R. Belk, G. Guliz, and S. Askegaard, "The Fire of Desire: A Multisited Inquiry into Consumer Passion," *Journal of Consumer Research*, 30(3) (2003), 326–51 (p. 330).

102 Ibid.

103 E. Fein and S. Schneider, *The Rules: Time-Tested Secrets for Capturing the Heart of Mr Right* (New York: Warner Books, 1995), pp. xvii–xviii.

104 For a description of the transgressive quest for sexual pleasure and renewed desire within "peer marriages," see Schwartz, *Love between Equals*, ch. 3.

105 *http://dating.about.com/od/datingresources/a/SecondThought_2.htm*, last accessed February 15, 2006 (no longer available online).

106 *http://www.uncommonforum.com/viewtopic.php?t=15806*, last accessed October 11, 2011.

107 H. Frankfurt, *The Reasons of Love* (Princeton: Princeton University Press, 2004), p. 46.

108 The choice of a partner can involve different and sometimes contradicting sets of criteria for the same object of evaluation. For example, a partner can be evaluated using the criteria of attractiveness, consumption habits, character, emotional or psychological match, or his/her status.

109 A. MacFarlane, *Marriage and Love in England: Modes of Reproduction, 1300–1840* (Oxford: Basil Blackwell, 1986), p. 296.

110 Or any other sort of couple relationship, for that matter.

111 T.D. Wilson and D.T. Gilbert, "Affective Forecasting," *Advances in Experimental Social Psychology*, 35 (2003), 345–411.

112 T.D. Wilson, "Don't Think Twice, It's All Right," *International Herald Tribune*, December 30, 2005, p. 6.

113 G. Klein, *Sources of Power: How People Make Decisions* (Cambridge, MA: MIT Press, 1999).
114 T.D. Wilson and J.W. Schooler, "Thinking Too Much: Introspection Can Reduce the Quality of Preferences and Decisions," *Journal of Personality and Social Psychology* 60(2) (1991), 181–92 (p. 182). Similarly, Chezy Ofir and Itamar Simonson demonstrate that expecting to evaluate a service or a product leads to less favorable quality and satisfaction evaluations and reduces customers' willingness to purchase and recommend the evaluated services. The negative bias of expected evaluations is observed when actual quality is either low or high, and it persists even when buyers are told explicitly to consider both the positive and negative aspects. The findings are consistent with what they call "the negativity enhancement account," indicating that unless buyers begin the evaluation task with low expectations, they tend to focus during consumption primarily on the negative aspects of product/ service quality. See C. Ofir and I. Simonson, "In Search of Negative Customer Feedback: The Effect of Expecting to Evaluate on Satisfaction Evaluations," *Journal of Marketing Research*, 38(2) (2001), 170–82.
115 Wilson and Schooler, "Thinking Too Much."
116 Similarly, Ravi Dhar suggests that there is a greater tendency to select the no-choice option (i.e., the option not to choose any of the offered alternatives) when the choice set offers several attractive alternatives, but none that can be easily justified as the best. See R. Dhar, "Consumer Preference for a No-Choice Option," *Journal of Consumer Research*, 24(2) (1997), 215–31. There is research that suggests that consumers avoid making any choice when confronted by too many or too few options. See D. Kuksov and M. Villas-Boas, "When More Alternatives Lead to Less Choice," *Marketing Science*, 29(3) (2010), 507–24.
117 According to Larry Bumpass and Hsien-Hen Lu, the percentage of marriages preceded by cohabitation rose from about 10% for those marrying between 1965 and 1974, to over 50% for those marrying between 1990 and 1994; 55% of cohabitations end in marriage, and 40% of these relationships dissolve within five years (most in the first two years). See L. Bumpass and H.-H. Lu, "Trends in Cohabitation and Implications for Children's Family Contexts in the United States," *Population Studies: A Journal of Demography*, 54(1) (2000), 29–41.
118 G. Kline, S.M. Stanley, and H.J. Markman, "Pre-engagement Cohabitation and Gender Asymmetry in Marital Commitment," *Journal of Family Psychology*, 20(4) (2006), 553–60; G. Kline et al., "Timing Is Everything: Pre-engagement Cohabitation and Increased Risk for Poor Marital Outcomes," *Journal of Family Psychology*, 18(2) (2004), 311–18.
119 W. Axinn and A. Thornton, "The Relationship between Cohabitation and Divorce: Selectivity or Causal Influence?" *Demography*, 29(3) (1992), 357–74; R. Schoen, "First Unions and the Stability of First Marriages," *Journal of Marriage and Family*, 54(2) (1992), 281–4.

120 H. Simon, "Bounded Rationality in Social Science: Today and Tomorrow," *Mind & Society*, 1(1) (2000), 25–39.

121 B. Schwartz, *The Paradox of Choice: Why More is Less* (New York: HarperCollins, 2005), p. 163.

122 D. Spechler, "Competing in My Own Reality Show," *New York Times*, June 11, 2010, *http://www.nytimes.com/2010/06/13/fashion/ 13love.html?emc=tnt&tntemail1=y*, last accessed October 11, 2011.

123 E. Lawler, T. Shane, and Y. Jeongkoo, *Social Commitments in a Depersonalized World* (New York: Russell Sage Foundation, 2009), p. 26.

124 D. Pugmire, *Sound Sentiments: Integrity in the Emotions* (Oxford: Oxford University Press, 2005), p. 175.

125 A.J. Weigert, *Mixed Emotions: Certain Steps toward Understanding Ambivalence* (Albany: SUNY Press, 1991), p. 34.

126 Ibid., p. 34.

127 Quoted in ibid., p. 22.

128 A. Sen, "Rational Fools: A Critique of the Behavioral Foundations of Economic Theory," *Philosophy and Public Affairs*, 6(4) (1977), 317–44 (p. 329).

129 J.-L. Marion, *The Erotic Phenomenon* (Chicago: University of Chicago Press, 2007 [2003]), p. 174.

130 R. Craig, *Promising Language: Betrothal in Victorian Law and Fiction* (Albany: SUNY Press, 2000), p. 6.

131 A. Seligman, *Ritual and Its Consequences: An Essay on the Limits of Sincerity* (Oxford: Oxford University Press, 2008), p. 115.

132 Bellah et al., *Habits of the Heart*, p. 90.

133 Z. Bauman, *Consuming Life* (Cambridge: Polity Press, 2007).

134 T. Kreider, "The Referendum," *New York Times*, September 17, 2009, *http://happydays.blogs.nytimes.com/2009/09/17/the-referendum/ ?scp=3-b&sq=Light+Years&st=nyt*, last accessed October 11, 2011.

135 The temporal and ontological segmentation of the self structures commitment as a situational, differentiated, and temporary action.

136 J. Derrida, *Mémoires: For Paul de Man* (New York: Columbia University Press, 1986), p. 94.

137 A. Giddens, *The Transformation of Intimacy* (Cambridge: Polity Press, 1992).

138 In this utilitarian model of love – as a short-term relationship – as described by Bellah et al., "love becomes no more than an exchange, with no binding rules except the obligation of full and open communication. A relationship should give each partner what he or she needs while it lasts, and if the relationship ends, at least both partners will have received a reasonable return of their investment." *Habits of the Heart*, p. 108.

139 *http://www.urbandictionary.com/define.php?term=commitment-phobe*, last accessed October 11, 2011.

140 See Hannay, *Kierkegaard*, p. 155.

141 P. Regan and C. Dreyer, "Lust? Love? Status? Young Adults' Motives for Engaging in Casual Sex," *Journal of Psychology and Human Sexu-*

ality, 11(1) (1999), 1–23; M.B. Oliver and J.S. Hyde, "Gender Differences in Sexuality: A Meta-Analysis," *Psychological Bulletin*, 114 (1993), 29–51.

142 R. Fisman, S.S. Iyengar, E. Kamenica, and I. Simonson, "Gender Differences in Mate Selection: Evidence from a Speed-Dating Experiment," *Quarterly Journal of Economics*, 121 (2006), 673–97; P.C. Regan, L.S. Levin, S. Sprecher, F.S. Christopher, and R. Cate, "What Characteristics Do Men and Women Desire in Their Short-Term Sexual and Long-Term Romantic Partners?" *Journal of Psychology & Human Sexuality*, 12(3) (2000), 1–21; S. Stewart, H. Stinnett, and L.B. Rosenfeld, "Sex Differences in Desired Characteristics of Short-Term and Long-Term Relationship Partners," *Journal of Social and Personal Relationships*, 17(6) (2000), 843–53. Historically, however, men and women came to value physical attractiveness more in the second half of the twentieth century.

143 L. Cubbins and K. Tanfer, "The Influence of Gender on Sex: A Study of Men's and Women's Self-Reported High-Risk Sex Behavior," *Archives of Sexual Behavior*, 29(3) (2000), 229–55.

144 Collins, "A Conflict Theory of Sexual Stratification," p. 7; W. Burgess and P. Wallin, *Engagement and Marriage* (New York: Lippincott, 1953).

145 For a different strategy, taken by middle-class women who separate marriage (or any other form of dyadic relationship) and motherhood, see Hertz, *Single by Chance, Mothers by Choice*.

146 *http://www.nytimes.com/2008/05/04/fashion/04love.html?pagewanted=2*, last accessed October 11, 2011.

147 *http://parents.berkeley.edu/advice/family/committment.html*, last accessed October 11, 2011.

148 L.S. Stepp, *Unhooked: How Young Women Pursue Sex, Delay Love and Lose at Both* (New York: Riverhead Books, 2007), p. 10.

149 Ibid, p. 4.

150 C. Townsend, *Breaking the Rules: Confessions of a Bad Girl* (London: John Murray, 2008).

151 *http://www.nytimes.com/2008/05/04/fashion/04love.html?pagewanted=3*, last accessed October 11, 2011.

152 E. Jong, *Fear of Flying* (New York: Signet, 1974), p. 11.

Chapter 4   The Demand for Recognition: Love and the Vulnerability of the Self

1 E. Dickinson, *The Poems of Emily Dickinson*, ed. R.W. Franklin, Reading edition (Cambridge, MA: The Belknap Press, 1999), pp. 352–3.

2 H. von Kleist, *Penthesilea* (New York: HarperCollins, 1998 [1808]), p. 104.

3 R. Descartes, *Discourse on the Method and Meditations on First Philosophy* (Cambridge, MA: Hackett Publishing Company, 1998 [1641]).

4   C. Taylor, *Sources of the Self* (Cambridge: Cambridge University Press, 1992).
5   J.-L. Marion, *The Erotic Phenomenon* (Chicago: University of Chicago Press, 2007 [2003]), p. 22.
6   Ibid.
7   One of the first examples is Plato's *Phaedrus*.
8   J.W. Goethe, *The Sorrows of Young Werther* (New York: New American Library, 1962 [1774]), pp. 50–1.
9   D. Hume, *A Treatise of Human Nature* (Oxford: Oxford University Press, 1888 [1739–40]), bk II, pt ii, sec. 11, p. 394.
10 S. Blackburn, *Lust: The Seven Deadly Sins* (Oxford: Oxford University Press, 2006), p. 82.
11 S. Freud, "Being in Love and Hypnosis," in J. Strachey (ed.), *The Standard Edition of the Complete Psychological Works of Sigmund Freud*, vol. XVIII (London: Hogarth Press and the Institute of Psycho-Analysis, 1953 [1922]), p. 112.
12 Quoted in A. Carson, *Eros: The Bittersweet* (Princeton: Princeton University Press, 1998), p. 39.
13 Blackburn, *Lust*, p. 83.
14 L. Boltanski and L. Thévenot, *On Justification: Economies of Worth* (Princeton: Princeton University Press, 2006 [1991]).
15 J. Browne, *Dating for Dummies* (New York: Wiley Publishing, 2006).
16 J. Gray, *Mars and Venus on a Date* (New York: HarperCollins, 1997).
17 N.C. Warren, *Date . . . or Soul Mate? How to Know If Someone Is Worth Pursuing in Two Dates or Less* (Nashville: Thomas Nelson Publishers, 2002).
18 Gray, *Mars and Venus on a Date*, p. 179.
19 Warren, *Date . . . or Soul Mate?*, p. xviii.
20 E.S. Person, *Dreams of Love and Fateful Encounters: The Power of Romantic Passion* (New York: Norton Company, 1988), p. 38.
21 Ibid., p. 59.
22 T. Kenslea, *The Sedgwicks in Love: Courtship, Engagement, and Marriage in the Early Republic* (Boston: Northeastern University Press, 2006), p. 46.
23 E.K. Rothman, *Hands and Hearts: A History of Courtship in America* (New York: Basic Books, 1984), p. 98.
24 Ibid., pp. 98–9.
25 Ibid., p. 19.
26 Ibid.
27 S. Harris, *The Courtship of Olivia Langdon and Mark Twain* (Cambridge: Cambridge University Press, 1996), p. 96.
28 D. Karlin (ed.), *Robert Browning and Elizabeth Barrett: The Courtship Correspondence 1845–1846* (Oxford: Clarendon Press, 1989), p. 124.
29 Ibid., p. 218.
30 Ibid., p. 229.

31   W. Littlefield (ed.), *Love Letters of Famous Poets and Novelists* (New York: The J. McBride Co., 1909), p. 29.

32   Kenslea, *The Sedgwicks in Love*, p. 156.

33   S. Shapiro, *Five Men Who Broke My Heart* (New York: Delacorte Press, 2004), p. 29.

34   Person, *Dreams of Love and Fateful Encounters*, p. 44.

35   This stands in contrast to another type of romantic interaction in which one's worth need not be re-affirmed, precisely because one's social worth and social standing are both known to all parties and non-negotiable. To refer again to the world of Jane Austen, when Harriet, Emma's charming friend, aspires to marry men who are of a higher social status than she is, and when she is, as we would say today, "rejected" by them, her feelings of rejection do not affect, let alone crush, her sense of self; rather, she is simply embarrassed because she committed a social mistake in evaluating her own and others' social position. Her sense of *worth* is not affected, only her sense of appropriateness. In contrast, in modernity, social value does not precede interactions as such but is constituted in and through them.

36   Person, *Dreams of Love and Fateful Encounters*, p. 38.

37   A. Honneth, "Personal Identity and Disrespect," in S. Seidman and J. Alexander (eds), *The New Social Theory Reader: Contemporary Debates* (London: Routledge, 2001), pp. 39–45 (p. 39).

38   U. Beck and E. Beck-Gernsheim, *The Normal Chaos of Love* (Cambridge: Polity Press, 1995); M. Evans, *Love: An Unromantic Discussion* (Cambridge: Polity Press, 2003); A. Giddens, *The Transformation of Intimacy* (Cambridge: Polity Press, 1992); E. Illouz, *Consuming the Romantic Utopia: Love and the Cultural Contradictions of Capitalism* (Berkeley: University of California Press, 1997); L. Stone, *The Family, Sex and Marriage in England, 1500–1800* (New York: Harper and Row, 1977). My current book takes a different stand toward this problem, as will be demonstrated in the following pages.

39   R. Collins, *Interaction Ritual Chains* (Princeton: Princeton University Press, 2004); R. Collins, "On the Microfoundations of Macrosociology," *American Journal of Sociology*, 86(5) (1981), 984–1014.

40   L. Fraser, "Our Way of Saying Goodbye," *The New York Times*, May 30, 2010, *http://www.nytimes.com/2010/05/30/fashion/30love. html?emc=tnt&tntemail1=y*, last accessed October 12, 2011.

41   A. Honneth, *The Struggle for Recognition: The Moral Grammar of Social Conflicts* (Cambridge: Polity Press, 1995).

42   Marion, *The Erotic Phenomenon*.

43   B. Jacobson and S.J. Gordon, *The Shy Single: A Bold Guide to Dating for the Less-Than-Bold Dater* (Emmaus, PA: Rodale, 2004), pp. 4–5.

44   A. Honneth,"Unsichtbarkeit: zur Epistemologie von Anerkennung," in *Unsichtbarkeit: Stationen einer Theorie der Intersubjekvität* (Frankfurt: Suhrkamp, 2003), pp. 10–27.

45   Jacobson and Gordon, *The Shy Single*, p. 15.

46   Ibid., p. 17.

47 V. Van Gogh, *Complete Letters* (New York: New York Graphic Society, 1959), p. 254.

48 C. Townsend, *Breaking the Rules: Confessions of a Bad Girl* (London: John Murray, 2008), p. 283.

49 J. Franzen, "Liking Is for Cowards. Go for What Hurts," *New York Times*, May 28, 2011, *http://www.nytimes.com/2011/05/29/opinion/29franzen.html?_r=1&pagewanted=all*, last accessed October 20, 2011.

50 *http://www.glamour.com/sex-love-life/blogs/smitten/2009/02/the-one-thing-not-to-say-to-a.html*, last accessed October 12, 2011.

51 P. Paul, "A Young Man's Lament: Love Hurts," *New York Times*, July 22, 2010, *http://www.nytimes.com/2010/07/25/fashion/25Studied.html?_r=1&emc=tnt&tntemail1=y*, last accessed October 12, 2011.

52 Islamic culture had privileged this motif, as exemplified by the famous story of Leyla and Majnoun, from the seventh century.

53 I. Singer, *The Nature of Love: Courtly and Romantic* (Chicago: University of Chicago Press, 1984), p. 25.

54 Quoted in A. Clark, *Desire: A History of European Sexuality* (London: Routledge, 2008), p. 55.

55 The French brothers Goncourt could write that "la passion des choses ne vient pas de la bonté ou de la beauté pure de ses choses, elle vient surtout de leur corruption. On aimera follement une femme, pour sa putinerie, pour la méchanceté de son esprit, pour la voyoucratie de sa tête, de son coeur, de ses sens [...]. Au fond, ce qui fait l'appassionnement: c'est le *faisandage* des êtres et des choses." Quoted in M. Praz, *The Romantic Agony* (New York: Meridian Books, 1956), p. 45.

56 Quoted in ibid., p. 74.

57 Quoted in ibid., p. 72.

58 C. Nehring, *A Vindication of Love: Reclaiming Romance for the Twenty-First Century* (New York: HarperCollins, 2009), p. 232.

59 Quoted in M. MacDonald, *Mystical Bedlam: Madness, Anxiety, and Healing in Seventeenth-Century England* (Cambridge: Cambridge University Press, 1983), p. 90.

60 J. Ferrand, *A Treatise on Lovesickness* (New York: Syracuse University Press, 1990 [1610]), p. 273. I want to thank Michal Altbauer for drawing my attention to this text.

61 MacDonald, *Mystical Bedlam*, pp. 88–9.

62 Ibid., p. 100.

63 J. Butler, *Subjects of Desire: Hegelian Reflections in Twentieth-Century France* (New York: Columbia University Press, 1987), p. 77.

64 Ibid., p. 49.

65 Ibid.

66 O. Schwarz, "Negotiating Romance in Front of the Lens," *Visual Communication*, 9(2) (2010), 151–69 (p. 157).

67 Ibid.

68 R. Bellah, W. Sullivan, A. Swidler, and S. Tipton, *Habits of the Heart: Individualism and Commitment in American Life* (Berkeley: University of California Press, 1985).

69 *http://www.enotalone.com/forum/showthread.php?t=152843*, *finneganswake*, last accessed October 13, 2011.
70 Person, *Dreams of Love and Fateful Encounters*, p. 45.
71 W. Shalit, *Girls Gone Mild: Young Women Reclaim Self-Respect and Find It's Not Bad to be Good* (New York: Random House, 2007).
72 C. Bushnell, *Sex and the City* (New York: Warner Books, 1996), p. 222.
73 Townsend, *Breaking the Rules*, p. 179.
74 *http://www.nydailynews.com/lifestyle/2010/02/16/2010-02-16_online_dating_grows_in_popularity_attracting_30_percent_of_web_users_poll.html#ixzz0fmImu6AT*, last accessed October 14, 2011.
75 R. Norwood, *Women Who Love Too Much* (New York: Pocket Books, 1985), p. 3.
76 J. Austen, *Sense and Sensibility* (Harmondsworth: Penguin Books, 1994 [1811]), p. 172.
77 S. Neiman, *Moral Clarity: A Guide for Grown-Up Idealists* (London: Bodley Head Adults, 2009).
78 J. Austen, *Northanger Abbey* (Chenango Forks, NY: Wild Jot Press, 2009 [1818]), p. 125.
79 A. MacIntyre, *After Virtue: A Study in Moral Theory* (Notre Dame, IN: University of Notre Dame Press, 1984), p. 123.
80 H. de Balzac, La Femme Abandonée, Project Gutenberg, *http://www.gutenberg.org/catalog/world/readfile?fk_files=1630285&pageno=15*.
81 *http://www.medhelp.org/posts/show/670415*, last accessed October 14, 2011.
82 S. Schlosberg, *The Curse of the Singles Table: The True Story of 1001 Nights without Sex* (New York: Warner Books, 2004), p. 55.
83 T. Russell, "Alone When the Bedbugs Bite," *New York Times*, November 21, 2010, *http://www.nytimes.com/2010/11/21/fashion/21Modern.html?_r=1&emc=tnt&tntemail1=y*, last accessed October 14, 2011.
84 H. Fielding, *Bridget Jones's Diary* (London: Thorndike Press, 1998), pp. 167–8.
85 Compare A. Honneth and A. Margalit, "Recognition," *Aristotelian Society, Supplementary Volumes*, 75 (2001), 111–39.
86 *http://www.naughtygirl.typepad.com/*, last accessed October 14, 2011.
87 *http://www.helium.com/items/477586-ways-to-avoid-emotionally-unavailable-men*, last accessed October 14, 2011.
88 *http://www.therulesbook.com/rule10.html*, last accessed October 13, 2010 (no longer available online).
89 *http://www.simplysolo.com/relationships/love_strategies.html*, last accessed October 14, 2011.
90 Susan Anderson, "Where Did My Self-Doubt Come From?," *http://susanandersonlcsw.wordpress.com/tag/self-esteem*, last accessed October 14, 2011.
91 *http://www.ynet.co.il/articles/0,7340,L-3320096,00.html* (in Hebrew) last accessed October 14, 2011.

92 H. Arendt, *The Human Condition* (New York: Doubleday Anchor Books, 1959), p. 252.

Chapter 5   Love, Reason, Irony

1 J.M. Coetzee, *Disgrace* (Harmondsworth: Penguin Books, 1999), p. 13.
2 J. Barnes, *Love, etc.* (New York: Alfred A. Knopf, 2011), p. 115.
3 Quoted in M. Berman, *All That is Solid Melts into Air* (London: Verso, 1983), p. 109.
4 Quoted in ibid., p. 95.
5 L.A. Scaff, *Fleeing the Iron Cage: Culture, Politics, and Modernity in the Thought of Max Weber* (Berkeley: University of California Press, 1991).
6 E. Illouz and S. Finkelman, "An Odd and Inseparable Couple: Emotion and Rationality in Partner Selection," *Theory and Society*, 38(4) (2009), 401–22.
7 U. Doyle (ed.), *Love Letters of Great Men and Women* (Basingstoke: Pan Macmillan, 2010), p. 76.
8 V. Nabokov, *Lolita* (New York: Vintage, 1989 [1955]), p. 39.
9 Doyle (ed.), *Love Letters of Great Men and Women*, p. 51.
10 Ibid, p. 57.
11 W. Shakespeare, *Romeo and Juliet*, Act 1, Scene 5.
12 Doyle (ed.), *Love Letters of Great Men and Women*, p. 78.
13 See, for a good example, S. Zweig, *Letter from an Unknown Woman* (New York: The Viking Press, 1932).
14 In the Middle Ages, the religious rhetoric was often mixed with the amorous rhetoric, presenting the loved one as a divinity, which had the effect of further strengthening the view of love as a total experience, in which the subject of love aims to fuse with and even be absorbed in and by the object of love. The nineteenth-century bourgeois novel presented love as the main narrative crux of one's domestic and (for women) social life. To a certain but definite extent, this model is also present in modern cinematic culture, with love, sex, and romance constituting the most widespread *telos* of characters' actions and psychological longing and the crucial knot of plot structures.
15 C. Bushnell, *Sex and the City* (New York: Warner Books, 1996), p. 2.
16 M. Dowd, "Tragedy of Comedy," *New York Times*, August 3, 2010, *http://www.nytimes.com/2010/08/04/opinion/04dowd.html*, last accessed October 17, 2011.
17 M. Weber, "Science as a Vocation," in H.H. Gerth and C.W. Mills (eds), *From Max Weber: Essays in Sociology* (Oxford: Oxford University Press, 1970 [1946]), pp. 129–56; M. Weber, *The Protestant Ethic and the Spirit of Capitalism* (London: Routledge, 2002 [1930]).
18 K. Lystra, *Searching the Heart: Women, Men, and Romantic Love in*

Nineteenth-Century America (Oxford: Oxford University Press, 1989), p. 50.

19 Wordsworth, in "Influence of Natural Objects" (1799), describes it thus:

By day or star-light, thus from my first dawn
Of childhood didst thou intertwine for me
The passions that build up our human soul;
Not with the mean and vulgar works of Man;
But with high objects, with enduring things,
With life and nature; purifying thus
The elements of feeling and of thought,
And sanctifying by such discipline
Both pain and fear, – until we recognise
A grandeur in the beatings of the heart. (emphasis added)

See W. Wordsworth, "Influence of Natural Objects," in *Poems* (London: Ginn, 1897), p. 70.

20 W. Shakespeare, *A Midsummer- Night's Dream*, Act 2, Scene 1.

21 B. Tierney and J.W. Scott, *Western Societies: A Documentary History*, Vol. II (New York: McGraw Hill, 2000), p.185.

22 R.W.B. Lewis and N. Lewis (eds), *The Letters of Edith Wharton* (New York: Charles Scribner's Sons, 1988), p. 152.

23 A. Bartels and S. Zeki, "The Neural Basis of Romantic Love," *Neuroreport*, 11(17) (2000), 3829–34; H. Fisher, *Why We Love: The Nature and Chemistry of Romantic Love* (New York: Henry Holt, 2004).

24 A. Aron et al., "Reward, Motivation, and Emotion Systems Associated with Early-Stage Intense Romantic Love," *Journal of Neurophysiology*, 94(1) (2005), 327–37.

25 D. Marazziti, H.S. Akiskal, A. Rossi, and G.B. Cassano, "Alteration of the Platelet Serotonin Transporter in Romantic Love," *Psychological Medicine*, 29 (1999), 741–5; D. Tennov, *Love and Limerence: The Experience of Being in Love* (New York: Stein and Day, 1979); A. Tesser and D.L. Paulhus, "Toward a Causal Model of Love," *Journal of Personality and Social Psychology*, 34 (1976), 1095–105.

26 Marazziti et al., "Alteration of the Platelet Serotonin Transporter in Romantic Love."

27 T. Curtis and Z. Wang, "The Neurochemistry of Pair Bonding," *Current Directions in Psychological Science*, 12(2) (2003), 49–53; T. Insel and L. Young, "The Neurobiology of Attachment," *Natural Review of Neuroscience*, 2(2) (2001), 129–36; K. Kendrick, "Oxytocin, Motherhood and Bonding," *Experimental Physiology*, 85 (2000), 111s–24s.

28 Fisher, *Why We Love*.

29 C. Townsend, *Breaking the Rules: Confessions of a Bad Girl* (New York: John Murray, 2008), p. 241.

30 D. Evans, *Emotion: The Science of Sentiment* (Oxford: Oxford University Press, 2001).

31 One should perhaps nuance this claim because psychology still viewed the experience of love as singular, and somehow tried to explain it in terms of the private history of the subject.

32 Weber, "Science as a Vocation," p. 139, quoted in N. Gane, *Max Weber and Postmodern Theory: Rationalization versus Re-enchantment* (Basingstoke: Palgrave Macmillan, 2004), p. 53.

33 Gane, *Max Weber and Postmodern Theory*, p. 53.

34 M. Berman, *The Politics of Authenticity* (New York: Columbia University Press, 1998), p. xvi.

35 This chapter deals with heterosexual love. Unless otherwise specified, our use of the term "love" should be understood in this sense.

36 S. Firestone, *Dialectic of Sex: The Case for Feminist Revolution* (New York: William Morrow and Company, 1970), p. 126.

37 B.M. Dank, "The Ethics of Sexual Correctness and the Cass Case," in *Book of Proceedings, Seventh Annual Conference on Applied Ethics*, 1996, pp. 110–15, *http://www.csulb.edu/~asc/post9.html*, last accessed October 18, 2011.

38 Coetzee, *Disgrace*, pp. 52–3.

39 HGSE Student Handbook, p. 45, *http://pdca.arts.tnua.edu.tw/reference/Harvard%A1Ghandbook.pdf*, last accessed October 18, 2011.

40 *http://www.upenn.edu/affirm-action/shisnot.html*, last accessed October 18, 2011.

41 S. Crichton et al., "Sexual Correctness: Has it Gone Too Far?" *Newsweek*, October 25, 1993, *http://www.soc.umn.edu/~samaha/cases/sexual%20correctness.htm*, last accessed October 18, 2011.

42 L. Hunt, *Politics, Culture, and Class in the French Revolution* (Berkeley: University of California Press, 2004).

43 L. Boltanski and L. Thévenot, *On Justification: Economies of Worth* (Princeton: Princeton University Press, 2006 [1991]), p. 283.

44 *http://www.revolutionhealth.com/healthy-living/relationships/love-marriage/couples-marriage/sharing-housework-equally*, last accessed October 18, 2011.

45 J. Matthews, *Lose That Loser and Find the Right Guy* (Berkeley: Ulysses Press, 2005), p. 21.

46 A. Giddens, *Modernity and Self-Identity* (Stanford: Stanford University Press, 1991), pp. 70–108; A. Giddens, *The Transformation of Intimacy* (Cambridge: Polity Press, 1992), pp. 49–64.

47 E. Illouz, *Cold Intimacies: The Making of Emotional Capitalism* (Cambridge: Polity Press, 2007).

48 L. Stone, *The Family, Sex and Marriage in England, 1500–1800* (New York: Harper and Row, 1977).

49 A. Macfarlane, *Marriage and Love in England: Modes of Reproduction, 1300–1840* (Oxford: Basil Blackwell, 1986), pp. 160–6.

50 G. di Pagolo Morelli (exact original year unknown) in M. Rogers and P. Tinagli (eds), *Women in Italy, 1350–1650: Ideals and Realities* (Manchester: Manchester University Press, 2005), pp. 116–17.

51 L. Dolce (1547) in ibid., p. 118.

52 A. Macinghi Strozzi (1465) in ibid., pp. 117–18.

53 Certainly in the pre-modern period there were many cases of local matches in which actors relied on long-term, in-depth information about prospective partners, yet as the examples here illustrate, in the cases that paralleled the modern acquaintance with previously unknown prospective partners, the information gathering was significantly less detailed and elaborate than in online dating.

54 F. Gies and J. Gies, *Marriage and the Family in the Middle Ages* (New York: Harper and Row Publishers, 1989), pp. 242–3.

55 L. Dolce (1547), in Rogers and Tinagli (eds), *Women in Italy, 1350–1650*, p. 118.

56 B.J. Harris, *English Aristocratic Women, 1450–1550: Marriage, Family, Property and Careers*, Oxford University Press, 2002), p. 55.

57 Gies and Gies, *Marriage and the Family in the Middle Ages*, pp. 242–3.

58 It should be clear that this observation is not a moral one. As Lawrence Stone suggests, in the period from the end of the seventeenth century to the beginning of the eighteenth century in England, a new "a-morality" or even "immorality" seems to have taken hold of court-ship and marriage. "Story after story, whether about the making or the breaking of marriage, provide evidence of an abnormally cynical, mercenary, and predatory ruthlessness about human relationships, which is deeply offensive to modern sensibilities." L. Stone, *Broken Lives: Separation and Divorce in England 1660–1857* (Oxford: Oxford University Press, 1993), pp. 27–8.

59 For examples of other rational methods of modern partner selection see: A. Ahuvia and M. Adelman, "Formal Intermediaries in the Mar-riage Market: A Typology and Review," *Journal of Marriage and Family*, 54(2) (1992),452–63; R. Bulcroft, K. Bulcroft, K. Bradley, and C. Simpson, "The Management and Production of Risk in Romantic Relationships: A Postmodern Paradox," *Journal of Family History*, 25(1) (2000), 63–92; S. Woll and P. Young, "Looking for Mr or Ms Right: Self-Presentation in Videodating," *Journal of Marriage and Family*, 51(2) (1989), 483–8.

60 According to researchers of digital technology at comScore Networks, in December 2006 the leading US online dating site was Yahoo! Person-als with over 4.5 million hits, and US online dating sites received a total of 20 million hits from US visitors per month. With monthly packages costing between $9.95 and $49.95 (*http://www.onlinedatingtips.org/faq/online_dating_cost.html*, last accessed October 18, 2011), online dating is also a lucrative business. In 2006, online dating was the second largest online paid content category, with revenues of over $1 billion in that year (A. Wharton, "The Dating Game Assessed," *Review Today* (May/June 2006), *http://www.revenuetoday.org*, no longer available

online). While market growth seems to be slowing, JupiterResearch predicted that revenues for US online dating sites would reach $932 million by 2011 (*http://findarticles.com/p/articles/mi_m0EIN/is_2007_ Feb_12/ai_n17218532/*, last accessed October 18, 2011).

61 The analysis below is a reprint of the third 2004 Adorno Lectures.
62 *http://www.match.com*, last accessed October 18, 2011.
63 *http://personals.yahoo.com/us/static/dating-advice_romance-predictions-07*, last accessed October 18, 2011.
64 *http://www.eHarmony.org*, last accessed October 18, 2011.
65 Illouz, *Cold Intimacies*.
66 Weber, "Science as a Vocation."
67 N.J. Smelser, "The Rational and the Ambivalent in the Social Sciences: 1997 Presidential Address," *American Sociological Review*, 63(1) (1998), 1–16 (p. 2).
68 Weber, "Science as a Vocation" and *The Protestant Ethic and the Spirit of Capitalism*; also on Weberian rationality, see: M. Albrow, *Max Weber's Construction of Social Theory* (Basingstoke: Macmillan, 1990); W. Schluchter, *The Rise of Western Rationalism: Max Weber's Developmental History* (Berkeley: University of California Press, 1981); and S. Whimster and S. Lash, *Max Weber, Rationality and Modernity* (London: Allen and Unwin, 1987).
69 W. Espeland and M. Stevens, "Commensuration as a Social Process," *Annual Review of Sociology* 24 (1998), 313–43 (p. 316).
70 G. Klein, *The Power of Intuition: How to Use Your Gut Feelings to Make Better Decisions at Work* (New York: Currency, 2004), p. 293.
71 E. Katz, *I Can't Believe I'm Buying This Book: A Commonsense Guide to Internet Dating* (Berkeley: Ten Speed Press, 2004), p. 103.
72 P. Bourdieu, *The Social Structures of the Economy* (Cambridge: Polity Press, 2005), p. 6.
73 For examples of the consequences of utility maximization on satisfaction and motivation see B. Schwartz, *The Paradox of Choice: Why More is Less* (New York: Ecco Press, 2004); S. Iyengar and M. Lepper, "When Choice is Demotivating: Can One Desire Too Much of a Good Thing?" *Journal of Personality and Social Psychology*, 79 (2000), 995–1006.
74 J. Alexander, *The Meanings of Social Life: A Cultural Sociology* (Oxford: Oxford University Press, 2003). See also Smelser, "The Rational and the Ambivalent in the Social Sciences."
75 H.B. Edgar and H.M. Edgar, *Internet Dating: The Premier Men's Resource for Finding, Attracting, Meeting and Dating Women Online* (Aliso Viejo, CA: Purple Bus Furnishing, 2003), p. 22.
76 Ibid., pp. 21–2.
77 J. Derrida, *Deconstruction in a Nutshell: A Conversation with Jacques Derrida*, ed. J. Caputo (New York: Fordham University Press, 1997), p. 14.
78 C. Nehring, *A Vindication of Love: Reclaiming Romance for the Twenty-First Century* (New York: HarperCollins, 2009), p. 79.

79　L. Dumont, *Homo Hierarchicus* (Chicago: University of Chicago Press, 1970 [1966]), p. 4.

80　Ibid., p. 16.

81　L. Dumont, *Essays on Individualism: Modern Ideology in Anthropological Perspective* (Chicago: University of Chicago Press, 1986 [1983]), p. 249.

82　R. Barthes, *The Pleasure of the Text* (London: Jonathan Cape, 1975 [1973]), pp. 9–10.

83　R. Shusterman, "Aesthetic Experience: From Analysis to Eros," in R. Shusterman and A. Tomlin (eds), *Aesthetic Experience* (London: Routledge, 2008), pp. 79–97 (pp. 92–3).

84　Ibid., p. 89.

85　Quoted in Gane, *Max Weber and Postmodern Theory*, p. 143.

86　Ibid.

87　G. Bataille, *The Accursed Share: Volumes II and III: The History of Eroticism and Sovereignty* (New York: Zone Books, 1992 [1946–9]).

88　P. Rieff, *Freud: The Mind of the Moralist* (Chicago: University of Chicago Press, 1979), quoted in W.I. Susman, *Culture as History* (New York: Pantheon Books, 1984), p. 278.

89　J.-L. Marion, *The Erotic Phenomenon* (Chicago: University of Chicago Press, 2007 [2003]), pp. 69–70.

90　C. Townsend, "Why Some Men's 'Hot' Sex Scenes Leave Me Cold," *Independent*, January 7, 2010, *http://catherinetownsend. independentminds.livejournal.com/17943.html*, last accessed October 19, 2012.

91　R. Greene, *The Art of Seduction* (New York: Viking Press, 2004).

92　S. Bartsch and T. Bartscherer, "What Silent Love Hath Writ: An Introduction," in S. Bartsch and T. Bartscherer (eds), *Erotikon: Essays on Eros, Ancient and Modern* (Chicago: University of Chicago Press, 2005), pp. 1–15 (p. 7).

93　J. Alexander, "Iconic Consciousness: The Material Feeling of Meaning," *Environment and Planning D: Society and Space*, 26 (2008), 782–94 (p. 789).

94　W. James, *The Will to Believe: and Other Essays in Popular Philosophy, and Human Immortality* (New York: Courier Dover Publications, 1956 [1897]), p. 77.

95　M. Dowd, *Are Men Necessary? When Sexes Collide* (Harmondsworth: Penguin Books, 2006), p. 40.

96　R. Pippin, "Vertigo: A Response to Tom Gunning," in Bartsch and Bartscherer (eds), *Erotikon*, pp. 278–81 (p. 280).

97　"Structure of Feeling," in M. Payne and J.R. Barbera (eds), *Dictionary of Cultural and Critical Theory* (Oxford: Blackwell Publishing, 1997), p. 670.

98　C. Townsend, "Romance and Passion," September 28, 2008, *http:// sleeping-around.blogspot.com/2008/09/romance-passion.html*, last accesed October 19, 2011 (no longer online).

99   Schlegel, quoted in A. Hannay, *Kierkegaard: A Biography* (Cambridge: Cambridge University Press, 2001), p. 145.
100 S. Kierkegaard, *Either/Or*, Vol. II (New York: Doubleday, 1959 [1843]), p. 21.
101 D. Halperin, "Love's Irony: Six Remarks on Platonic Eros," in Bartsch and Bartscherer (eds), *Erotikon*, pp. 48–58 (p. 49).
102 Plato, *The Symposium*, eds M.C. Howatson and C.C. Sheffield (Cambridge: Cambridge University Press, 2008).
103 V. Gornick, *The End of the Novel of Love* (Boston: Beacon Press, 1997), p. 158.

Chapter 6   From Romantic Fantasy to Disappointment

1   R. Barthes, *A Lover's Discourse* (Harmondsworth: Penguin, 1990 [1977]), p. 137.
2   J. Keats, "Ode on a Grecian Urn" (1820), in *John Keats: The Complete Poems* (Harmondsworth: Penguin, 1988), p. 344.
3   J. Schulte-Sasse, "Imagination and Modernity: Or the Taming of the Human Mind," *Cultural Critique*, 5 (1986), 23–48.
4   Quoted ibid., pp. 26–7.
5   Quoted ibid., p. 27.
6   J. Alexander, *Cultural Trauma and Collective Identity* (Berkeley: University of California Press, 2004), p. 9.
7   J.-P. Sartre, *The Psychology of Imagination* (London: Routledge, 1995 [1940]).
8   Quoted in E. Scarry, "On Vivacity: The Difference between Daydreaming and Imagining-Under-Authorial-Instruction," *Representations*, 52 (1995), 1–26 (p. 1).
9   Ibid.
10   W. Shakespeare, *A Midsummer Night's Dream* (1600), Act 5, Scene 1.
11   Ibid., Act 1, Scene 1.
12   C. Taylor, *Modern Social Imaginaries* (Durham, NC: Duke University Press, 2004).
13   *Don Quixote* (1605–15), for example, parodies chivalrous romances which distort readers' minds with an exaggerated rhetoric of amorous devotion. The novel was an attempt to poke fun at these romances which had flooded the European book market, and at their influence on the minds of aspiring lovers and knights, and thus pointed to the institutional basis and systematic, rather than chaotic, character of the imagination.
14   Thomas Jefferson, for example, argued in 1818 that "when this poison infects the mind, it destroys its tone and revolts it against wholesome reading. [...] The result is a bloated imagination, sickly judgment, and disgust towards all the real businesses of life." Quoted in H. Ross, *The Sentimental Novel in America, 1789–1860* (Durham, NC: Duke University Press, 1940), p. 4.

15 A critic condemned what he saw as the free use of romance novels, claiming that "their only tendency is to excite romantic notions, while they keep the mind devoid of ideas, and the heart destitute of sentiments." Quoted in ibid., p. 5.

16 A. Pushkin, *Eugene Onegin* (Princeton: Princeton University Press, 1964 [1833]), p. 139.

17 Ibid., p. 152.

18 Quoted in S. Mitchell, "Sentiment and Suffering: Women's Recreational Reading in the 1860s," *Victorian Studies*, 21(1) (1977), 29–45 (p. 32).

19 G. Flaubert, *Madame Bovary* (New York: Bantam, 1989 [1856]), pp. 31–2.

20 Ibid., pp. 140–1.

21 Ibid., p. 94.

22 Quoted in R. Girard, *Deceit, Desire, and the Novel: Self and other in literary structure*, Johns Hopkins Press, pp. 63–4.

23 C. Campbell, *The Romantic Ethic and the Spirit of Modern Consumerism* (Oxford: Basil Blackwell, 1989).

24 Ibid., p. 89.

25 B.H. Boruah, *Fiction and Emotion: A Study in Aesthetics and the Philosophy of Mind* (Oxford: Oxford University Press, 1988), p. 3.

26 K.L. Walton, "Fearing Fictions," *Journal of Philosophy*, 75 (1978), 5–27.

27 E.A. Holmes and A. Mathew, "Mental Imagery and Emotion: A Special Relationship?" *Emotion*, 5(4) (2005), 489–97.

28 A. Breslaw, "Casting Call: Bit Player, Male," *New York Times*, March 13, 2011, *http://www.nytimes.com/2011/03/13/fashion/13ModernLove.html?emc=tnt&tntemail1=y*, last accessed October 20, 2011.

29 A. MacIntyre, *After Virtue: A Study in Moral Theory* (Notre Dame, IN: University of Notre Dame Press, 1984), p. 212.

30 K. Oatley, "A Taxonomy of the Emotions of Literary Response and a Theory of Identification in Fictional Narrative," *Poetics*, 23 (1994), 53–74 (p. 64).

31 September 23, 2008, *http://sleeping-around.blogspot.com/2008/09/culture-of-love.html*, last accessed October 20, 2011(no longer online).

32 As Reinhart Koselleck puts it: "My thesis is that in modern times the difference between experience and expectation has increasingly expanded; more precisely, that modernity is first understood as a new age from the time that expectations have distanced themselves evermore from all previous experience." Quoted in J. Habermas, *The Philosophical Discourse of Modernity* (Cambridge, MA: MIT Press, 1990 [1985]), p. 12.

33 More specifically, intense romantic love that idealizes a particular partner is tied to serotonin, dopamine and norepinephrine.

34 M. Berman, *The Politics of Authenticity: Radical Individualism and the Emergence of Modern Society* (New York: Atheneum, 1970), p. 90.

35 C. Bushnell, *Sex and the City* (New York: Warner Books, 1996), p. 6.

36 B. Anderson, *Imagined Communities: Reflections on the Origin and Spread of Nationalism* (London: Verso, 1991).

37 J. Delumeau, *History of Paradise: The Garden of Eden in Myth and Tradition* (New York: Continuum, 2000 [1992]), p. 117.

38 Ibid.

39 D. Kahneman, B. Fredrickson, C. Schreiber, and D. Redelmeier, "When More Pain is Preferred to Less: Adding a Better End," *Psychological Science*, 4(6) (1993), 401–5.

40 D. Kahneman and D. Redelmeier, "Patients' Memories of Painful Medical Treatments: Real-Time and Retrospective Evaluations of Two Minimally Invasive Procedures," *Pain*, 66(1) (1996), 3–8.

41 J. James, *Terror and Transformation: The Ambiguity of Religion in Psychoanalytic Perspective* (London: Routledge, 2002), p. 14.

42 S.A. Mitchell, *Can Love Last? The Fate of Romance over Time* (New York: Norton, 2003).

43 J.-C. Kaufmann, *Gripes: The Little Quarrels of Couples* (Cambridge: Polity Press, 2009 [2007]).

44 L. Stafford and A.J. Merolla, "Idealization, Reunions, and Stability in Long-Distance Dating Relationships," *Journal of Social and Personal Relationships* 24(1) (2007), 37–54.

45 Harriet Beecher Stowe to her husband in 1847, quoted in C.N. Davidson, *The Book of Love: Writers and Their Love Letters* (New York: Plume, 1996), p. 73.

46 S.W. Duck, *Meaningful Relationships: Talking, Sense, and Relating* (London: Sage Publications, 1994), p. 11, quoted in Stafford and Merolla, "Idealization, Reunions, and Stability in Long-Distance Dating Relationships," p. 38.

47 L. Berning, "I Call Your/His Name," *New York Times*, January 27, 2011, *http://www.nytimes.com/2011/01/30/fashion/30Modern.html?pagewanted=2&tntemail1=y&_r=1&emc=tnt*, last accessed October 28, 2011.

48 D. Johnson, "The Marrying Kind," *New York Review of Books*, August 19, 2010, p. 24.

49 P. Kennedy, "Breathe In, Breathe Out, Fall in Love," *New York Times* November 4, 2010, *http://www.nytimes.com/2010/11/07/fashion/07Modern.html?pagewanted=1&tntemail1=y&_r=2&emc=tnt*, last accessed October 20, 2011.

50 C. Townsend, *Breaking the Rules: Confessions of a Bad Girl* (London: John Murray, 2009), p. 183.

51 D. Black, "Online Dating Grows in Popularity, Attracting 30 Percent of Web Users: Poll," *New York Times*, February 16, 2010, *http://articles.nydailynews.com/2010-02-16/entertainment/27056462_1_new-poll-web-users-internet*, last accessed October 20, 2011.

52 D. Jones, "Modern Love: College Essay Contest," New York Times, April 28, 2011, *http://www.nytimes.com/2011/05/01/fashion/01ModernIntro.html?emc=tnt&tntemail1=y*, last accessed October 20, 2011.

53 D. Jones, "You're Not Sick, You're Just in Love," *New York Times*, February 12, 2006, *http://www.nytimes.com/2006/02/12/fashion/sundaystyles/12love.html*, last accessed October 20, 2011.

54 E. Illouz, *Cold Intimacies: The Making of Emotional Capitalism* (Cambridge: Polity Press, 2007).

55 E.S. Person, *Dreams of Love and Fateful Encounters: The Power of Romantic Passion* (New York: Norton, 1988), p. 43.

56 Ibid., p. 115.

57 Ibid., p. 92.

58 A. Bolte and T. Goschke, "Intuition in the Context of Object Perception: Intuitive Gestalt Judgments Rest on the Unconscious Activation of Semantic Representations," *Cognition*, 108(3) (2008), 608–16.

59 Mitchell, *Can Love Last?*, pp. 95, p.104.

60 Here Updike is referring to an act of imagination, grounded in experience: that is, with someone one has actually met. Quoted in J. Updike, "Libido Lite," *New York Review of Books*, November 18, 2004, pp. 30–1 (p. 31).

Chapter 7 Epilogue

1 E. Dickinson, *The Poems of Emily Dickinson*, ed. R.W. Franklin, Reading edition (Cambridge, MA: The Belknap Press, 1999), p. 411.

2 J. Franzen, "Liking Is for Cowards. Go for What Hurts," *New York Times*, May 28, 2011, *http://www.nytimes.com/2011/05/29/opinion/29franzen.html?pagewanted=all*, last accessed October 20, 2011.

3 H. Frankfurt, *The Reasons of Love* (Princeton: Princeton University Press, 2004).

4 Ibid., p. 65.

Index